CELEBRATING THE VOID

NOVEMBER 6, 2020

ANGELIQUE BUCKINGHAM

Angeliquemcadam@gmail.com

Foreword

I have always known since the day I was born, that I have a message to carry through to the world. I was born to this world as a woman, a daughter, a sister a mother. My mission was to understand, to experience and to acknowledge how to serve the children that keep on being born.

The reason for sex of birthing yet another child that doesn't understand why. But now that child breathes and have to make SOMETHING of the world they are born into. If my work on this plane has taught anyone anything, then bless it. If my work on this earth has taught no one nothing, then it is Not my problem. All I know is that I have learnt what I needed to have learnt. Release me from these shackles as I am done!

I know that I have through my influence and my journey changed the mind set of Welfare. From the flat based structure of purely statutory to - governance, statutory, programs, psych-social, as the internal structures of social development. I know through my persistence have had welfare restructure to that of a disseminated franchise structure. Sometimes you need not be at the top to make a difference.

I know that through me being a step-mother, a mother, an adoptive mother, and opened my home to many children. I have made a difference in changing not only my own children's lives, but also the lives' of many other children.

I know that through serving as madam chair, I have not changed 1 social worker's life, but many social worker's lives' to inspire them to make more of a difference, in the world of many vulnerable and abused.

I know that through my messages, talks, social media presence, I spoke out about my abuse. I have inspired many women, men, children. The courage to speak out about their abuse.

Building, supporting and understanding!

#unitethefight, #rapeculture, #inhumanecapital - It happens in 3s

Biological – Adopted – Abused = charity begins at home! My Trinity has been created! I wanted the children, but never the man! I manifested that prayer early on in my life.

I write this book to show you, how your whole life actually revolves around exactly that, which you have manifested.

"The wheel of life turns, just make sure you are sure you are not at the bottom when the shit pours from the top" - (one of my mottos and sayings)

I want to live the balance of why I am on this plane a rejoiceful journey to the end.

I love and embrace everyone!

Thank you for making my last journey to this plane a wonderful and amazing realisation –

My message to you is

Love is – "Celebrating the Void"

3 + 3 + 3 = 9

Love you my children – never apologise for who you are!

Mama Ange

Celebrating the void:

"Pappa, I am sorry, please come and fetch me, I love you" – I replace the handset back on the ticky box with tears in my eyes, making my way back to the ward where I pack my bags and wait from him to walk through those doors in his white golf-shirt, white jeans and white sneakers.

∞

'Let her die'

∞

'Tears role down my cheeks in the dark, I hope he doesn't know, as he keeps pounding away at me like I am a piece of meat'

∞

'You will be bare foot and pregnant at the age of 18'

∞

'My measure of success – is the day I have a children's home, without having to beg for money'

∞

'our new Miss College 1991 …. Is'

∞

'do you want a baby'

∞

'you are proper missing it babe'

∞

'show me you belly'

∞

'don't worry, it's all taken care of, you will never have to deal with him again'

∞

'Models of me' – models of you

I am now starting my book, after many years of mentally, emotionally and physically attempting to do this. I have decided. Why wait when all I need to say is right here. Totally relevant to what I am going through and experiencing right now.

Being married to a man that is frustrating me right now. Again in a situation where trust is completely broken. As I had gone through this journey, of what I hoped I would not have to go through… the universe had a different plan - obviously...

I hate him right now, as I am sitting here… without having any means of saying it to anyone. I don't want anyone to discredit my emotions. To tell me that he is good to me. Try to give me any advice!!
I am angry with him. Angry at myself for being in this situation…

I have a choice. I can leave, but am I prepared for the consequences? Do I want to destroy my children, through having to be just another statistic in today's families of divorced parents?

No, I am not an – "every second weekend, and every second holiday Mom".
After all, I had always said 'I want children but do not want the man'!!
Look at how that turned out for me?
I got the man, and ended up struggling to have children.
My first born being an IVF baby, one of the lucky few that fell pregnant first time around. And then having to go through hell for the second. Until that knock on the door.

Why did I go ahead with the marriage in the first place?
O hell, because I felt guilty about breaking up his marriage, the home of his two sons. His first marriage. How could I put them through that hell tears, misery and do not pull it through… Walk away??? I could not do that to them.

The signs were there right from the beginning with this man. But I chose to ignore it. I took that first step to take him in. Leave my house, him leaving his house and family, to move in together.
The signs, even when I phoned my mom, she said: 'oh my child just look the other way… '!! Why did I not make the decision to leave then??

I had a Bartholin cyst the size of a marble, I was in such pain.
We went out to 206 in Louis Botha avenue with my brother and his girlfriend. I tried to be fun, but the pain was excruciating, I wanted to go home… After arriving home, he still tried to have sex with me. Seriously? My vagina was throbbing and not for him, but with this damn cyst that was bigger than life!!
(Do you know what the Bartholin gland is? It is that tiny little gland at the opening of your vagina, that lubricates your vagina, that pumps even more juice when you are aroused… That little opening is the smaller then the dot on an 'i') ….
Now imagine that being blocked with a marble being stuck behind it… You can't sit, you can't pee, you can't walk, let alone dance under the low set light in the middle of the dance floor…
Then he still wants me to have sex with him – holy shit, what do I look like?

When I asked him if we can rather leave it, his word to me was: "fuck you" ….
Turns around and falls asleep…

I am in tears, delirious with the fever. All I can think of is I need my Mommy…
I take my old Siemens cell phone that was on charge in its charging station.
"Mamma, ek is so seer, ek weet nie wat om te doen nie"
"Waar is hy?"
"Mamma, hy slaap" …snot snot snot…
"Ag my kind hy is seker moeg, laat hom maar slaap, drink 'n Disprin, more sal dit
beter wees"

The story of my life… the conversations – many, had with my Mom…

The following day – we went to the Gynaecologist. With a quick slice of the scalpel in
the Doctor's rooms ... Oh, the relief …… when that cyst drained!
He actually drove me and stood by my side. Off to surgery to have the Bartholin
tube reconstructed.
Throughout this whole process, he was so good to me, nursing me, serving me hand
and foot.

I lived in my own house which I bought in Newlands. At the time the area was filled
with promises and dreams that Newlands will be the future Westdene / Melville. An
upbeat funky, arty area, in Johannesburg. But still till today it is just Newlands,
nothing much has changed.
I bought the house when I was a mere 21 years old. A beautiful old house, which I
wanted to renovate. 191 Waterfall street, the corner house, right behind Ganis. I
had big plans.

Only to have a Dad the handy man that knows everything about construction.
I had a vision for my old house. To renovate to its original beauty of Wooden floors,
pressed ceilings, Oregon pine window frames and doors.
Then – Dear Dad, (whom had been threatening to divorce my Mother for as long as I
can remember) took on a job in Durban. We started with the renovations, making the
house inhabitable.
Dad meets Poppie, that works behind the sunglasses counter in a chemist on the
Bluff. (Needless to say, this has now become Dad's new project, leaving mine in the
dry.)
Building materials being stolen, furniture being stolen, building sand getting rock
hard. While Pappa kindly engages with his new project in Durban.
Who bears the short end of the stick as a young girl, with this vision and dream of
her first house?

When he comes home, in between catching a "sunglass tan", he insists on building
my house. I have a full time job so can only pop in over lunch times and after work,
to find my dream home turning into a Dad's modern vision of open plan living area.
Out goes all the old fittings. Replaced with cheap builders plumb and tile crap. Steel
windows, hollow core doors. My money just being drained by this "semi-daddy's-
can't-wait-to-get-back-to-Durban" new project of his.

My dream house, everything I don't want and hate. But what can you do? You never argue with Dad or go up against him. He was a hard working good Father.

In the meantime, I have to pacify my Mother, with the story that I am 'letting' the house. I won't move out of home or leave her alone. I am the last one still left in the parental home. My sister being married and both my brothers living on their own. Yes - I was there when Dad finally moved out and down to Durban. My mom was shattered, screaming, crying, collapsing as he drove off.

Oh he angered me so! I had arranged with my brothers, who then lived in Durban, to go visit. Dad said he wants to go down with me in my car. Yes, My car!! The first brand spanking new out of the box car, that I bought with my hard earned money. A Metallic Blue Mazda Midge!! (Completely unaware the Sunglasses was in high demand on the Bluff at that time…)

Luckily, I ended up having so much fun with my brothers, smoking weed, going out every night, experiencing the night life in Durban. Meeting all their gorgeous friends. Going to the trans parties in the mealie fields.
Oh my, do I remember one particular guy. Long black hair, quite the continental look, a gangsta – jip wheeling and dealing, in diamonds, drugs and anything that could be dealt… oh my!! I had such a crush!!
My hair was shaved at that stage, doing the Sinead O'Conner look. Michael had a hot blonde babe. We only hooked up way later, when he came up to Johannesburg with my brother… (let me think the song – "party something---- will find the song and capture it right here – can't think of it now!!)
We all went to dinner. Michael and I decided to take a detour to Delta Park on the way home. Low and behold, that wonderful gorgeous boy, just needed to come to reality …
Oh we sang, we danced and yes we had sex!! Under the trees, in the car park! It was just so liberating for me! (Who says that you need to be blonde with long hair to have a man want you?)
Later I found out that he was killed by gun shot during one of his underhanded dealings a mob kill, I was told! Very sad news indeed because he was fabulous! So gentle, so considerate and so special, only in a way that a woman can understand. When a man touches you with such adoration (he is supposed to be so scary gangster, with what he is involved with from day to day). Yet, when he is with you, you are his only thought feel and caress! Gentle even if it is on the bonnet of your car! Singing to the music, and admiring the moon … the dream man he was! But yet, still so young!!
Funny it was when got home, we walked into the house, pretending nothing happened.
"We just stopped to buy cigarettes." (I knew my brothers would kill me if they knew.)

Which is what I need to do right now, as mine is done and I am on a roll writing these stories of my life! – so pardon me for a moment… I need to put my kids to bed …

(The reason why I never wanted to write my book, and publish it while I am still alive.)

How do you write a book about your chronicles, if your children are still around, need to respect you, as they will not understand where you were, at that point and time in your life? They still have to write their life story, sometime.

So that was Michael and my moment with him.

Do you think this is where my passionate hate for lies and deception started?

Oh my, did I tell you that we were Old Apostolic that had to go to church 7 days a week and twice on Sundays?
Mom and Dad went off to church. We are now older, and allowed to stay at home if you had homework or needed to study…. What do you think? We always had homework and we always needed to study. On our own though, because church comes first!
We had to be in bed on their return, which was always around 20:30 or later. Dad happened to always be in 'The Office' of the church, which meant he was either Under-deacon or Priest.
Being Priest meant that you needed to interpret those dreams and visions for the church members. Console all the sisters of the church…. You were allowed to console the single sisters, only at your home, or when your wife was with you. Somehow, the Priests managed to wangle their way past the rule that "no Priest is to visit a single Sister without the wife being present", which was often upheld. However, till there is an attractive single Sister – oh no – heaven forbid the children can't be left alone at home. The House Priestess (the Mother and Wife) needed to stay with the children. Lucky Priest!! Again here I was, in the middle of all this Dad, "the Priest" needing to console those Sisters.

For some reason or another, I was cursed or blessed with a maturity, that was just – I don't know? Sometimes I think it is a curse, but I have learnt, it is a blessing to others!! But for me, a curse it was…

Started working when I was very little, thinking that my parents are burdened with 4 children. How are they going to pay for all of us?
I Started working as a packer aged 13, at fruit and vegetable shop in Hans Strydom Drive. Oh wow, this is when I met George, the Greek boy, with his small and gentle hands. What a lovely boy! I had a crush on this so sweet and innocent young man, who taught me how to work a till. George, was so lovely, such a gentleman. He took me to meet his Mom. (You know that in a Greek family, this is a big step for any boy, let alone the girl!)
Who do I meet, Costa, his brother! Oh whoopee twang!! He was wild, he had a mullet, Greek style, with a lazy eye, and you could see, 'the Rebel' man oh man! But I was with George, gentle soul he was, and although Costa winked at me, made my heart skip that beat, George was my boyfriend.

Oh this book brings back way too many memories!

Luv it!!

Dear Lucy

I am currently going through a process of cleaning house, my house. As you have also become a Christian you would understand the importance behind such an exercise in cleaning your spiritual house. I used to do this on a regular basis, but since my life had become a little bit hectic with my new family, I have not done this in a while but the time has come.

The reason why I am writing to you, is that you have become a part of my life and there are still a lot of things unsaid between us, which I need to say now, to help me in my healing process. First and foremost, I need to thank you for the coffee we had, it was very pleasant to sit face to face and be able to talk to you. (a bit nerve wrecking at first, but we parted with a hug)

Secondly, I need to thank you for being more understanding towards the children. Compared to other persons whom experienced similar pain and loss to that of yours. For raising such wonderful children, and for always being there for them.

You know there are so many stories, so many scenarios for our situation that we are in, some with negative impact some with positive, but we should see ours as being unique in its own.

I have to apologise for the past. For the pain and sorrow I bestowed upon your family. I never meant for any harm to be done to anybody. In the beginning it was hard on everybody involved. A major change in all our environments. You lost your nest egg, your husband. The children lost their dad. He was in fear, and agony for what would happen. I felt like a traitor, but we were all very scared all five of us. The future looked bleak and shady. But we all survived, we all where we once thought this was the end of the world. Will we ever see the light at the end of the tunnel? Now, seem to come out pretty okay. Yes, it went with a lot of tears, a lot of arguments things better left unsaid, but now we are all managing and on the path to recovery.

The children are starting to settle, and accept their new life. We are certainly very happy, and from what I can see and judge, you and Samuel seem to be very well suited and very happy too.

When the children are with us they are reassured of the fact that, all I can ever be to them is their friend. They are supported and reassured of the fact that their Mom is a very important figure in their lives, and very special for that matter. Samuel is also a very important figure, and they should see him and treat him with respect, although he will never be their Father, but he makes Mommy happy. When the children are with us, the only role I fulfil is to ensure they have a clean place to sleep, a comfortable bed, food to eat, nice juice to drink, their clothes are washed, ironed and on occasions they have the good old spoil, which is important for every person in life, everybody needs to be spoilt. I drive them around, fetch them, carry them, haircut, help them with their school work, pack their bags etc. but there is a very special place in every child's life and heart for their Mom. I can never have that with them, that special place is only for you, their Mom.

There are a few things that I am in charge of now. To ensure that we can all live, that is the financial side of things, which is quite a difficult item to control, when you have to take care of two households. As we would all like to give the children the best of both worlds. Sometimes money runs tight, and sometimes I need to talk about it, should I need to talk to you about the issues at hand I don't want you to feel offended by it. I also don't want us ever to argue about that. I know things have been said before like 'he will not be allowed to see the children' more because you are afraid of losing maintenance, but I am sure this was said off the cuff in anger.

But there are certain things that I need to talk about financially, and I don't want you to feel offended if we discuss it, because nothing is about us, it is for the children and about the children. After all money is a materialistic item and spiritual happiness and peace of mind is worth more at the end of the day

I have recently bought him a book called "Fathers after divorce" to help him through his process of guilt and hurt. One always forgets about the person who made the decision of separation and divorce. This was a big decision for him to make too. He had to leave his kids behind, leave all that he built up for 17 years behind, for his own personal happiness. He misses his children daily, when they are not with him, talks about them all the time, and when days go by when he has not seen them he does sit with tears in his eyes. He has a constant guilt burdened on him. It is starting to improve a bit, as we talk about things every night, and he sees them more regularly. However, here is still a lot of healing that he needs to go through, as he is the proud man, protector and fixer of all, he still feels as though he betrayed his kids. The only assurance is the love he has for them and the love they in turn have for him. When they see their Daddy they run to the garage to wish him welcome. They sit on top of him when they watch TV together, they play Cricket together, swim together, play pool together. At night he takes them milk and sits for hours just talking to the boys, they really have a special bond, they are best friends.

There's a little thing as well when you collect the children, can I please ask you not to hoot but rather to phone and say you are here? Just because the taxis always hoot when the have to go to town and sheep herders whistle to call their sheep, so very big please?

The kids have also said to me, that they feel guilty if they don't go to see you, or if they want to spend time with their Dad. We need to find a way to not burden them with guilt, whether they want to spend time with Mom or with Dad, it is not healthy for them to feel that way. This is something we should both help them with, as they have gone through so much already. Still have to deal with school and being teenagers, we can't still have them feel guilty. They have the full right to love their Mother and their Father and should be free to do so at all times. I will do whatever I can from my side to console them, not let them feel guilty for loving you and wanting to be with you or loving their dad and wanting to be with him.

The last little thing on Thursday you had the children deliver the Lawyers letter to me with the Attorney stamp on the back. Please could we not have the children involved in any of the legal matters, which we hopefully will not have again in future? We can't have them get wound up in adult matters like that, if there are any such letter in future, please call me I will rather collect it them have the boys involved.

But over and above my little bits that I just voiced, I still want to thank you for being so understanding throughout the whole divorce and for being such a good Mother to the kids

To our happy and peaceful future as real Mom and step mom.

Love Ange

∞

Oh fuck I am falling! I am screaming inside! I am trying to keep it together but I am falling apart! I feel like I can just run, run, run so far away! Give everything up and sit somewhere – nowhere and scream and cry and shout! I can't anymore!

Business is: Ange to design, Ange to quote, Ange to finance, Ange to make a showroom work, Ange to sell – Ange Ange Ange – and I can't anymore!

House – keep house clean, food, clean, decorate, Ange can't anymore
Kids – mom, homework, school, food, love, play
Daughter – mom and her issues
Sister – Sally her stuff, Martin and Joe and their stuff
Staff – Bella, Sam, Kora, Pete, Kevin, Victor, Stella, Bongani, Rachel – I can't
Friend – be there, phone, be happy, be cool
Husband – wife, friend, food, sex, love – I can't

I am losing it! I don't want to take any medication. I want to cope on my own! Without being drugged up!

Myself – hair, clothes, the pill, eat, smoke, happy, meditate, exercise – do things, money, maintain, sleep – be happy, cope!

I am finished – done! I need help! Where do I start? When I can't even get myself up – I can't get going! I am listless, I am demotivated!
I want to cry – but there's no tears!
I want to scream – but there's no voice!

I hate where I am at and feel that I am about to lose it!
I am about to run, run, run!
I feel guilty about everything!
Guilty about not being there for my kids! Guilty about not being there for my husband! Guilty about my house not getting done! Guilty about not sorting out the showroom!
Guilty about feeling like I need to run! Guilty about having to think about myself!
Guilty about not doing anything for myself! More so the thought: that I might have to do something for myself, makes me feel even more guilty, because I could be doing something for my kids, or family or clients!
I feel Guilty about everything!
I feel so God damn wrapped in this constant feeling of Guilt that I am stuck and

going around in circles!

I want to get out of it immediately!

Then I think, maybe I must just go to a Doctor! But if I go on any meds, I won't know the emotions I have been going through – I don't want to be numbed out by drugs – I want to feel!
But I am screaming right now! I am not coping and falling faster then I know – think or thought.

I feel I need to take some time out – but feel too Guilty to leave my kids – even if it is just for a short while.
But I am so stuck in this stupid fucking rut! So what do I do and where do I start?

Baby steps:

Its destroying my soul!
My everything is being sucked out by this family – soul destroying – I am getting too close and too involved – I am taking it too personally!
I have to remove myself form it all, it is sucking the life out of me, I cannot fix the years of pain, I cannot fix their shit.
I am there to do a job. My job is to do interior decorating, to furnish their place and to move away. They have killed my creativity with their negativity and pitiful behaviour. I can't and don't have the strength right now to deal with it! Fuckit, I can't cope with it and by the same token I cannot walk away from it. If I do I fail, if I don't – I will be destroyed!
I will not do more! I can't do more; it is not my problem!
The fact that the family is a fuckup and they are dysfunctional is not my problem!
I can't fix it; I also can't work there anymore! It hurts me, it freaks me out to be there. To see such complete and utter fucked up household!
I can't! The man is dying, the wife is absent, only sees the money, the kids just see the money, while the son is on drugs…

Focus Ange:
Tomorrow Tuesday 27/07/2010:
- Wake up at 6 o'clock
- Shower and get dressed
- Get kids ready for school
- Take kids to school
- Go for a cup of coffee next to Emmerentia dam
- Go to work at 8:30
- Go to Paco for carpets
- Take delivery of bedroom furniture
- Toby to arrange – PJ Stuart, Paul Head interiors, Steve security
- Fetch kids from school
- Take the kids for a bicycle ride at Zoo Lake!

One day when I grow up do you think I will fulfil my dreams in being who and what I want to be?

I am sitting here peacefully on my stoep, sipping my wine. Legs curled up on the couch, having the odd smoke, watching my children playing, whilst the crickets are calling out to a friend to join them in their celebration of summer.

The green grass all around them, the smell of Jacaranda blossoms filling the air. Whilst cricketing to their hearts content, in the hope to friend that special friend that will assist them in continuing their race in completing their cycle of life.

What is it about the simplicity of their life – nothing really – but the sound that they make that brings so much peace and tranquillity to light.
Quite a contradiction in terms.
Here they are desperately seeking Susan, or is it Mike, who would know? However, to us that sound brings about peace, to them the desperate search for fulfilment.

What a strange world we live in … everything that we have, we do, everything that surrounds us all just has this innate yearning to serve a purpose.
Some or other need to make a difference, to belong, from the smallest grain of sand to the highest mountain.
What purpose does one grain of sand serve? But in multitude it can, whether be the source of life to plants, grass, trees, a home for bugs, earthworms, animals.

What purpose does on cricket serve? A friend or mate to another cricket? But in multitude a chorus that sounds in the ears of many a human that needs to find peace.

…. My thoughts are now interrupted….

∞

Ward 4 – JG Strydom hospital 1988

So my pa kom kuier:

"Ek is so kwaad so ontsettend kwaad hoe kan jy as 'n Pa weg stap van jou dogter wat jou nog altyd hoogagting gegee het, not for the benefit of the doubt so as very few kids, I probably did more than anyone else did, I am so angry but got to keep going"

The fucking old man has hurt me so much in my life!! Has lied so much about who he really is and what he is doing when he goes out to church, business or work…!!!

∞

Is it 1 thing or 20?
I cannot say. Nothing I can really put my finger on!

All I know is I have had enough. Enough of only being good enough if people want something or need something.

13

I need to focus on me and my children my family and husband.
So until I feel satisfied that my relationship with them are okay – everyone else need to move on, and stay on the side-line! That's that!

So for now I am making my shopping list for the weekend:
blits, brickets, long-life milk, ice lollies, cold drinks, eggs, bacon, rolls, mieliepap, shebo, meat, chips, sweets, cheese, butter, muffins, toilet paper, dishwashing liquid, sugar, tea, coffee, cold meat

– we are going camping

∞

THE JOURNEY UNFOLDS

Innocence removed

1984

Liewe mamma

Mamma I have thought about this (about everything). Mamma I realise that I was and am wrong. Mamma I am really sorry about everything. If I say everything, I mean the way in which I spoke to you, the guitar and all the other things. Mamma I am really sorry about everything. Mams I just want you to know Mamma you can always trust and depend on me. 'Marmie remember that I love you and sorry again.'

Love Anne

Ps – I will do anything to repay you for your guitar.

∞

1985

Mamma must get better. I am trying to get along with my sister. If only she also just wants to try, then it will be heaven. But please nothing to worry about, if I have to clean one more dirty nappy I am going to scream!! Come home now please, get better soon.
I love ya lots and lots Angelique

∞

1986

Liewe Mamma

I am actually too scared to tell Mamma what happened to me last night, because I know Mamma will never trust me again. Last night I French kissed another guys by the name of Louis. He tried to do other stuff with me, but is told him no, that we must rather go into the house. I now feel so disgusted in myself, I feel like I have lost all self-respect. I feel dirty and like a whore and a slut.

I don't know what Mamma thinks of the idea that came up in my mind, that I on Monday I want to go to him and tell him that I have lost all my respect for him, and that I don't think anything of him anymore and that he must forget about me completely.

Mamma I am really sorry for what happened on Friday night, I promise it will never ever happen again, because I know now how it feels and it is not meant for me.

I am also sorry that I treated you bad, I did not mean to be nasty, but I hope that we will understand each other again in live together in peace and harmony.

Met liefde Angelique

I love you

∞

1986.06.17

Liefste Mamma

Oh please get better soon and come home, I miss Mamma a lot. Because there is no one here to talk to, and no one to argue about, to bath with me at night, now I am forced to bath with my sister in the mornings. There is also no one here that can reprimand us and tell us what is right and what is wrong. There is no one here to sign our tests, and no one to congratulate us when we won at Netball. I miss Mommy lots… "You are my refuge and safety my God on which I can depend on. It is you that keep me from the bird catcher's trap and protect me from deadly harm. You protect me beneath your wings and give me a safe haven. Your trust protects me from every side, and I want to thank you for that"

Lovies

Angelique

∞

1986 September 09

A very interesting story about myself – do yourself a favour and read it:

I am Angelique, and I am a girl. I am 13   years old, my birthdate is 1972.12.12. Many people like me while other dislike me. Sometimes I can be very cute and loveable, friendly and bouncy. Then you get the days where I am ha huge big bitch, irritating and irritated as well as frustrated and miserable. If I don't like someone I am very nasty and snobbish. Many people get the wrong impression about me, but I don't care for I always think that he or she is very childish.

I love school but I just have to study harder, because I know that I can do better in exams. I also know it is in my power to become a leader, and I know I can be an example for other and open the ways for others. BUT, yes a big BUT, I am afraid I will lose my popularity with the children, although I know that friends won't bring me where I want to be, I have to fight for my own future.
And then you get this big problem in life, and that is men! Maybe I inherited that from my Mom, but I always seem to fall for them, they always seem to come my way!
I actually hate them; no I love them but in anyway.

I want to set a goal in life, actually I had already done that. I want to be sporty as well as cultural next year. They say that the more you do the more you are able to do, maybe that will improve my marks. Maybe then I will reach my goal and set an example for others. I shall do anything in my power to reach that goal. It was difficult to do that this year, because it is a big change and huge step from std 5 – primary school – baby little pupils to std 6 - high school – grown up – two thousand pupils. You know that is a 'moerse' big change.

And to come back to my house-life. I don't know whether I am wrong, but this is only what I think.

I think that Mom and Dad don't trust me. They don't think that I am able to stand on my own two feet, and to know what is right and what is wrong. What I am concerned,

I think that I am able to judge from what is right and what is wrong. They don't to give me a chance to show them what I am able to. If only they'd give me a chance. But they don't want to let me go out to show them that there is no need to worry about me.

I was in the drain; I mean nearly down the drain. That was in the beginning of the year, and I don't want to be there again. I struggled to where I am now, and want to stay here, and now I just want my parent's trust.

I want to go to this Disco but I'll have to do anything that I have to go there and show everybody what I can do. And what I am. If only they would say yes. Maybe then, when they don't hear stories about me like they are used to, I can win their trust. I don't want people to spread stories about me now like they used to do in the beginning of the year. Or like they spread about my brother. I want to show them that I am not like that anymore. I want to show them that there is no need for them to spread stories and gossip about me anymore! Because I have changed, and I am still changing.

Lovies Angelique.

∞

The many letters found In a box that my Mamma preserved. As I wonder what had happened to make me, who I am today. Many more little letters of love and gratitude to my parents written. Letters to my Ouma and Oupa for being a part of my life, when I so desperately wanted to be adopted by them.

I love writing, I love singing, I love praying and playing. Never a day went by that I did not kneel by my bed giving thanks for the blessings I received. Never a night I go to sleep without apologising to those, whom I might have disappointed or hurt through my actions, that could have hurt them.
My belief till this day: "never go to bed angry".
When you ask for forgiveness, or apologise, it is up to the other person to either accept or reject it. You know from your side you have cleared your conscious.
Falling asleep every night with the thought, 'what more could I do today?'
The answer remains, nothing, as the day has ended.

I remember the nights that myself and my sister who shared a room, used to fall asleep with our arms crossed over our hearts.
Our last words being, 'Goodnight God'. Yes, we did that as we wanted to be Nuns.

Open letters written to my parents. Sometimes it was difficult to have to talk to them. Reverting to writing letters, was a way of avoiding conflict. There was a certain amount of fear, or was it respect? I can't exactly tell you, I just know that having open discussions was not how we raised.

Writing letters was a way of releasing, giving them the time to read, think, and understand where I am and what I think.
Letters and writing has always been a mechanism of release.

Understand me.

∞

1986

"Hey little girl is your Daddy home, did he go and leave you all alone, with a bad desire… I am on fire" – Bruce Springsteen

I hate this song. But the priest always plays it in his car. It is okay, because he is young and funky and we are all driving in his car. I baked my very special chocolate cake for everyone. We went to watch Wimbledon with all the other church youth, I am so glad I don't always have to stay at home anymore.
I need to shave my legs I can't stand this stubble all the time. I know he likes to touch my ankles every time we drive in his car. Heaven forbid it is prickly, how embarrassing.

∞

Still so innocent and so impressionable.

∞

18

.... 1987 ....

'I think that God's got a sick sense of humour, and when I die, I expect to find him Laughing' – Depeche Mode

3 Jan 1988

Liewe Mamma en Pappa

I am sorry if I disappointed you! But you need not worry anymore, because from now on there will be no one for you to worry about. You do not have to hang your head in shame. I won't be there anymore.

Pappa this what you have been waiting for so long, I really hope that you enjoyed every second of it. But do remember: it only hurts that body from the outside, but from the inside it only builds up hatred! Why did you really have to do that? You don't care about us anymore?

Don't ever ask why I am how I am. It is all your fault! Do you think that I enjoyed it every time when I had to hear how terrible and bad I am. To stand by and hear how terrible my Mamma is, unfortunately I was there every time when you told Mamma how little you feel for her! Then you still have the audacity to be so hypocritical to sleep next to her in the same bed, to also finally buy her a present. Did it give you such pleasure to see your wife and children, that has such respect for you and that look up to you, get hurt and live in hell every day?

I hope you enjoyed every second of pain that you caused everybody!

But after last night I just decided I have had enough!

I have had enough of standing by and watching how you destroy Mamma and hurt her, and how you hurt us children. My respect for you has dropped so low. The same way you broke her down with your hurtful words, I have now gone through exactly the same.

But thanks for reminding how bad I am at least I know now what others think of me and what I have to think of myself! You hypocrite, first cast out the beam out thine own eye; and then shalt thou see clearly to cast out the mote of another's eye.

Do anything you like and say anything you want. But leave my mother alone! I hope you enjoy watching others suffer! But I surely had enough of suffering! Remember that at the age of 15 I suffered more emotionally than what you think! But I am sorry for all the trouble I caused you but don't ever ask what I have done that's wrong, rather ask the question: what have I done wrong as a parent? But to save you the trouble I'll tell you – lack of communication!

∞

'Thank you Dad, now I how who I am'

∞

∞

'Let her die'

∞

My ideals: - 1988 – ward 4 JG Strydom hospital

- Become feminine
- Be loving again
- Look after your skin
- Look at your posture
- Look at your manners
- Look at your behaviour
- Look at the manner in which you speak
- Start doing exercise
- Start going to decent places
- Be careful of who you mix with
- Look at the way you treat your parents
- Look at the way in which you walk
- Look at the way in which you dress
- Look at the way in which you sit
- Don't allow yourself to be influenced by others
- Stick to what you say and don't change it
- Be spontaneous and friendly
- Live for the future
- Be obedient to Dad
- Pass every grade with distinctions, you have the brains, you can
- Aim for a scholarship
- Go study after school and become something
- Don't ever place yourself in a difficult situation with a man
- Don't create opportunities with a man
- Show self-respect and dignity
- Try support mom and dad in everything
- Don't be stubborn
- Listen when your parents speak to you
- Build up trust in your parents
- Try and get to the fashion and modelling world
- Start looking for a casual job
- Start being independent in a way
- Save some money for your studies
- Work really hard at getting scholarship
- Don't be ashamed of being yourself
- Start to rebuild your faith in Jesus again
- See Gerrit regularly, so that you have someone that can help you hold it together (emotionally)

- Don't ever try to take your own life again, you have too much to live for
- There are many that care for you, although it does not always seem that way.

Come on, pull yourself together, be the Angel you used to be. Be Gods child again. Be what your name means an Angel. Go for it, you can. You have a very strong personality, everybody knows you can, I know that as well. Go for it and make the best of life. Life is a ball; depends on what you make of it. So go for it and be what you want to be. You must help yourself, before you can help others.

"if we could learn to divide by two
half for me and half for you
all our cares would seem much less
and greater would be our happiness
for cares that are shared
just dwindle and die
while joys will simply multiply"

'I didn't really have the time
to knock upon her door
to sit and listen whilst she
told me the talk I'd heard before
I didn't think I had the time
to step out of my way
but I'm so glad I made the time
to cheer her lonely day'

Look well to this day
yesterday is but a dream
and tomorrow is only a vision
but today well-lived
makes every yesterday a dream of happiness
and every tomorrow a vision of hope
look well therefore to this day'

'who builds a church within his heart
and takes it with him everywhere
is holier far than he whose church
is but a one-day house of prayer's'

∞

"Pappa, I am sorry, please come and fetch me, I love you" – I replace the handset back on the ticky box with tears in my eyes, making my way back to the ward where I pack my bags and wait from him to walk through those doors in his white golf-shirt, white jeans and white sneakers.

∞

Sitting in the lounge on the floor, listening to.

"You little slut, you sleep with married men…!!"

No words could come through my mouth, as yes perhaps I am guilty of doing that. Perhaps I am that slut. I know he is married, I was in his house and met his wife and children. I know his brother. He was older than me and I worked for him.

How do I say this? I am a disappointment. I failed my Parents. I failed God. I am not worth anything anymore.

Let me go find that NT cutter in Pappa's panel van, in the tool box. If I lie in my bed and cut my wrists they won't find me. I will lie under the duvet, so they think I am sleeping…. Oh my god the blade is so blunt….

I can't go without writing my last letter…

Tablets, Mamma, just came out of hospital again with her knee operation. It's all in her bedside table. I will go to the bathroom and swallow all her tablets… Looking in the mirror.

Who are you? What have you done?
You are disgusting!
I hate you!

Bottle after bottle. Water, more water…

Here's Mamma's lipstick – let me write a message on the Mirror.

I am starting to feel dizzy, I better go to my room, just now they find me…

……. Angelique….

……Vomit….

….. Wakeup….

…. The pipe down my throat….

Waking to bars in front of the window. Closed in behind a locked gate. Tears running down my cheeks. Crazy people all around me.

NO – I can't still be alive!!

∞

1988 - continued

My liefste mamma

Ek weet nie mooi hoe om dit vir mamma te se nie, maar ask ek piepie dan brand dit, end it is seer. Ek weet nie wat aangaan nie. (I don't quite know how to tell you this, but when I urinate it burns. I don't know what is going on.)

Liefde Angelique

∞

Mamma

I am sorry I called you a bitch last night, but I do feel that you are extremely unreasonable to say the least!

Throughout this story of Pappa, I have tried my utmost best to stand beside you every possible moment and to keep you strong. I stayed strong to be therefore you!

You often asked me what do I do to be so hard. But it is not for being hard it was more hurt than hard. That is why I accepted every job offer I could get, every invitation to go out! I just wanted to get away from home. It hurt me every day to see everyone crying, the tears and how everyone hurts. To see my Mamma hurt me, to see Pappa hurt me, to see my sister and my brothers, hurt me just as much. I hated every minute of being at home.
Remember I am not made of stone, I too have feelings and emotions, and I am only a child of 15 years, that still has a whole lifetime ahead of me. It is also not nice to have to hear how bad and terrible I am the whole time and how bad and terrible my Mamma is. And a Dad that I would do anything for telling me that he doesn't care about me. That is not a nice feeling, now is it? This is the reason that want to go out every night, and times that I do go out, I don't want to come back home, because it is too nice to see how others enjoy themselves and laugh and smile. This is the reason why I come home in the mornings, times when everyone is asleep, and I want to go to work early and come home late. Things have just become too much for me.

But what hurts me even more, is that you stood back every time and watched how is was busy cracking and being hurt by Pappa. And now you telling me that I deserve it, I asked for it. Do you really think so? And then you still ask me why I reject you! Do you really think I deserve what I am getting?

Lovies Angelique

PS – is this your way to thank me for what I have done for you?

∞

07.07.1988

Dear mommy

To begin right at A:

The night I chased you out of my room: Conrad phoned and said that he wants to tell me something, but he is afraid I might not be friends with him anymore. Anyway, I jumped to the conclusion that he is going to kind of drop me. I just thought to myself that I can't keep a guy, is there anything wrong with me or what is the problem, am I stupid, childish, ugly etc.? Why can't I be as lucky and happy with a guy like other girls. I also want a boyfriend; someone I can be proud of. I felt down and depressed.

When you came into my room, I was on the verge of crying, and I did not need any criticism from anybody. You know I smoke in my room, and I know as well as you don't like the smell, but I can't sit with a can of spray and every time I take a drag, spray the smoke away. By you hammering on the fact that my room smells of smoke, isn't going to change anything except for you wasting your breath and me getting irritated and our relationship breaking down. I will open my windows and door every day and night till I go to bed (if it is not too cold). But you going on like that is just like and old lady. It won't make me stop smoking. I will take you into consideration as to open my windows, but please stop nagging. Don't take this up as a confrontation, but take it up like we are two friends, please? Cause what I am telling you now is to me like you are my friend.

Next: the story at school:

That was a plain common joke we made. Everybody took it up as a joke. Maybe you don't, but it is different at school. I wish you could be there just for one day to see what children do, and hear what they talk about. Times change, I know you think it is not proper for a girl, or maybe any child to talk about the facts of like and discuss it openly, but we do. We often sit in our groups and talk about sex, drugs, alcohol and all that stuff. It is normal. That is what everybody talks about. I know as well as you, maybe those things should be discussed at home or in private, but it is not just like that anymore. Nobody can do anything about it, that is the way things change day to day. The whole world is going to pieces, the youth is scattering to bits and pieces.

I want you to be my friend, someone whom I can talk to, and feel free and open to tell everything to. You always tell me you feel the same way. But every time I tell you something that is not even that bad, you think it the worst. You make a whole scene about it. In some ways, come what may, you are still a little conservative. Face it, that as much as you try, the pace sometimes gets too quick for you. It always this time of each month, that you feel down and depressed, and everything is getting too much for you. If you feel like that, come and talk to me, I am quite prepared to listen. I mean that's what friends are for.

But Mom let me tell you one thing – you are the best Mother and friend a child could ever ask for. By crying now and being cross about something that already happened is useless. I can't go back and change what I have done. As hard as I try I can't be perfect and do just the right things in life. Everybody is entitled to make a mistake. I am not all that grown up to know exactly what is right and what is wrong. Sometimes you do things you regret afterwards.

And please another thing is:

I feel guilty and filthy enough with this "story" of mine, as it is. It hurts if you make such jokes and pass such nasty remarks the whole time. It is nice to know that you walk around with a disgusting disease in your body. Please stop it?

Luv ya stax

Your friend Angelique
xxx

∞

Dear mom - 1988

There is something I have to tell you, I should've actually told you this weekend, but I could never find the right time to hand it to you.

Thursday night when I went to Nelle, she told me that we should slip out, and go out with our older friends. Because her parents are very strict, and doesn't like it if she goes out. So, we slipped out at about 9 o'clock and we all went to a restaurant named Godfather in town. We enjoyed ourselves very much. Although I wasn't very keen on the idea of doing things behind her parents back, because I want to lead a straight life without having to do such things.

We came back at about 1 o'clock, but when we came back her doors were open and lights were on. We panicked on hell of a lot. Because I had that feeling the whole night that her parents are going to find out. And I knew that doing stuff behind someone's back, again is going to rest on my subconscious mind, and I am going to feel guilty and horrible again. Her dad came into the room after we switched off the lights and go into bed, and she had to go to their room.

But now her parents don't approve of our friendship and they kind of blame me for what happened. What she told them to save her skin, I don't know?

But thinking about what happened: everything happens with a reason, and I think that the reason is that God doesn't approve of our friendship, and maybe if this didn't happen, I could've ended up as the same little shit I used to be! BUT GOD HAS HIS REASONS FOR LETTING THINGS HAPPEN.

And also thinking back to our friendship we had: she tried every possible thing to break up my relationship with Sam, and in a way she makes me think of Sally. Because she has a few ways of being just like her. And this fighting between me and Sam was mainly because he found out in some way that I went out with Dan that night, and he doesn't like the idea. Although nothing happened between Dan and me. Still, just the thought that I went out with other guys.

Thanks for reading, and I hope you understand.

Lovies Angelique

∞

1989

1989

So shall my paean be

I'll string you a dream of wooden beads
a bracelet of affection and sacrifice
and perhaps lay marble bricks on foundations of burning bark
resorting to find the essence of devotion in return
oft times was I clawed by a soaring vulture
advent of expected destruction
hoping that the flight would be to set me free

∞

Being a teen somewhere when I was 16:

Dear Mom

I'm really sorry that I freaked out at you so much this afternoon. But I really feel that although I know you are always right what judging people is concerned. But I also think you should try and understand others a little bit more. Everybody is not the way you want them to be and you'd like them to be. Each person's got his own way of living and his own way of life. Paul is really a very nice guy, once you get to know him he is very quiet and a strange character. Although he might seem a little queer to you he is actually a very nice person to talk to and he always try to help where ever he can. You must just get to know him. Alfred — I know he is a freaked out character but he is going to the army and I hope and believe the army will pull him together. It is only till Tuesday! he has always like me and now eventually I became friends with him, and that is how far it goes. I don't like him that much that I would have something going with him! And ONE THING I will never even think of getting off with him because he doesn't attract me in that way because he is sooo sloppy!

Mom I met this nice guy this Len that Jenny introduced me to on Saturday night! He is really very cute! It is he that phones me every day! He has got longish hair which I'm afraid you won't like but doesn't do anything to his character! He will come and visit me sometime so you can meet him. He is 21 and also did what Deandre did but the only difference is, he did his for 8 months and not 10. He is going with me to the ball! He is really gorgeous. He has glass green eyes that looks like ice, brown hair. He is half Afrikaans half English (mom Afr dad Eng.) he lost his dad 3 years ago. He started work last week at a computer and technology firm as a rep. Now, his hair is not very long — he wants to cut it but I begged him no to because as you know I love long hair. I think you might just like him (depends)

Mom we never get time to talk so that is why I decided to write this letter. I hope you understand a little bit more and you know a little more about what is going on in my life at the moment.

Love Ange

∞

∞

30 Mei 1989

Dear mom and dad

I haven't written you a letter for a long time and I actually realised that after you have left for church.

I would like to thank you both for everything you have done for me through the past 16 years. We had a couple of differences but as they say, a relationship without arguments is false. Having arguments and torments brings you closer to each other. It proves how much you care for one another. Francois and I actually talked about it on Friday. We talked about parent and child relationships and I realised again how grateful I should be for the parent I have. I realised how wonderful you both are.

I would like to thank you for treating me like an adult and letting me do the things I want to do for example: the modelling

I have always wanted to do that, but I didn't have enough confidence to do such a thing, for I always thought they'd laugh at me. But you made me realise what I can do. I promise you I am not wasting your money. I am going to make it real big in my life. It is not everybody that gets the opportunity to do modelling although it is every girl's dream. If it wasn't for you I would never have done it. Thank you very much.

Working:

To me working and earning one's own money means a lot. Learning to be independent and know how to work with money at an early age is very important. Learning to meet people and how to work with them is also important especially in my future career as a Psychologist or PRO. Whatever I am going to do in future, I know now that I am going to work with people. I enjoy working. It gives me self-confidence, maybe a little too much, but I believe it is necessary for every person to have that, and believe in themselves for every person has a right to live, and every person has a say in life. I know what I am going to say now, you won't like much, but it is true whether you like it or not it is a fact. Why I also work and why I worked at Alexanders and Scotts, was because I know how much you suffer to make enough money each month to keep everybody happy. To give to my sister to buy food, pay rent, keep my brother and me in school. That is why I hate asking you guys for money, because I know you don't have it. Seeing I am a girl and growing up I need clothes and cosmetics and a decent room, and you can't afford giving me all that. I hate asking you for money unless I don't have any, and I know I will be able to give it back.

I appreciate the fact that you come and fetch me from work although I hate keeping you from the rest you need so badly. That is why I invite my friends to the restaurant, and ask them to bring me home. As a matter of fact, I hate asking you to do anything for me. The word hate might sound a bit harsh, but you already do so much for me, that I don't like to burden you with another thing – please don't interpret what I said now the wrong way. I might have said it a bit harsh, but I hope you understand

I don't have much of a social life, seeing that I work over the weekends, which is actually good, it keeps me away from doing bad things, but when I do go out (and that happens very little), I enjoy myself. Because I hardly ever get a change to socialise, I hardly every go out, because I work. Not that I hate it, don't get me the wrong way, but you know for a fact that it is true. To me whether I go out or work, time is not factor. Whether I work till one, two o'clock in the morning or whether I go out till that time, it makes no difference. When I work, you know where I am. When I go out you know where I am, because I have stopped lying to you about where I go when I go out. I know the time I have to be at home is twelve o clock, and I see that I am at home round that time. To tell you the truth, I hate going to clubs and discos because I have been to everyone in town, I know what it's like, and there is simply nothing that attracts me to such rubbish clubs. First of all, you have to scream at the top of your voice to talk to someone, all the people are so common, and they see a girl just as another pick up or slut!

To tell you the truth, I'd rather go to a decent restaurant or a pub and have a good conversation, or else go to a good movie, or to someone's house where everybody acts like human beings. I enjoy myself more than in a pathetic disco. If you are worried that I don't behave myself, I do. Why do you think people say I am older than I say I am. Maybe because I act more maturely than a normal 16-year-old. I behave like and adult and not like the other sixteen your olds that get absolutely drunk and fall around the place.

I mean, I know what it is like to have a name dragged through the mud, all because of the way you appear to others in public, and that is why I act sophisticated and I enjoy being like that. Because of what had happened in the past, I understand if you are still wary about trusting me. But I know everything, or should I say basically everything in life. I know what the consequences will be if I do things I shouldn't do. The last thing I want to do is to disappoint you again. I have done enough harm and I do not want to go through that again.

Dad, I feel so bad about things I have said in the past that caused our differences, but I love you very much, have always had a very big tender spot in my heart. There are things that you have done and said that hurt me very much, and things I have done and said. I am sorry about what I have done, and I appreciate it if you talk to me and tell me how you feel and think. The days you took me to modelling and you talked to me in the car. It really meant a lot to me, if only it would happen more often. One day I'll take you for coffee somewhere where we can talk. I'll let you in on my secrets and you can let me in on yours. I know you want to talk Dad, there are a lot you want to tell me, but you don't know how, but that day we'll talk like friends. I want and love to know a bit more about you. I love you Dad!

Mom, I would like to thank you for understanding me so well. It means a lot to me to be able to talk to you without hesitation. I know I have hurt you quite a bit in the past, but I would love to better on that. One day I'll take you for a Diet Sprite and we can talk like old friends, for we are old friends. Mommy I love you very much and I want you to know that I will always be there for both of you. I love you Mom!

Thanks for everything!

Love Angelique

PS – there might be things in this letter that you might interpret wrongly, but please don't, read with a positive eye!

My Fun Faith Brother:

This is the name I call him. Down the road from us they lived. Myself and my little brother would oft escape to their home to get away from home, when it became unbearable.
He still is a friend of mine, that with heart still wishes to console me. He cannot get the image of my beatings that still haunts him.
One night I went out with friends of mine to watch a film in Sandton. Instead we chose to go to the Dome, (a club in Johannesburg CBD at the time). My friends chose to leave me there. I had to find my way home. Took a lift with a Portuguese couple that brought me home. Quietly, not making a noise, I got out the car. The gates opened…. It was my Dad…

Oh my God, I went cold…

"Waar was jy!"

Pulling me by my arm into the house.

"Jou klein slet, gaan slaap! Ek deel more met jou!"

The fear that night. I never slept. What do I say? I messed up! Please God help me!

The bed room door opened the next morning…

"Ek is jammer Pappa, ek is jammer"

With now further words exchanged, he took off his belt. Just starting beating and beating….
"Staan still…. Ek is nie klaar nie!"
"Pappa … ek is jammer!"
"Jou klein slet, ek slaan jou mors dood!"

"Liefling – hou op!!"
My Mom runs into the room…
"Liefling – jy gaan haar dood slaan!!"

My mom jumped in the middle, lying on top of me to protect me from the ongoing lashes….

Yes, my fun faith brother saw me the next day when I walked down to their house. The welts had drawn blood. My back, my bum, down my legs….

For weeks I had to use foundation to try cover the marks. Mom fortunately wrote PT teacher a letter to excuse me from participating in PT.

Oh my Dad's favourite words:

"I would rather see you dead by my own hands, then see you in the gutter."
∞

1989 was a brilliant year. I had settled into my new school. Everyone had forgotten about the 'nervous breakdown' I had in the beginning of last year.

The marks on my shin has healed nicely. I had little warts on my leg that I wanted to have removed. Pappa had a plan to use light gas to burn it off. Fortunately, the warts were removed, as well as a big part of my skin which left me looking like a wild girl that burnt her leg on a hot exhaust pipe of a motorcycle.

The school camp in 1988 also gained me a lot of respect amongst my friends. Everyone clubbed money together, and supplied me with their empty Tampax boxes and empty shampoo bottles. In the 80s there were no restrictions, and I looked more mature. My Mamma and I had a more open relationship by now, as she accepted that I am not going to stop smoking. After all I was the eldest child left in the house. With all the money collected, I bought Benson and Hedges cigarettes, Vodka and Cane at Solly Kramer's the liquor store up the road from us. Mamma and I sat on the floor in my bedroom, packing the boxes full of smokes. Decanting the alcohol in the shampoo bottles. Off we went to school camp. Happy Campers.

At the school camp there were girls from the other school that joined us. Items of clothing and underwear started going missing. Inspector Ange did some investigation until I found the culprits. In the bathrooms, whilst I was pushing the one girl up against the wall, my friends searched the bags and found all the missing items.

Yes, there were times that I was a bully too. When calling the shy kids out into the middle of the school quad and making them sing to the school. Teasing a girl, because she never shaved her legs, her hair always greasy and long braids that really made her look like a Viking, with her long skirt down to her ankles. (how terrible I felt, years later when I found out that she was adopted)

I knocked a boy out once. On the stairway to the top classrooms, he lifted my dress, for the whole school to see my panties. With one swipe, I know the bejesis out of him. Another one received an honorary 5 fingers and palm through the face for saying to me to close my legs, because my breath stinks.

Many of my friends, were afraid of their parents. I used to go to the Family planning clinic in Windsor. I was also on the Pill since beginning of last year. I had extremely bad pains, and periods that was uncontrollable. The doctor recommended I go on the pill. So I arranged to get extra packets for my friends, that I took to school and gave them their daily dose. They were already sexually active. The last thing for them was to fall pregnant. Condoms were not an option in those days.

In 1987 I was in the Art Ballet and Music School, which was right next to Johannesburg Hospital. We had to make use of the public transport bus services to get to school and back. I learnt the ropes of catching the bus, and the Roads of Johannesburg CBD, Hillbrow and Braamfontein.

I had my first interview for modelling school. My friend wanted to have her hair braided. So off we went to town on the bus. I took her to the Tony Factor building in Eloff Street to have her hair braided. Off I went to my interview near Hillbrow. We met up again, at the hairdresser. Walking back to catch the bus back home, crossing

Bree street…. I looked left and saw the Minibus Taxi was not going to stop… I woke up in the ER in Johannesburg Hospital. Jaw dislocated, Neck fractured, arms, back, ankle grazed. What a wonderful start that was to April Easter school holidays…

I spent more time in the Principals office than in class. To such a point that when I arrived at the office if was offered tea by the Admin lady.

My visits to the office was not without good reason. I had a letter written by my mom, for the reason for my nails to be longer, as I was a Nivea hand cream model. A letter for my hair being permed and coloured, as I was a hair model for L'Oréal. A letter for eyeliner and mascara on my eyes, as I was a waitress at night, sometimes during the week.

Teachers:
- the one I told to please close her brief case, and teach us. As she had a mirror stuck inside her brief case and used to perform to herself, to her own image. Not even listening to the answers we gave her in class.
- the one, for shouting like a banshee at the top of his voice, at a child for not understanding what he needed to do.
- My best performance was, when the Biology teacher, looked under the girl's dresses when we sat on the tall chairs in the Laboratory. Oh how liberating it was to walk up to him in smack him so hard that his glasses broke.

This was also the last year of being in a School. The Principal called me in, as he was going to be leaving the school. Told me that he does not think I would be understood by his colleagues. So if I should wish to stay, my Matric year might not be fun.

With this, I left for College.

∞

10 May 1990

Dear mom

Please forgive me if I have done or said anything to offend you in some way or another? If it is that am very touchy and nasty the past few day, it has been because I haven under a lot of stress, I am going to be for the next 4 weeks, because of all the tests, exams and projects we have to do. I write up to 3 tests every day. Next week I have to prepare 3 speeches. A practical mark on Monday and office practice, I am writing short hand on Tuesday, Wednesday I have to hand in a project, Thursday I am writing office practice, Friday I am writing my big communication prelim exam. Projects. Monday I am writing Afrikaans prelims, Tuesday office practise and so it goes on till the long weekend. Monday after that final exams start.

Mommy please understand I need you more now, to stand by my side than ever before as I have told you before, the only friends we have is each other, please be my friend, I don't need this fighting right now, Simon doesn't understand me all that well, and I don't want others to know I am stressed, you are the only one who understands me. He does not know what it feels like to just want to cry and for no particular reason, and I haven't had time to talk to you about it, but I am telling you now. Please understand I need you now more than ever.

∞

Cactus flower incorporated:

My first true love that I met. I was truly convinced that we would marry someday. "Could I ever explain, this feeling of love, it just lingers on…." – Japan.

When I was in std 5, standing outside the main gate of Unika, after netball practice. There was this young man, on his black motor bike, dressed in black with a black helmet. All I could see was his blue eyes. Day after day, he used to park he would wait across the road. Just staring at me. Years later, a black GTI drove past me whilst walking down the road with my friend. The same eyes met mine. It was that boy on his black bike, that stood outside the school gate. It was surreal. Inseparable we were from that day.

The character I needed to portray was the girl in the film "Unbearable lightness of being". Unaware of the visions of what he had for me. Photographs, crawling around on the floor, blind folded…. Actions became more violent, that turned into fights. Physical and verbal fights.

This was later exasperated, when he had to go through a self-finding journey of a course. The course that would break him down to a raw open being, to then rebuild the self. Each participant had a partner allocated to assist them through the journey of break and build. The love of my life, arrived at my house late one night. Clothes crumpled and creased. The smell of sex still lingering on his person.
"No, nothing happened. I love you. You are the only one for me. We just talked."

"I want to know the truth. Why are your clothes creased? What is that smell?"
"It was nothing, really, it was part of the course, of finding what we want."
"So you had sex with her?"
"I am sorry, it was not meant to happen. Please forgive me."
"Leave."

I was torn apart. The hurt was excruciating.
The next day, I asked him to fetch me. Near sunset. I found the gun in my Dad's
bedside drawer. I told him to drive us to West Park Cemetery. We sat on a grave.
"Tell me everything…."
Listening to the whole story, of being broken down to complete vulnerability during
the course. Weeks of being left alone as this was part of the course is to distance
yourself from everyone and everything. Being told how he had grown close to his
partner… I could not listen any further…
Not knowing anything about the working of a gun. What to do with it, I pulled it out,
pointed it at him…
"You leave this course now! You ever do this to me again. Ever cheat on me again.
This is your destination!"

Many gifts, many letters, many cards followed. Flowers, more flowers.
He collected me one day from home. Before entering his house, he blind folded me.
Sat me down on a chair, Night porter playing. Confessions of love, devotion and
eternally being mine and I his. The blind fold was removed….
The before my eyes, was 'The Dress'. Oh the dress that had caught my eye in
Paloma in Rosebank. Beautiful Black Satin and Velvet bust with Red and Pink Roses
flaring out at the bottom below the waist. Netting and Big Satin bow… Oh how I
desired to one day wear a dress like that. Here it was, displayed in front of me! It is
mine, he had bought it for me!
"Will you forgive me?"

∞

1990

THE GIFT

In her moment of content, although seeking answers to the unknown
he then arrived at the door, not knowing what to expect
as setting expectations prior to that of the first meeting.
he then arrived at the door, trying to paint a picture
matching that of the voice,
but will the painting be distort upon the first meeting
he then arrived at the door, all preconceived ideas fade
as he brought her a gift
the gift that answered all those questions
he gave her that gift expecting nothing in return
he gave her the gift wrapped in newspaper clippings
still to be read
they laughed and they talked, they laughed

a brief projection of happiness that only a friend can offer
please can we continue laughing ?

∞

1990

To two very special people:

A matter concerning my heart,

God gave me two special people and he told me to call them Mother and Father. I gazed up at them and to my surprise I saw two perfect faces, smiling as they look at me. I closed my eyes and thank the Lord for entrusting me into the hands of two such beautiful perfect beings.

They laid me down on a white satin pillow and dressed me like a fairy-princess. They gave me the most beautiful name and name that made me feel as if I was a gift from God. They taught me how to walk, they taught me how to talk, they taught me to be just as perfect as they are. They taught me what love is, the kind of love that only a parent can teach a child. They taught me the righteous path of God, a path that they have straightened for me, so that I may follow.

They have always lent me a helping hand when I needed one. They lifted me up at times when I stumbled and fell. At time when I sought no reason to live, they gave me new meaning to life.

Now I am almost grown and ready to fight my own battles, and looking back, I can only thank God for giving me such wonderful parents that taught me what I know today and for giving me such exquisite moral standards.

Thank you Lord for my parents

AMEN

∞

20 – 10 – 1991

Dear mom

You know that so many times one feels low, down, hurt, unappreciated, left alone and one basically feels worthless.

Every person has a stage that they have to go through when they feel emotionally very low in one self, but therefore one has a friend, someone to speak to someone who understands what you are going through, someone who is prepared to listen, to help and to advise, and that someone is right in your own home, although it doesn't always seem that way but that person has been through all that pain and suffering herself, and that person is me.

I understand that you might find it difficult to talk, but you know that if you come to me with a problem that you need to discuss, I am always there to listen, it does not help to sit in your room and cry, and think about that problem the whole time, because when you think of that problem, the more you think and the more that problem is repeated in your mind the bigger the problem becomes. You cannot always solve the problem or understand the problem without the view or understanding or advise you get from others. Being able to get another's points of view about a certain subject, or even talking about your problem with another, it will definitely give you a better understanding and perspective about such a situation or subject.

As you have so often told me, that one cannot carry one's burdens all by oneself, and that one needs to talk to others about it. Now it has come to a point where I am telling you to talk when something is bothering you.

I know you think or feel that we think you are just feeling sorry for yourself, but to be very honest, we do think that way, if you just sit in your office and cry, and that is all we see is you crying, and you aren't prepared to talk. Please Mom, speak when something is on your mind.

Another thing that we also understand, is that you are going through your mid-life menopause, and as you have so many times told people, you cannot go through it alone, because you make life unbearable for others, you need to talk to someone.

Now things will go as follows: when you have a problem, come speak to me. I will always listen, I am not going to ask you what is going on when I see you cry, because I am going to take it that you are not ready to talk. Don't sit in your office and cry, because one wants to scream if you sit there and cry, we come in and see you if you talk about your problems, you won't find the need to sit and cry and feel uncared for and worthless.

PLEASE MOM TALK TO ME!!!

Love Ange

∞

1991

Dear mom and dad

I am writing this letter because I am afraid that if I might talk to you about this it might end up in an argument, I don't want that.

I am not going off the right road or anything like that, I know my responsibilities especially what church is concerned. As you very well know that a few years back, I was totally off the right track and I have had enough experience in the wrongs of life, and I know what the wrong road is like. I am definitely not planning to land in that dark pit again.

As Mom said to me not long ago, that it is not easy for you to trust me after what I have done, but every person changes, and I am sure that you have noticed that change in me. But you still don't trust me – do you know what it feels like, if your own parents don't trust you? – an absolute hell! All I ask of you is to trust me, I will never do what I did before because I know what it is like!

I know you don't want your children to grow up, but we are. Because of everything I have done before, I now have the ability to judge between that which is right and that which is wrong – which is a sign of maturity. I honestly think I am a bit more mature than others my age.

You know how much I hate being treated as a child – and therefore, I would like and appreciate it if you don't treat me as one anymore.

I see the whole situation as follows:
If I had to finish Matric at school, I would have been a 1st year student in reality, just like my sister was, and my brother. The only unfortunate thing, is that I am still living at home (don't take it up wrong I love living at home, just keep on reading) where my sister was in Bloemfontein, where you couldn't see what she was doing. Whether she was going out during the week, not going to class, going out with who knows, you didn't know what she was doing. At least you know where I am going to and with whom, you never had that with her, but yet you didn't mind.

Now – don't you think it is unfair to me, if I don't receive the same adult treatment? When she came home she never had to ask if she could go out, neither did the guys who took her out, yet you trusted her. Just like her, I don't waste your money at college indeed, I am a straight 'A' student. You never knew what she was doing, but with me at least you know. I also have the eye to distinguish right from wrong. I know when to do what, for e.g. I know what is going on at college, and if I want to take off one day, I can judge whether it will do me harm or good.

All I am asking of you, is to please treat me like and adult, trust me and give me the same treatment you give and gave my sister. Please don't get me wrong I am not throwing her in your face, or saying that there is any favouritism, the only thing I am asking of you as my parents and best friends, is to treat me as an adult.

If you have to think about it – at my age Mom got married and was working long before. Dad was working and if I have it correct, living in Brixton. My brother was in the army, doing his own thing. My sister was in Bloemfontein doing her own thing. What is wrong with me?

Please this is really a very serious matter, and I don't want us to argue, or have any disagreements I only think it is fair.

Love you stax

Ange

Ps – I would like to ask you now, I will go to church every night, but my friend is leaving on Friday night, and I want to be seeing her, I know we haven't been friends for long, but she is very special to me and like a sister. She will not be having friends where she is going and therefore, we would like to go out every night to give her a farewell – we won't be going to Discos or anything, we just want to have a good time – on Wednesday I don't have college – it is a fun day. Please start treating me as an adult and trust me – as from today ….

∞

This all goes to a wonderful person called my mother. It might look expensive mom – because it is, but for someone like you, no present big enough or no money could make up for the pleasure you have brought to me in my lie. You once sent me a card saying I am the best friend you have ever had, but mom I don't think you realise how much of a friend you have been to me. You are my bestest and greatest and most wonderful person. Mom I really think you are absolutely groovy – my best.

Love Angelique – what more can I say but that I love you!!

∞

'You are a conniving little bitch'

My Cactus flower incorporated shouted at me whilst standing in the front garden.

The love of my life that I thought to be my ideal man, my husband. I could not find it in me to trust him again. Not only did he cheat on me that day. The continuous visuals of posing for photos. Being blind folded. Having to enact 'unbearable lightness of being'. Having to wear Opium that reminded him of his previous girlfriend. Her photo still hanging above his bed. The fights and arguments that became physical. Photographs of specific models that I reminded him of. Then there was the Airforce. The reasons for him having nightmares. Still holding on to a steel statue of Jesus that he found at a mine-field.

No – all the gifts. The cards. The flowers. Does not make up for the way you treat me behind closed doors. The promises that it won't happen again.

Who am I to you? Am I a vision? Am I a Model in a Photograph? Am I an Actress in a film?

No – I am Angelique. I will not be that image in your head of another woman. After all I cannot trust you anymore. You betrayed me. Then I found out that you never lost contact with her. You gave up your career to sell the course that broke you down. You are not the same person anymore.

Yes – I am wearing your dress that you gave me. I asked you to escort me to the event. You refused to. We are still friends. Just because we broke up, does not mean that we cannot remain friends. You had the opportunity to walk me into the Wanderers Club, me wearing my dress. Hooking into your arm. Be proud of me.

Running up and down like a lunatic. Calling me a conniving bitch.

This is my big night!

!!!! 'Our new Miss College 1991 …. Is …. Angelique Buckingham'!!!!

3 years I dedicated to you, to us! In the hope that things would change. Now sitting alone in the lounge. Going through my prizes. Holding my crown! I Did it!

I am Miss College!!!

I will wear my Crown!!!

26 March 1996

These are thing one does not say to those who mean the most to you. One tends to forget how important it is to utter them. To remind yourself and the people around you what they really mean.

One falls into the trap of thinking that when you are around and when you speak that this defaults to that which you really feel, but is that all? One often would announce to a stranger that enters into your life those words, forgetting that those whom were there before them and those that made a difference before them, will still be there when they're gone, are the people that really need to hear these words.

By uttering those words, the reassurance that you give, means far more than it does to the stranger for the stranger does not understand but the others do.

How difficult can it then be to say I Love you to someone that understands...

Mom – I Love You

∞

Allow me to draw you a picture:

A picture was painted, words were spoken, a story was created in the mind of the archer. The lion walked into her life creating a thought, and idea and painted a picture in her innermost though, with his boisterous, powerful first roar, he drew her attention and captured her mind. The picture – painted in beautiful shades of green. He followed up the story by creating chapter 2 and chapter 3, but how can something end when it's not complete?

A thought, a word, the first steps to the deed was taken now what happens to the fulfilling steps to finish this journey? Does and artist then stop painting when his creation is not complete? Did God stop creating after the 3rd day?

I compared this to the King of the jungle:

He cordons off his humble domain under the greenest tree, close to his fleshly feedings – onto of the greenest, softest grass. Surrounded by lionesses – he flexes to impress, he strides to impress, he projects his mantelpiece to impress. Yet, when a thorn hurts him, he becomes weak, pain he cannot stand, losing a battle he cannot face, yet the lion under all that muscle and main will not hurt another. The softest nature, the most caring features are hidden behind the windows of the soul. In adoration the lionesses follow the King, but for one and one only he lets go of that absolute front and becomes likened unto a kitten once she notes his windows giving freedom to his soul.

Oh lion when will this creation be fulfilled? I do not ask commitment; I do not want to create restrictions. I just ask freedom of the soul.

∞

20/04/1999

Hello this is me I am back

Back because who do I talk to about this?

We have come as far as moving in together, getting divorced, a document / settlement not be discussed – something setup to just live with.

Got married, had the vasectomy reversal, children tolerating me so – now, where are we? After all of this?

A divorce agreement – something that was set up – which has never and could never be discussed, what happens should any mention be made, major fight major argument even physical abuse.

Work – me - I was forced out of my job, which I enjoyed – I excelled, I loved the people, work environment and company. What did working together do to our relationship – fucked it up – we argued, could never talk about the day – could never go to functions together, because all I end up doing is either stand on my own, I am not allowed to know what he was talking about. Or the other option is to follow him around like a lap dog in his shadow. So I had to leave.
Working for another Corporate would destroy us even more, as he would never handle it. Knowing I need to travel or work late or company functions, he is to jealous and possessive of me to allow that.

∞

29/11/1999

The sanity checklist the landscape after one year of marriage:

1 got married

2 forced to leave corporate

3 started the art school

4 fixed the house

5 have to make up my salary

6 child personal school issues

7 fetch child from school

8 child going into puberty

9 have to be a friend to child

10 have to fetch other from school

11 cart other back and forth to friends

12 other child going through puberty

13 be treated like shit by other child

14 keeping peace between the brothers

15 be a friend to other child

16 buy food for the house

17 make supper

18 make school lunch

19 help the children with homework and study

20 ex-wife

21 children's emotional issues

22 wasting money on ex-wife

23 living in a lie

24 taking 3rd place when the children are around

25 husband's operation – vasectomy reversal, testicular biopsy

26 my operation – ovarian cysts

27 more laparoscopies

28 infertility

29 adoption

30 my mother's issues

31 my brother and nephew's issues

32 ordering and supervising house renovations

33 gardener's issues

34 Domestic training

35 art classes

36 building animal farm

37 watching animals die

38 Genghis sickness

39 Goldy's sickness

40 looking after animals

41 student's accident in classroom

42 babysitting ex-wife's new step daughter

43 keeping peace with husband

44 be sexy

45 be a friend

46 be a lover

47 sort out house

48 work on my marriage

49 look good for my man

50 make supper

51 look after my man

52 car issues

53 investing in wrong car

54 car theft

55 new car

56 sort out the papers

57 domestic's trouble

58 contract

59 policy

60 cleaning

61 spastic colon

62 periods painful

63 painful sex

64 bronchitis self

65 bronchitis husband

66 studies

Main categories:

1. Husband – marriage – food – lover – friend – wife – clothes, household, share in monies, peacemaker
2. Mother – children
   Child – friend, taxi, teacher, clothes, food, peacemaker, money pouch, advisor, decorator
   Child – friend, taxi, money pouch, advisor, decorator, punch bag, teacher, clothes, peacemaker
3. Housekeeper – domestic, gardener, house manager, grocery shopper, food shopper, bill payer

4   Art school – build customer base, prepare classes, fetch children, build property, responsibilities of other children, build stock, problem children, creative tots, parties, workshops, art classes
5   Renovate house – paint, design, buy, order, build, supervise
6   Ex-wife – take orders, console children, share life, maintain house, phone calls, hate
7   Study – Montessori, psychology
8   Baby – infertility, adoption, living in a lie
9   Personal – hair, pain (colon, ovaries, period), smell nice, look good
10 Farm – animal feed, animal care, vet
11 Advisor to others – mothers, mom, peacemaker
12 Babysitter

∞

Babe;

I know we can't talk finance or money as this results in a huge argument.

The reasons are as follows, you say I am negative, which is absolute bullshit, because I am actually very positive, but we have now come to a point in the house where as much as I hate it – just like you do – we actually have done everything this house and property of ours that to date, did not require any money.
Now the next steps unfortunately require money to be spent, unless we want to continue living or walking through property where everything is more broken and half done than being complete.
I just would like us to budget…

∞

Chapter 2: - Pappa

Let me return to my fabulous time in Durban with my brothers, it had to be intercepted by having to return home with Pappa. He had never asked me to help him look for an apartment nor spent one minute with me.

As he came to fetch me in my car, to go home, we needed to make a stop!! Seriously, we needed to go past his work he said, but it was an excuse for him to introduce me to 'Jorsie-my-ding', the Sunglasses girl.
I don't want to be introduced to your 'floozy' dad!! But I sucked it up and was so friendly, and acceptingly wonderful, (well I thought it was).
She was not introduced to me as his 'girlfriend', no, she was introduced as his friend that supplied him with Degorans when he had a sniffy nose - really? I ask you, with tears in my navy blue eyes?
Oh oops, it was her birthday, so please wish her a happy birthday!! That was the actual reason for him driving with me to Durban, it was for her birthday!!

Driving back, I asked him:
"Why the hell did you even want to come down to Durban at this time? We never looked for your apartment! I am sooo angry with you right now, I don't want to speak to you! As a matter of fact, I don't want to look at you!"

(In the back of my mind, I am playing down the whole scene of back home, my Mom, my half built house, the lies, the deception…) Why lie to me, you bastard when I am the one that have been with you for so long watching how you are with other women and how my Mom sits day in and day out crying!

Dad wanted to leave mom in 1987 when I was in std 7!
Living in Barkston Drive in Blairgowrie, the house of all truths and parties, parents always saving the worlds of other people.
My mom was a Day Mother (that's what it was called), when you had a Crèche filled with children from near new born till age 3 with a stretch 4year old. She looked after 20 to 30 children per day, from 6 o'clock in the morning babies started crying everywhere till 6 'o'clock at night.
In the mornings you would have to go to school saying goodbye to your Mom in the kitchen where at least 10 kids were sitting on the potties being fed Mealie pap or Pro-nutro for breakfast with parents dropping off more and more babies, nappy bags and bottles.

Dad is in his car ready to go to work, but hell no, he would agitatedly ask

 "Meis waar is my tee"
"ag Liefling ek maak dit gou warem vir jou, en hier is jou lunch"
"Mamma – ons is laat ons moet by die skool wees"
"..Morning, here is my baby"

She did it all my Mom, every morning. Every afternoon after school, we would arrive home to Peanut Butter and Syrup sandwiches for lunch with Tea. She would be there, supporting us at all or most of our sports and cultural extra-mural events. She would ensure that my Dad had his supper when he arrived home, where he just sat and watched TV for the hour before they needed to get ready for church, she would serve him on a tray. She also managed his diary and appointments for his electrical business.

So the church is all about, you need to tithe, according to the Bible. Which meant in real terms, you need to give to the church 10% of your earnings (don't know if that was quite before or after tax, or what you had left after actually living, but be it as it may), this was your financial contribution to maintain the buildings and church grounds. In addition, you also have to give your time, (also don't know if it was 2.4 hrs of 24hour day, or 1,2 hours of your 12-hour wakeful day) but we were raised in this Church. Christian it was with the St James version of the Bible. (also don't know why his version was any better than any other?) (also a little weird when Saints Are Catholic, and the Catholics are also not saints when it gets to all their corruption, in paedophilia and wars and twisting the governments). Bottom line is, that you have to sacrifice something of yourself, in other words you have to give to receive. But hell no – belong to a sect, a body, a club, a church… you need to offer up something.

Pappa was a hard working man. He never stopped working. Even when his electrical business went into liquidation. We arrived home from school one day with most of our furniture gone. The cars all gone. Stereos, Televisions, Microwaves gone. This was replaced by a little blue Mini panel van. Mamma still having the crèche, now having to be Pappa's secretary and administrator.

Still being the Priest of the community. The young sister, whom became my friend, also became Pappa's best friend. She got me the job at the glazing shop that she worked at. I helped with the filing. One day she slipped and fell. Breaking her arm. She had a little daughter, just the two of them living in the apartment opposite where we worked. Pappa offered that I stay with them to help her. As this friendship developed, every morning I would be fetched for school. Having to wait in the car down stairs, while "the Priest" does an early morning prayer with the "sister".

Back home we would be sent to the shops, when Mamma was out shopping for food. My little brother would hide under the window sill, right there where the phone was. Listening to the sweet little conversations that "the Priest" had with the "sister".

I worked with her. Stayed over to look after her. I knew her male friend, he had an American or Canadian accent. He worked across the road at the window tinting company that he co-owned with his brother. I even went to her male friend's home with her one night for a braai. He lived in the house with his brother who was married at the time and had two little children. My friend even taught me to drive her white Stanza.

Not long after eves dropping on the phone calls, my mom stopped me from going to stay and look after my friend.

The arguments started. On the little porch, just outside the front door of our house in Barkston Drive. Mamma's knee operations from years ago had failed. She had to go for more knee operations. For many years, she struggled with her knee. Every time she went for operations, my Ouma used to come stay with us. I had to help with the children in the crèche. Cook Supper, make tea, Iron clothes, help clean the house.

Anyway, that is where I assume I learnt my domestic bliss. It also worked out well for me, because I was asked by many of the parents to baby sit their children. This brought me some extra pocket money. I also started cleaning other people's houses, ironed their clothes and did their cooking for extra pocket money.

Days and nights when Mamma and Pappa argued, they would call me to be their sounding board.

Tell Mamma ….
Mamma, Pappa says …
Tell Pappa …
Pappa, Mamma says …
The words that stuck:
"Liefling, you made love to me last night"
"that was sex, that was not love, I needed to relieve myself"

Yes, they were actually standing right opposite each other, with me still in my school clothes in the middle of the two.

As this all unfolded. We had the big family meeting when my sister returned from University for holiday, my brother from Army pass. All sitting in the lounge. Pappa announced that they are getting divorced. Everyone was shattered. This was also the first time that Mamma was given the news of his decision.

Anyway, they never divorced. They tried again.

The Sister, my friend, still worked with me at the glazing shop. It was difficult to work there and still know what was happening at home.

It was then that I was asked to help out at the Window Tinting company across the road.

∞

'show me your belly'

Klara S my vrou

I often think about what happened to me when I was a little girl visiting the farm (the plot as they called it). I have memories of so many good days when I played in the garden and amongst the life stock, cows, chickens, pigs, dogs. Climbing the many fruit trees and up the stairs of the pump house. I had a strong woman figure in my life, my Gran Marie, that was always alone on the plot. With oupa working on the mines, leaving at 3 am for his shifts and returning for lunch to a hearty meal that Ouma stood in the kitchen preparing for him.

Yet, there were times when I have blocked certain things that I cannot vividly recall, however things that irk me, for what it is worth – the old man with the pipe and the hat with the beard above the chair in the lounge where Oupa used to sit, when he was not under the open garage roof at his table watching the road as people drove by, and he waved to everyone. The fake leather of the pull out chair. I remember the words "show me your belly" that still haunts me to this day. Questions and memories that I cannot place together and cannot phantom other than the uncomfortable feelings. I still despise a Lazy chair.

My uncle going through his identity crisis and sexuality of being gay and not allowed to live this, and taking it out on me "Angelique" chasing me through the house with a belt, me hiding under his bed in fear of being hurt punched and bullied, he was only 12 years my senior yet, I relive that fear on many occasions by feeling claustrophobic and hating cleaning or going under a bed in case I might not come out.

My pet pig being slaughtered – and giving me the fear and hate for eating pig.

I wonder if my Oupa ever found peace in his soul – as on earth he always seek the love and attention of many others instead. Clara he never found again – he seeked this empty hollow in many other vessels – do I hate him for hurting the one and only brilliant Woman in my life that meant so much to me, that have taught me so much – my Ouma? Or do I hate him for my pig, or did he really touch me in places I cannot recall?

As a small child not understanding most of this plane – what on earth happened? What is reality, and what is un-explained memories that don't tie together – that the pieces of the puzzle one cannot explain? Do they fit or don't they fit?

I know I was his favourite and yes we had so much fun, he taught me to smoke, he always had competitions going and challenges amongst the cousins and kids – I was competitive and always won. Every challenge that was set out, was this the reason for me being so competitive now? For not sitting back and waiting for others approval and taking on the world?

Was it him that made me fall in love with Tretchikoff and his story?

Was it him that made me believe that there is only one person in your life that you love and you should never give up on seeking for that 'one true love' – which you will probably meet, but never live with or love but probably never meet?

Was it him that created little pet hates?

Show me your tummy – haunts me ----- why? Was it him or was it the creepy old man that sat on that chair and made me feel uncomfortable? They both had lost a finger … I know who ever it was, sat on that fucking fake leather chair – with the old man with the grey beard and the pipe and the hat – my haunting memory.

However as haunting as it seems – it started my passion for not wanting any of that to happen to any other child!

∞

My little Peachie,

I shall never forget when we came back from Durban when Mamma received the call. 'there was an accident'. Then the investigations and that photograph of your little burnt body lying on the cold steel mortuary table. Only 18 months old. Your little body was cooked from the waist down. Signs of acid burning your little mouth and tongue away. And the whole of a hot poker through your back. I met you when you were a tiny little angel of three weeks old, with your little red cheeks, we named you peachie, as you looked like a little peach.

Yes, your parents got away scot free from doing this to you. But you always remain in my heart. I shall do whatever I can to change the system for no other baby to die like this.

Then you had two little friends that also shared in our home. That little 4-year-old boy and his sister. Being exposed to their mother's life style of drugs and prostitution. The little boy that we had to watch all the time, to make sure he was not playing sex games with other children. The little girl of 2 years with her amputated leg and scars all over her little body, from a drunken mother that got behind the steering wheel.

The other phone call we received late one night, with the towelling nappy that had our landline number on it. He was sitting blocks away from his parent's home with only a dirty, wet nappy in the middle of winter. His parents both high on cocaine, having a party in their fancy double story house. Sometimes he would arrive with beer in his bottle. This after we had managed to build up his little body, as when he first arrived at my Mamma, he was so malnourished he looked like an Ethiopian with a huge head and swollen tummy.

The little friend with this little smile and half paralysed body, as his mom tried to self-abort with a knitting needle. Now having to live his life half paralysed.

The little girl that was dropped off for Crèche on the Thursday, with only the bottles, clothes and nappies packed for the day. Without a word, arriving the next Tuesday, after they had a lovely weekend away in Durban.

But my peachie, I promise that I will make a difference someday, for you and all your little friends.

Love Angelique

∞

'You will be bare foot and pregnant at the age of 18'

These were the words when we sat on Mamma's bed whilst she was recuperating from her many operations. My sister would be the lawyer, the success. I will be the one that will be barefoot and pregnant.

When we walked through the school gates one day when my sister was in grade 12 and I in grade 6, she asked me, how do I be sexy like you. We walked through the gate in Ash street. I helped her to roll up the top of her skirt, to make it shorter, and folded her socks down to her shoes, loosened her top button on her shirt and her tie.

I thought she was the most, amazing girl all the time. She was a top athlete. She was a drum majorette. She was popular. She was a prefect. In my eyes she was the perfect person. I wanted to live to fill her shoes.

Then she went off to University in Bloemfontein. I found letters she wrote me in the box Mamma kept.

She was not around when Pappa decided to have an affair.

She was not around when I was raped.

She was not around when we had to say goodbye to my brother going off to the army.

She was not around when my younger brother got beaten by the teacher, and we had to go to court to stop corporal punishment from schools. (yes, it was my brother's case that brought the court ruling to stop corporal punishment against the Department of Education)

But I was compared to her, being the one that would end up being bare foot and pregnant.

We laughed a lot. We had such fun. We wanted to be Nuns. Then we created our own language called "gabriancha". We used to lie at the Blairgowrie Swimming pool, tanning and reading Afrikaans books, with the covers off. Every time a boy walked past, we spoke "gabriancha" … oh we sounded so international.

In 1990 – I was meant to have been Matriculating in the "normal education system" but I was at College. From a child that used to meet up with her Principle for tea to discuss her future, I moved to College. I excelled, I was a straight 'A' student.

In 1991 – I was nominated as "Head of the Student Council". And crowned "Miss College"

Commencing my career, as I always said: I will start as a secretary and work my way up in a corporate so that I can study child psychology. My measure of success will be the day I own a children's home.

1992 – I was employed at Goodbrand Architects. I learnt about architecture, interior designing, managing a small business… we worked on a retirement village in Scottburgh KZN. Still working on floppy discs. Lotus 123.

1993 – I was employed at Nedcor. I worked for the IT strategic department. (my boss ended up being my husband). I was a secretary for a whole 6 months. Taking minutes of the meeting as Microsoft was just introduced. The whole concept of Server versus workstation was an absolute strange phenomenon. E-mail was extremely strange. Till the day I asked them to allow me the opportunity to explain how it works. Wiping out the white board and showing them how LAN to WAN worked.

I was then promoted to "the Email Female" as I called it. Yes, I was one of the first Microsoft Certified Engineers in South Africa.

Microsoft never had a user manual for email, so I wrote one for the secretaries to work with Microsoft exchange to book their bosses diaries, and trained them. Making fly leads to go through the walls. Working in the first server to workstation testing station and then introducing online printers.

Then I was asked to manage the disaster recovery project for IT. This meant that if the bank's live system goes down, there is a backup to continue running all systems. I knew nothing about this.

Yes, I was one of the first students at Damelin to complete Project management course.

I took on the project with 11 sub projects. We Switched over live!! From our main system to our backup system.

Intranet was built. I was nominated to assist with the security build on that.

Branch rationalisation – to remove many workstations to dot matrix printers to centralised printing – was my concept (claimed by my boss)

Implementation of Information security and incident management data base systems.

Printers and ATMs project management and testing.

Facilitation courses, Microsoft Courses, Dale Carnegie Courses (god I was bad at remembering people's names… still am #justsaying, Dale only taught me to connect a nickname, and not the person's name … hahhahahahhah)

Bronze awards. Gold Awards ... I walked that stage… (such a pity the CEO whilst I was on the stage put his hand down the back of my dress and said I am gorgeous... wtfff)

Yes, I chose my man above my career. I was offered to move to Business. I was offered a position at Unisys. I was offered a position at IBM. I was offered a position at Dimension Data. I was offered a position at Percitel.

I thought to myself: Okay, if you are in such demand, you can always return if the next step doesn't work.

I started 'My Art School' – an art school for children. It was a brilliant concept. I could not stay ahead in the bookings I received for children especially during school holidays.

My school I taught art therapy at was Casa do Sol. What Angel Children, all down syndrome children.

My one student, was a 4-year-old boy with such anger issues, because his Mom was badly physically abused by his dad. The other little girl through her art showed me how her uncle was sodomising her.

I enrolled into UNISA to commence with my studies in Psychology.

Tutoring my eldest step son in home-schooling. Second step son going to school. Both of them dealing with divorce and their friends going through their various issues of their parents going through divorce and issues of new women.

My husband and his colleagues regularly meeting to start a Business.

Me now going through IVF and running Art School, Studying, Home-schooling.

The business is found – thanks to both my brothers being in the film industry.

The Set building company in Cape Town.

My Pappa, is the man to help do the physical work. My brothers will recruit the work. My husband will initialise the finance. I do the administration. The partner will do the accounting. Game – Set - Done…. Everything is set up in My name as I have NOTHING to lose (it's called Anti-nuptial agreement) The Birth of SAPW.

My son is born. Art school and SAPW is running. I can't keep up with Art School and baby and home-schooling and studying. Family comes first.

I stopped the Art School. (later the concept was taken over by my sister, she needed extra income so Arty Tots was born and still running)

My son is now 18 months old. SAPW still operational. Studying at UNISA on the back burner. Home-schooling now moved towards Cambridge.

I started a playgroup for my son. I need an income. Party venue…. SAPW is being built for my husband to move into and generating income for my Pappa and brothers.

What do I need to do to start a playgroup… Aha… Montessori...? I studied Montessori teacher diploma. (also one of the first in south Africa)

For 3 years I had the best playgroup! Managing SAPW remotely from Johannesburg whilst the Workshop was in Cape town. The set building company had many items in commercials and films…

THE RECESSION … THE MOVE…

We needed to review. The set building company became the timber factory. Everything had to move from cape town to Johannesburg.

We are now going to manufacture, skirting, dado rails, decking and flooring.

My step sons are now being trained by my brothers to be art directors and set builders in the film industry.

My baby boy is at pre-primary school. My new baby has just arrived.

I am now enrolled back into UNISA to continue my studies.

I am the administrator, accountant, sales person, Human Resources, designer, Director of this company. I have to start a factory, sales brochure, client list, set up policies, safety regulations, employ, accounting, sell, buy, distribute, stock, staff, quality check, deliver, site manage, install, measure, learn timber, learn learn learn a completely new industry. Thank god for my year at Good Brand architects. I can read plans. Thank god for art ballet and music school for seeing perspective in being creative. Thank god for my mother, I have a vision in seeing the ultimate picture. thank god for Nedcor and project management. Thank god for my Pappa that thought me what a tool and measuring tape is. Thank god for my father in law that taught me accounting.

Then I created a show room, the first of its kind. People don't have vision. So you have to put things in a visual perspective for them. 2D is different to 3D and 4D. yes you can see and hope it fits your needs. But when you are part of the experience, it is not real. People are multi-sensory. See, hear, feel, smell, taste… you will NEVER take that away … they will always seek what is missing…

My show room appeared in magazines... woman and home, conde naste, my works where displayed in print ... before social media was the claim to fame…

In hind sight, I created an up roar in Social Welfare, being interviewed for opening up cans of worms in welfare. Being interviewed by newspapers for being the new chairperson, and not standing for Good Governance in Non-profits.

Changing the way welfare for children and the social structure from already being abused, abandoned and raped, to being prevented from being harmed. It was being preventative, rather than reactive. I know I should've copy written my Intellectual property. But too late she cries. From the flat Statutory intervention when it was too late for that child. I developed the structure of programs, psycho social, statutory and governance. The Social development white paper is based on the blue print. But does it really matter? Does my name have to be attached to this re-structure? No – because the impact to saving children is far greater than my name.

The constitutions that rule Non-Profits are so whimsical that anyone can get away with murder. Hence I instituted the re-write of the Non-profit constitution, and was instrumental as co-author in aligning a 65-page constitution that is aligned with the King IV principles of good governance. So many still say NGO which irks me. But that is another book on its own.

Running the Show room, In the back ground the Factory, being an attentive and active mother to both my two sons. Being a Friend/Step mother and employer to my other two sons. Employer and daughter to my Pappa. Business Partner, sister and baby sitter to my younger brother. Financial guardian, employer and sister to my older brother. Wife, lover, mother to his 4 boys, household manager, friend, business partner to my husband. Employer, accountant, sales person, marketer, strategic planner. Then still maintaining friendships with friends. Making friends and playdates, for my children. Attending all sports and extramural school events. Doing homework, cooking, shopping, managing household.

The phone call again. Angie please help me; my babies are being taken away. Wow, this is when I found out that my son had more brothers. Thank god that through my business I met the mother that also desired children. Then the fight and struggle to assist in the adoption process of saving my sons two brothers. His biological mother. And now I am the proud God mother of two beautiful boys. There was a little baby girl left abandoned, my Barbara had always desired to be a mommy. And now I am a proud mommy of a little baby girl.

Many Non-profits organisations were not being understood by business. Opening the doors for corporates to do a matrix, DG Murray. Women that needed to be recognised within their contribution to welfare work, giving them a footprint to develop themselves Women of Substance. Focus on only girl child, leaving the boy child with no means Boy child program. Disparity in social worker salaries, Non standardisation in the social welfare industry Legislative office. Introduction of Non-profits to business ROCCI. Centralisation of Administration, Writing off assets Nedbank. Media telling the story of good in the community.

Became the chairperson of Child welfare 1 then Child Welfare 2. Founded Child Welfare 3. The latter putting the small town on the map. Chairperson of Provincial child welfare, seating on National child welfare. First qualified Trustee on Pension and provident fund, as well as Monitoring trustee. Forcing restructure of National Child welfare. Turned child welfare 1 from closing down to one of the biggest affiliates. Assisted other welfares with governance. Re-instated Provincial Child welfare. Launched #INHUMANECAPITAL.

Woman of substance award. Rocci Women of the year. ROCCI Community Organisation of the year.

Founded AngelScouts NPO focusing on educating children in fauna, flora and animal welfare and conservation. Studied qualified as PSIRA B Grade Security Officer.

Continued studies in Social Work. Qualified as Auxiliary Social worker and currently 4th year in Social Work Degree. This is a little delayed due to COVID 19 and Lockdown, as the last 2 modules are practical interactive modules.

Qualified as Mediator in Family, Divorce and Restorative Justice. Oh hella no, when I found out how much it would cost to get divorced. I researched and found out how much it would cost to qualify. So instead of paying someone else to do the paperwork. I signed up, studied and divorced myself. 2 flies with one swat.

Oh and then at the same time, seeing I wanted to know how life would turn out. As we always look for answers and predictions. I studied astrology and qualified in astrology course.

COVID 19 and lockdown introduced a new dynamic of how to meditate, do yoga and exercise with so many children around. As my farm is now filled with children from varying ages. So I enrolled in a yoga instructors course. And am now qualified as a yoga for kid's instructor.

Developing yourself is endless. There is an infinity of wealth in knowledge and understanding.

The day I become over qualified. Oh blessed be that day.

As now, I am writing my book. And while I am doing so, I am learning and researching how to either self-publish, or be published by a media house, or publisher.

2012 January 25

The reason for getting involved with the welfare

I have prayed and asked for many years of being uninvolved and feeling unbalanced. Initially when I got involved, what was it that attracted me?

I saw for the first time from a different perspective, or perhaps I thought I saw what it is from a social worker perspective to being doing what they do. The version from their side. The message came across that they were hard done by, that they are working with so many children. Then speaking with so many people they all said they would like to get involved in some way, but how and where, where do they start? Well you have many ways of getting involved with changing those lives of many people

- Child that have a future
- Teenagers with a broken past – yet a future – drug rehabilitation, teen age pregnancies, juvenile delinquents, sponsorship etc.
- Middle-age – parents, single parents, drug addicts, alcoholics
- Old-age – with broken pasts and families
- Disabled – physically and mentally
- Mental health
- Education

And what attracted me was the impact that child welfare social workers have on babies, toddlers, children, pre-teens, teenagers

In reality if you do have a caseload of 150 files per 1 social worker, the recipe is keeping that 1 social worker happy, I can make a difference to 150 children's lives. The bottom-line to me was, do I make a non-emotional, non-financial, non-personal committed decision and involvement – that difference that does not affect my personal household, family and children- directly i.e. through adoption and foster care I bring that into my house.
Children is ultimately where my heart and passion lies, why?
A) they are innocent tiny beings which can either be influenced negatively or positively.
B) they have all the right to happiness, love and affection.

Although I have been molested somewhere, somehow by someone when I was a toddler, (it does not really affect me that much, but I have certain flashbacks or dislikes that have a bad taste).
What I choose to remember is my Mom, my Dad, My Ouma and Oupa, goddamn it FAMILY! I treasure that!!

I grew up in a family, love, food, care, protection, bed, house, clothes, school, education!! How many children can say that?
How many adults my age 39 can say that in this world?

Then you have the experience of being raped, that is still a . . .
You made semi-peace with your mother through writing, but never really in person!

You still believe your mother is too emotionally naïve to handle this.

Your father! Goddamn you – hate for not protecting you, not being there for you!
For not picking up the signs as a man!
For not looking out for his small Angel as you thought you were! You blame him!

YES, Fuck! I blame him because he was there, he was friends with those people, he
fucken dropped you off and picked you up and never saw anything wrong!!
He was everyone's advisor and your protector that even though you looked up at him
as your fucken idol, your perfect fucken man – he NEVER picked up this shit…
instead he blamed you!
He fucken blamed you!! Still you saw your dad as the wonder man!!
You still asked him for forgiveness!!!

This Ange… is not about Fucken JD – it's about why you chose to do what you do

---

I was committed to ensure that taking a staff count of 10 happy – the impact would
as a result make difference to 1500 children's lives….

What then happened was going into further investigation and close to the core, I
realised that I was sucked in to believing I was making a difference to 1500
children's lives – instead I was suckered into changing 1 person's life!
And that makes me very angry! As yet again I am being taken for an emotional ride!
Ange being emotionally raped!

The shit part is that this time I can! And will! stand up for myself and what I believe
in!

There are many kids – abandoned, sodomised, orphaned etc.! I will make it my
mission to help them! and not 1 Person!

The main reason why I am involved with Child Welfare:

- Being a parent, a mother that cannot naturally conceive
- Being and adoptive parent, going through the system
- Being fucken raped
- Being a child of divorce
- Being exposed to children in welfare
- Being interested in helping welfare children
- Being a mother of a biological child
- Being a mother of step children

The main thing – being in the system!

- System starting when I was little, being exposed to BAD parenting and on a
  secondary basis.
- Making a real difference !! damn it, kids need adult, because adults are the
  reason they are alive!
- They need adults to help them and adults need children to make them feel
  alive!
- Hand in hand we love it
- I want to be there to change the mind-set of social workers, as why do you
  become a social worker?

- Out of all the professions, why social work?
- What personal constraints do you have to perform your job as social worker?
- How do you feel about saving a child during working hours?
- What would you say if a police officer called you at 1:00 am? What would your reaction be?
- Howe would you feel about being on 24hour call?

I have been involved since I was a child. I love it! I love the challenge! I love what I am doing!

I have been hands on with social welfare, child related welfare whilst I am studying.
a) from a personal involvement as far as my own home, being the recipient of the system

b) coming from a corporate mind-set where I can provide my knowledge and input

c) from a distance I can see the change in the world without direct impact on my own children.

I need to balance it though, as I cannot allow it to affect my own biological children and their needs. I believe as I have grown to love my work, that my children will someday participate in causes out of their own. My passion is helping others, and through my passion and commitment I learn to help my own needs! I love what I am doing, I love being in the position that I am able to make that difference, the challenge of making a difference larger that myself and larger than life!

∞

I have come thus far to wonder why I am still doing this – my conviction of being involved has fallen away!
I keep trying to convince myself it is for the greater good, but every day it eats away at the core – humanity is no one's game!
What happened to people? What happened to everyone doing good for others? I know I have to be strong to make a difference and this too shall pass.
But walking into those offices to just find so much antagonistic behaviour!

Why do you become a social worker?
what drove you to choosing this career path?
going back – what changed you into a distrusting, antagonistic human being?
I want you to take out all that anger that you have and all the questions that you have – is it all e? or have you had that underlying anger and frustration before I arrived?

I tell you what I saw, that touched me and the reason why I got involved:
- I saw 13 woman working in a very unhappy environment
- the offices were in a state
- so cold and uninviting such and unpleasant environment
- you work in horrid conditions with a terrible client base
- how can I make a difference

Let start by making your workplace something to be proud of. As most of your day is spent there saving children's lives

The more I spend time with everyone, the more I realised that it was not only the walls that were damaged, but so was the soul and heart of the people that work

there. Being battered no only by their clients, but also by their superiors.
The culture was shocking, a culture of feeling unsupported, being cursed and shouted at, not feeling good enough and resulting in entitlement. That saddened me. So abuse from every angle – unfair treatment! Where do I start? How do I start? The only answer I could think of, is to start that the basics, to make sure that everyone is protected. To ensure that true transparency and compliance to all – HR/IR, health and safety, sponsorship, support, financial sustainability, insurance. Empowerment through training and knowledge. Recognition, Teamwork, Knowledge transfer, counselling and 360 support.

∞

Dear Social Worker

Your hurt form year of abuse run so deep that your trust in human kindness to you became non-existent. You no longer see the good in people, the good intentions that people still have!
Every person that enters into your life must have an agenda. An agenda to do you harm in some way or another and that saddens me to such a degree that I wonder where to start to make you realise that you are worthy of the good that life has to offer – the good that still exists in the world.
It is understandable that you would in a world that all you see, hear and experience is the evil of humanity.

"how can anyone do that to a little innocent child?"
"How can the world, the rich, the poor turn their backs on anyone, least or most of all a tiny kindred spirit."

So when someone walks into your life that wants to make you realise that you are worth more than a million stars, more that all the diamonds and gold in the world, for what you do for those hundreds and thousands of little being's day in and day out, when they cannot fend for themselves.
To thank you, to love and protect you to fend for you without an agenda, other than to stand up for you for what you do and who you are.
I pray that you stop seeing me as the enemy, yet I want you to know and to realise, start believing that you are worth every minute in my life that I spend here, to try make your world a better place.

You are the start, the beginning of my fight for all the special people like you as what you do for the children is worth more than life itself and its time that everyone realises that! But first I want you to believe you are worth it!

Because you are!

Love Angelique

26 July 2013

∞

2013

R15202.58 cents is what I own right now

My total nett worth after 40 years. I invested my time my hard work and my savings into a company which I believed in that would work for the sake and future of my children.

I suffered the turn of the economy, as many other companies have at this time. When it happened I was open and honest with all my creditors and believed in the process. These court proceedings, have proved to not be a fair and just process. As I stand before the court again, being undignified and reminded of my failures and (for what it's worth) my belief that:

a) I will make it work to provide a future for my children
b) that there is true justice and humanity that will prevail.

How wrong was I – the claimant with whom we had the best relationship with – reciprocal, is now the one that has me before the court and in public humiliation. For failures I did not expect, but was indeed the recipient of the injustices that are dealt by others that you believed in.

I have learnt through this process, not only, to not ever trust in business – but how it scares me, to have to turn to my children and teach them to follow their dreams but trust no one.

Turn to them and say be nice to the person, but don't ever trust him! – it's insane – its inhumane.

I still think that I am not a victim, yet a survivor, for many people took their lives, however looking at my children, yes I am a survivor of many wrongs – but those wrongs opened my eyes to see, and believe in myself.
To reach out and build others, to not haphazardly enter into a venture without understanding that it might go wrong. If so, what do you have to back you up? Are you strong enough to handle it?

The answer is no, you are never strong enough to handle it, until you have actually experience it. As Ange, the eternal optimist that should never put you off from trying!

The bottom line – I am not bringing my family into this - Dear Magistrate.
As a matter of fact I brought in my support, as my family is my support! And I thank you for that, as I need to have my support with me – that is my Mom!

That is how I am seeing it! Her and I have been through far too much shit for her not to be by my side, when I have to face the most difficult thing in my life right now. So – fuck you all – my Mom is by my side! As I have been by hers all these years! Middle finger right there!!

I am reliving it all – not paying people – because of economic turn, not paying people – because of the government – I love my people – I do!

What do you think it feels like to have invested R2mil of your savings in a company, your time, your everything, to lose it all in 1 day? To walk into a lawyer's office to just by 1 scribble sign it all away. To go through the process. Now being stood in front of 1 person, making a call on your life, and another making you feel like a criminal. Two complete strangers that have never been through the run and the dregs of any of what we have shared. Now having to stand here. I stand still facing the motion, whilst he backs behind a legal team I don't have! And can't afford been through that and will never put people through that siss on many levels!

And Ange! Why would you want to do that when it gets to kids?? Damnit I am now thinking twice!

Please God, the Angels and the Universe let this all please go away – may tomorrow be the end of this journey of the past. That we may move forward in the understanding that the battle which I am about to engage in is not a battle of person, but something that I will bring change and that will shed more light on Reality!
May tomorrow please not be about money or materials goods but indeed be about peace of mind!
I am ready to close the deal! Because I understand that people that put their lives into a passion, as much as I do, does not necessarily see it in the light that I do – but they see it in the light of just another hour! Just another cent.
We won't change humanity, but we will chip away at the rock – everything that is not a horse! What a beautiful analogy!

I have a children's home, as a matter of fact, I have a few children's homes. They all have a passion they all work together to make as one, and that is what I am not seeing, my dream has become a reality! Oh my! You will not take that passion away from me NO!

My Mother is here with me today, and I thank the court, as she is the person who taught me through my life! Never give up! Never give up! I look at her and I think to myself – Mamma you fought those nasty evils – yet you are strong! You are here! And you came out tops!

So in the end – does the ring make you? The car you drive? The house you live in? No- Ange you always said – "I will have the children's home that I will not have to maintain myself – that will be my measure of success" – you know what? You have many children's homes! That you are not maintaining – but you have to strive to maintain and fight for those children's rights and lives.
It is a job for them – a passion for us!

(I am so sorry, they are bringing a 9-month baby – and I have to go for lunch – you handle it …)

(April for registration as auxiliary worker)

(Substantial claim – 2005 new credit act, 2007 economic recession – R330k)

You know, through the business knowledge gained, through what you are putting me through right now, you have given me the opportunity to save many children's organisations! Shaun and Nick! I thank you! Because in hind sight, I would not have understood or have researched as much as I have done in this past while. This process in what I am facing, in my future it is just another learning curve! 'With every door closing there is another one opening' = a learning curve

Monday exam afternoon!

This has been my learning curve! And I am truly embracing it and loving it!!

∞

The Art of giving and the many angles if have been involved in giving!

The anger circums me! When I have been involved with the many forms of caring and giving. When at first you come to the oint of knowing and feeling the pain and anguish of those that suffer from some form of emotional deformity created by

a) The parent and be the self. Ehen in the beginning you have as the only frame of reference – the parent.
b) You read, research and learn. Start think and believing these is an external force that predicts our lives, our being. Be it alien, be it God, Christ, Allah, the Universe.
c) Be it personality predicted by the star signs.

We read books, we listen to stories. We actually hold on to every other bielief, hoping that someone else knows better than we do. But the bottom line is, Who really knows, other than actually we, ourselfves. We creat our own world's based on our own beliefs. As we continue our journey, albeit different, albeit the same. We all look for similarities somewhere along the line. As we meet many different species in the search for our own truth and belonging.

Whether we relate to the stars, or the moon. The animals or the human. Ther is still an inate passion and feeling of belonging and being part of something.

Taking myself as example. Oi!! I love life and love to live. However, I love to give. I love making everyone around me happy, special and giving them a sense of belonging. That is what I feed from. That is my soul food. I know not how to say thank you when things are done for me, but I know how to give. Be it my knowledke, advice, food, energy. My physical earthly riches, my kiss, tough, hug. My thanks come from seeing other's flourish, their smiles and happiness. My thanks is from them saying – thank you.

So when I receive something, as I have been overwhelmed with these past few weeks, I am already think of means and ways in which I need to return the gratitude to make others feel special. I hate the attention, because goddamnit, I need to do things for others, and not the other way around.

Now I am nervous... NO... STOP... I am trying to say to myself all the time, as I need to not be nervous right now, as I am receiving for a change! I am totally out of my comfort zone right now, I have you know.

So, yap, a new strage, a new phase! I am not done with fighting the battle. Noe done with my struggle where a statement needs to be made. I am sitting with my head in my hands, thinking… What is the statement you should make Ange?

Is it – "stop this thinking that men think they are superior?"
Is it – "stop this woman think they are submissive?"
Is it – "children shout out?"

CHILDREN SHOUT OUT

We are to start a march – Children for Children's Rights.
Children marching for better education.
Children marching against drug and acohol abuse.
Children marching for dignity.

That is my Mission! A National Campaign!
I Deserve Respect Education Love
12 December 2013

∞

16 July 2015

Ever felt that there is an imbalance in your life? That you need to not only focus on your material world and want to give back in some unique way that will make a difference? Give you that soul balance?

When I became a business owner in 2002, owner of a Timber Factory and Interior / Exterior finishes business in the Northern Suburbs of Johannesburg. Being married and having two step sons and a biological son of my own and then adopted a little baby boy, life had become so busy juggling time between my 2 businesses, my family and home life, that the spiritual, charitable side of my life was put on the back burner. The more successful my businesses became and the older my children grew, I felt an imbalance. There I was doing well, looking after me and my family, staff and clients, it was as though there was something missing … a void that needs to be filled … what happened to the soul food, the giving back, the charitable side of me?

Since I can remember, I have always been involved with the lives and caring for little babies and children. The day I received my driver's licence, I drove to find the nearest children's home, it was a home in the South of Johannesburg, where I befriended 5 little boys, whom I visited on weekends and took them out for the day to treat and spoil them.

I prayed, meditated and requested the universe to place the right opportunity on my path, where I can make a difference. A difference to not just one, but many. As I am now older and felt that I have the maturity, the knowledge and the life experience to make an impact far greater. I can transfer my knowledge and experience to uplift and assist on a bigger scale, and also in turn learn from my experience of giving.

Then ….

One morning walking down my driveway - I received a phone call to assist with saving the lives of two little boys, 3 months old and 2 years old at the time, who was reported to the welfare offices. I remember it so clearly in 2011 when my relationship with welfare commenced …. My prayers had been answered.

When I walked into this building, being introduced with the behind the scenes network. For the first time in my life I was introduced to the Social Workers involved with the process which not many people understand, the people behind the scenes who save the lives of so many vulnerable, abused and abandoned children. People working with such selfless passion in an environment that was so dark, so poor, with broken chairs, limited technology, broken vehicles, tripping over loose floor boards. And here I am upgrading the homes of the rich and affluent. Walking with a book filled with contacts in the interior and building industry. With contacts in the IT field. How can I turn my back on this?

My relationship started with each and every individual that dedicated their every second of their lives to save children.

Taking the time to listen to each person's needs and requirements that will make a difference in their lives in the work environment, to brighten up their days when they are faced with the sadness this world introduces to the many vulnerable children's lives. I learnt through listening and asking questions, the difference between a social worker and an auxiliary social worker. The process involved behind the scenes when a baby, a toddler, a child, a teenager is being removed from situations that pose a threat to their lives that they are found in need of care and protection. I listened to the process required on how to make the lives of the social worker/auxiliary workers easier, and the work environment flow. To enable them to focus on their work and not to balance on a broken chair or use their own salary (the little that they get) to pay for paper to print an urgent report to submit to court to save a child's life. I learnt what heartfelt passion for your cause really means. I listened to the harsh circumstances they have to enter, the life threatening environments they have to face, for the sake of saving a child. Through listening, and asking questions I learnt.

Then the question to myself – "Angelique, how do you make a difference? How do you take this knowledge and turn it into action?"

Hello little black book! Through listening and questioning, I could take this new knowledge I have just gained and seen with my own eyes, combine that with which I have learnt in my business and the contacts I have made and start by changing the work environment, redecorate the offices and implement technology to assist with the work flow.

This is how a long lasting relationship started, through listening, and taking heed, taking my past skills, knowledge and experience and developing a new strategy to help make a difference and change the lives of compassionate people to improve their work environment and in turn make a difference to the lives of the many children that they save.

On average the working person spends 8 hours a day, 22 days per month, 11 months per year in their work place. If you are faced daily with the devastation of this world and you still have to work in a dysfunctional office environment, how can you be effective?

Every Social worker has an average case load of 90 + ongoing cases, excluding short term cases and emergencies. A case refers to a family, which could consist of 1 to 6 children.

A new world opened to me. I became so passionate through understanding this new world, I gave up my carnal, materialistic world and dedicating my life to advocating for Social Workers and Auxiliary Social Workers and Children.

How amazing it is to establish relationships with the new, stepping out of your comfort zone and through listening to others, how much you learn. So much so that it could change the complete course of your life and fill your heart with passion. Such passion that you learn more about yourself, your abilities, which you take for granted in your comfort zone.

I have now formed such a bond with every individual worker, that we exchange 8 second hugs, they trust me with their life stories. Not only did I change others people's lives through listening, but my life, my outlook on the future of the country and the people of this country, has changed, through listening, and turning it into action with nothing other than through my knowledge and contacts.

I have found the balance, I prayed for … My business is now Welfare a Non-Profit Organisation which is being run and managed like a business just not for financial profit, but for the profit of saving little vulnerable lives.

Never stop listening as you might just find the answers in someone else's words…

∞

21 December 2016

When you ask the Universe and the Angels to assist in direction of your passions, to open up all the doors and the energies to come together – death happens to feed the living and through that a new world opens an epiphany, the answer to aligning everything to give you the answers!

- The governance lady
- Conservation education
- Conservation mediation
- Prevention through education and technology
- Aligning your taxes to give back to your passion
- Educating social workers in community development and education in conservation

- Using abandoned and abused K9 and training them in prevention and servicing – in turn – giving back and K9 have functions as humans do and wild does
- Existing organisations joining forces in conservation – rehabilitations and giving purpose
- Reasons for children abandon drugs and substance abuse and crime – lack of love, lack of belonging
- Rehabilitation – restorative justice takin the fallen and abused in given them new meaning to life a belonging
- Restoring broken – giving new purpose
- Expressive arts to raise awareness and education
- Making you tax work for you
- Bringing government to NPOs
- Conservation on the farm
- Snails for profit
- Training – figasa, tracking, bush craft
- Organic farming

(for my heritage – wrong angle – find new angle)

∞

Now for the journey ahead.

I have started a few projects, and it is time to put them into action.
To ensure that the seeds I have planted grow and develop to the extent that more lives are saved and impacted. That all the knowledge I have gained, everything I have seen and learnt now on comes together.
This be transferred for the sake of the future of many more to come! I am ready to accept the challenges that I need in my life to learn that which I have overlooked.

- Teach me what I have not learnt
- Give me the experience I have not lived
- Show me the paths I have not trodden
- Allow me to travel the journey that my future holds

'You lay before me – like and open book with riddles and rhymes with colours so bright
what do you hold in store for me
I am excited to open those doors
to take the paths
to turn the stones
to find you as you hide those gems I need to seek
to share with the world around me
My journey to date has been Soul fulfilling
with no negative karma
no lesson unlearnt
I look forward to what you have in store for me
my future journey'

```
43     1972 12 12   2016
7      0   3  3     9        4
44                  2017
8           6       10       6

∞
```

Yes, I have stepped down as chairperson of one singular APU as I believe I have laid the foundations of being a non-profit and wish them all the best in the future endeavours. The purpose for this was again reinforced that good governance – regardless of what you do is key to survival of all companies – regardless of being a cc, pty, trust, NPO

This all being led by my initial passion in investing in children, education for the future of this planet, its people, fauna and flora, wild animals and pets, environment, if we wish to exist we need to join forces and unite!

What is it with EGOs that forget what we are here for? Then Maslow creeps in with the simple "hierarchy of needs"

The "circle" "eat, pray, love" "bartering"

We plant seeds, to sell, to eat, to plant seeds again

"The mirror dance – that's a recovery exercise"

"My one-year visual- versary – Max and Marc– brilliant – tinder – stunning"

"in between we will establish work to make it work we will cross-pollinate #unitethefight – I need someone with security of their own to do this"

"Born with your penis as we are born with vaginas – get over it"
"a man has a heart – get over it"
"cry for fuck sakes cry"
"men are just as damaged as women"
"hence the whole ego thing"

∞

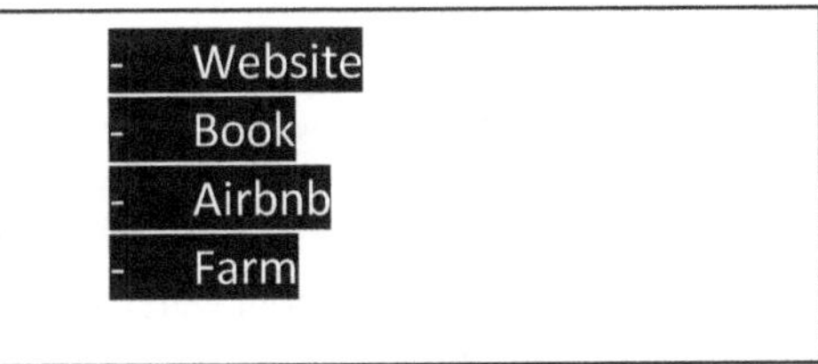

∞

Good day,
>
> I would herewith like to officially inform you:
>
> On 6 April 2017
> Sizwe sechaba principal, cooks, practitioner and cleaners and gardener
> ViTapson principal, teachers and gardener Dorothy Barber driver
> Childwelfare 2 x auxiliary social workers
>
> Stormed into the boardroom where we were interviewing for Chief Social
> workers
>
> They attacked myself as chairperson, Moira as vice-chair and Nastasja
> as board member. Intimidated the social workers that came for
> interviews and chased them off site. Forced Nastasja and Moira was
> physically pushed out of the gate.
>
> Sizwe sechaba principal pushed me and scratched me, forced me to get
> into my car. The teachers, principals, driver, gardener, cooks and 2 x
> auxiliary workers started smashing against my windows and started shaking my car.
> Screaming all sorts of false accusations and racist remarks.
> Sizwe principal screamed all remarks to the social workers who did not
> participate in the protest of intimidation.
>
> They locked the gate and refused to let me leave the premises,
> shouting, screaming, shaking and beating my car and windows.
> I was forced to call the police to come assist as they where
> threatening me and kept me in lock down.
>
> When the police arrived they at first would not let the police into
> the premises, but eventually gave police access.
>
> They demanded financial files and cheque books to be handed over. All
> files with financial history is in the office. When police arrived
> they allowed Moira back in whom joined the protest and she also
> condoned all false accusations and comments of racism towards me.
> False Accusations made of lying and stealing.
>
> I was falsely accused by a Sizwe practitioner for calling her a
> "kaffir meit"
>
> The police assisted me to show them the files in the office.
> Moira and 2 x auxiliary social workers kept shouting at me in front of
> police officer and falsely accused me of lying.
>
> I was forced to call the accountant to request the last year to date
> financial documentation and cheque books. The accountant delivered the
> above, which was handed over to Sizwe sechaba and ViTapson principals,
> auxiliary social worker, vice-chair and Board member.
>
> With police assistance I was escorted off the promises and out of Kagiso.

>
> This all happened during school hours.
>
> My concern:
> The traumatic experience to the children at Sizwe sechaba who was
> exposed to this Members of public, volunteers, other staff members,
> who were exposed to this Fellow board member exposed to this
> Vi-tapson children that where left unattended Acting chief social
> worker who is highly pregnant
>
> I as chairperson am therefore tending my resignation in fear for my
> life, as I was told that I am never to place my feet in Kagiso.
>
> The accountant's life is also threatened.
>
> The board members left on the board:
> Mummy
> Shadi
> Thsidiso
>
> The organisation is currently unconstitutional as there is not a
> minimum of
> 6 members
>
> Accountant function no longer performed
>
> It is with great sadness that I need to write this report.
>
> But as volunteer, I have to put the safety of my life first and have
> been severely traumatized by the situation.
>
> I wish you all the best in assisting the organisation for the sake of
> the children.

∞

PRIORITIES – ANGELIQUE

Future income:
Project community studies to form framework for #unitethefight
Donor application
Mediation – costing, outline, brochure

Boards:
Welfare4, 1, 2
Conservation

Studies:
Social work

NLP
Astrology

Personal:
Adoption
Finance budget
house

SAAM – mediation practices
Magaliesburg - Community development
Education and Training conservation
NPO Governance consultancy

∞

13 April 2019

I am at a new position in my place, where a lesson has been learnt again, to not allow anyone in your personal space.
That people are manipulative and hurt without feeling, care or emotions. There are various aspects to being in the epithetical realm, where you believe in that which you do and open yourself up to vulnerability.
Remain at arm's length with people. Remain at distance with those that see you as a commodity.
Yes, you do open up and allow and give humans the benefit of the doubt.

The moment you feel uncomfortable – step back and say no! Say NO to when that gut speaks, and there is doubt. You have doubt – you start asking questions, move away with immediate effect, and don't allow any further abuse and harm to the soul – walk away as it is not worth the hurt, the damage, the pain and disappointment, as you cannot and need not understand the psyche of another whom continue in life abusing others.

The question was asked during a meeting about your cause – which celebrity supports your cause – wow! It made me think and realise how fickle people are – would your heart only go with a true belief or cause for the sake of posing with fame? It amazes me just how this could be real?

Yes, you have a social responsibility – your responsibility lies with what makes you feel alive! When you walk out there and people are ignorant or are they are avoidant. Let's avoid the topic rather than having to face the possibility of thinking – this could happen to me.

Many adults today are survivors of crimes committed to them as children or even as adults – the re-occurring pattern that they face. Even in their current lives, behaviours and relationships. Could it be that the base of allowing manipulation and such abuse is that of being raised in a religion that subconsciously has brainwashed you in … I actually don't know...

No, is it that which you had grown up yearning for recognition for understanding…

No Angelique – this is what he has done

Given you self-doubt – questioning your integrity, your knowledge – your abilities, your intelligence… bloody toxic human!

Thank god the energy was short lived in the bigger scheme of things – but still – regardless of – made you question yourself!

Side tracking you from what it is that you have set out and prioritise! Regroup! Re-assess! Re-align!

So in the greater scheme of things – what has actually happened? Look at it! You have actually now aligned with the missing link to the bigger picture!

Triangle – 3s – band + application + missing children

Collaboration – create your own IP

Take the positive out of this negative situation

TM #inhumanecaptial + #MCSA + #SASOS

Child Welfare organisation + Corporate + Collaborating + missing children + schools

Fitness + security + politics + corporates + clocking systems

Sex + Drugs

Let people make money through protecting their own!

Part of the presentation will be creation of awareness – curbing the sex and drugs and slavery

Speak to:

Children's Act
sexual offences Act
Substance abuse
Parenting responsibility
social media, cell phone distribution, sales
educating Police force
anti-rape

To DO List:
how to register this?
Already registered NPO? – AngelScouts?

- Apple/Android Button
- Website
- Presentations
- Meet with MCSA
- IP Registration
- Contracts with #CWSAICETAGS #SASOS #MCSA
- Finalise the ice tags colours and styles
- Phases of roll out and upgrades
- 3rd party sales contracts
- Link all the education and training
- Link all the stakeholders in communities

Re-assessment! Re-alignment! – you can do it all Angelique!

You are feeling overwhelmed right now! STOP FIGHTING! Focus on what you are doing right now!

- Group work and community development
- Community is currently assisting you to write the business case and proposal for #INHUMANECAPITAL – so focus on that
- Research is the other that is working hand in hand with what you are doing
- Look at the diplomas and degrees you require for that
- You are not a caseworker
- CSI management, community work, fundraising, sales, Npo consultant, NPO Governance!!!

∞

The balancing Act:

2004 – things I have to do:

1 write my book

2 start tiling business

3 assist my husband in starting his business – phone all architects, developers, supply chain stores, interior decorators, interior designers

4 help my children reach their full potential in life

5 charity business – R10 p/p and functions

How to get started:

1 sort out current office: -

Filing, dissolving current business, look for premises, contact all potential customers, do more research to understand product

2 assist my child in his current crisis situation

3 clamber club for my child

∞

01/02/2012

You know I wrote him a letter hoping and believing it was going to make him understand?
Yet he doesn't!
I so hoped that the 12-year gap in age – good Lord – would have closed by now – oh my word it hasn't!
The response he gave me on a neutrally, non-accusatory, fabulous point, where I was extremely careful in not doing the direct 'he says, she says' bit – was so wrong in the end!!

In his eyes! When he read the letter! I was attacked the same night!

Are we now in some movie? As I am writing this, I am thinking, OMG, there is another side to this story!
But friggen hell I actually don't want to hear his story out right now!!
For fuck sakes my story is on my own fucking sleeve! Kids, study! Welfare!

He feels pressured somehow… WTF? I know him, he doesn't live his shit on his

sleeve but he feels fucked – why – he prefers not to share with me and quite frankly I prefer not to fucking participate!
 Why, because before when I did he got soo fucked off, he hates it!

Anyhoo my bottom line is – so many people have been done in somewhere.
Somehow along the line, their first premise in life is to be suspicious – why?
The mother figure – why?
It is scary!! Goddamn!! I am a mother, I am a woman, I am a wife!

Without the womb – no one can be!
So what is with woman and inferiority? What is it?

Woman, Mother, Wife there is no future, if it is not for us!!

Why do we choose to be inferior?
Why do we choose to be abused?
Why do we choose to …
(sorry that was quite funny cause I was being strong and pertinently a women's libber and had no final say)?

∞

I had a lovely day!
Do you know, or realise that my husband took me on again on his baby's birthday! I think we did well though…
My child wants a weekend away with his friends...

∞

15 June 2012

Ange is trying to make sure that we have a family unit continuously.
However – he is in 'How to break Ange down' mode!
So whatever Ange says – he breaks down!

Ange want to instate every 3rd weekend of the month as family weekend; either braai or whatever –
He goes off – finding every possible excuse, how can we not have this. Outright saying "Ange will fuck it up" – a family braai with all the children and family….

According to him – Ange will destroy it somehow…

∞

Aww Mammie my little Angel pie – he was so worried, that I was just to drop him off at an unknown place today! Not knowing how to tell me!

'Mom – don't just leave me here', he tried to be very tough to tell me that he doesn't like Debbie's car – and they don't stop talking…. and Dillan….
Shame he just didn't know how to say – 'Mom don't let me go to the party alone.'

Those little tears that just welled up in his eyes!
Shame – he wants to portray himself as such a strong tough persona, yet he is so little and vulnerable!

Its soo difficult to break through that barrier! The protective wall he has built!

It was a difficult and hectic week all round as we had a birth of my friend's baby, we had to look after Chris for the week!
His best friend went into hospital with appendicitis.
I was not necessarily emotionally stable and semi-absent!
Holy macaroni – what a week!

Therefore, tomorrow it is – projects!
Around the house projects to be attended to together – playing and being one again!
That is tomorrow – without any interference please God!
Just normality! No school activities – no work activities – no welfare activities just home!!

Mommy I don't like it when you don't fetch me!
My 12-year-old and 8-year-old don't like it when Mom is not at home!
My 52-year-old does not like it when Mom is not at home!

But Mom as a semi-thinking human being, can't just sit at home because she will go mad without mental stimulation.

∞

Just quickly want to write down this concept:

My two sons sleep in my bed, 1 is 5 years old the other is 9 years old. Both are emotionally not ready to sleep on their own in their own room and bed. Every adult keep telling me that I am doing an injustice to these little beings by not allowing them to stand on their own two feet. I feel this is absolute nonsense:

a) I have just read the book "Raising Boys" written by Steve Biddulph, written by a man, that explains how insecure a boy is, especially in their formative years. How important the arms of a Mother are?

b) I remember as a child how it felt waking in the middle of the night from nightmares. I was so scared, so afraid to get out of bed because those monsters are under your bed, and they will grab your feet as you get up, the crocodiles that where on the floor that will devour you. What made it worse is that as a little child, I could see the dead. Those ghosts or spirits would sometimes hold me down in my bed. My Great Grandmother used to stand at the end of my bed, holding out her hand saying "come with me, I am here to fetch you" (she always appeared to me just before something bad will happen)

You now have to sleep in your own bed as insecure, uncertain child with your Mother telling you: 'My child I am always there for you to protect you', but in the night when it is dark and that alone so much bigger than you. You now have to find comfort and protection in a doll, a blanket, a teddy bear, and in most cases a God that you have never seen or touched, a statue or a cross? This whilst your Mother and Father that are adults, are sharing a bed, and cannot sleep without that other body next to them, giving them security?

How does that work? As a child I must sleep on my own, yet, two adults must sleep together?

How so, I believe they call it sex, but from my child's eye, it sounds and looks like mom is getting hurt, because Mom is screaming and moaning when Dad, that I am quite afraid of because he is so much bigger and stronger than Mom is lying on top of her. When I want to come check if Mom is okay, I get shouted at – "Get Out!", or they just get a fright and go on as if I am not even there? I am so worried about Mom, because sometimes Mom and Dad shout at each other. Mom throws objects at Dad or anything she can lay her hands on. Dad sometime hits Mom or grabs her around the throat, screaming and cursing, and now they carry on like this in their bedroom? - Alone in the dark, I have to gather the courage woken by a nightmare and fears, I have to go find some solace, some help as they never heard my outcry for help.

What introduction to life do we provide our children with as adults? Regular or irregular – emotional or unemotional, consciously or unconsciously - so hypocritical - my children are my life?

Heaven is in the hands of children, protect your children, but where are we as parents when it comes to the biggest fear in every child's life – THE DARK.

Alone that child needs to sleep in the arms of a doll, while adults that are no longer afraid of the dark, sleep comfortably in another adult's arms, safely and securely listening to the comforting sounds of the other persons every breath and heartbeat, a warm body holding you tight.

My children will stay in my bed, thank you very much. Till they are ready!!

∞

26 august 2013

It is amazing that at a time when I feel so defeated and so worn that I ask the Universe to give me the strength to continue when so much is resting on my shoulders.

When everything that comes/falls in my way, whether it be books, or sayings, or just being, comes through and gives me messages of some sort to say:

'Ange you are stronger then this woman that have died.
Even the world, to the next book I pickup to say that regardless of, we still have the world.
Fascinating about our composition, although it is the thought that woman, are just there to open their legs.'

This is not true, as woman are the miracle, that at so many levels including ourselves need to learn from.

∞

Funny how I needed to be ill, when Dad needed to spend lone, uninterrupted time with his children, and not have anyone around to interfere with his time.
No phone calls, no nothing, just Dad and Kids…

Thank you God and the universe for giving me the strength, to not be ill when Dad wasn't around to spend beautiful time with the Kids.
What an amazing time.

On weekends, I feel I need to step back, as this is the only time Dad truly has to spend with his kids, and teach them Dad things.

I think perhaps one day is good and the next is family, somehow I need to work this out.
Perhaps Dad Saturday and family Sunday?

This will have to be the next year as I know that when the eldest reaches high school, Sundays might just be destroyed by projects and homework.

Much focus is placed on children's education and the future – the protest which was in the 70s 80s was inequality.

In the future: Education of children! We need to focus on that.

∞

I write a story of where I am at, so no one can ever say I did not write a story … the end.

Sitting at a table with wafer chocolate balls, Dunhill menthol cigarettes, short story book and I-phone 5, to my right sunglasses (my checkers specials for R50) and glass o wine.

Kids gone to bed, and husband 30 km away at some work function.
I have just finished reading the most amazing book about "The Hela", I am amazed, I am actually dumbfounded.
Yes, it was written by a woman, hence the drama, but hey, it was read by a woman. So really enjoyed the drama.

I washed my hands with Woolworths soap and put on Woolworths cream, smell absolutely amazing – need to buy it.

Flip I am just realising that I have a gran that's still alive. We want to know how, when and where we come from, what happened in our genealogy?
How much of it do we have left?
I better get going flip – we don't know much about our history, other than our memories as children the moments that we have.

Tinkie is still alive – so I should visit the old bat and ask her about my Pappa's history … goddamnit.
He was 2 years old when his Mom died…

∞

The usual always when trying to have a conversation:

'You just go on wharra wharra wharra – you should look at yourself.
You are the terrible on you are the sad one here.
You just don't get it.
You are just like your Mother and you have the logic of your Dad.
You are proper missing it babe.'

∞

2014

22 December 2014

So I actually managed to speak to Len today – he was shot in the stomach but seems like all vitals are okay and have been missed. Thank goodness, sad, but I know he is going to be just fine. He has faith, which is a good thing and my Khumbu will make sure all is well another lease on life.

My Child arrived on the farm, which had also given Dad another, something to keep his mind off having to find fault with me. Thank god, but now he has to try prove his masculinity / fatherhood and is shouting at the other children, which is not cool!

So just as I thought let the guard down it's - keep the guard up doubly hard to watch out for my little Children!

I however, had a fabulous day with my little baby, we went for lunch and shopped and played and laughed!
Another stunning, was getting all grounded by making herb, vegetable and flower beds, planting seeds and watering all the same.
Being able to meditate for a long undisturbed while, with dog pissing on me marking his territory whilst breathing in light, exhaling darkness and blessing the four corners with my guardian angels, Michael, Uriel, Gabriel and Raphael.
My gates with the other angels of the universe.

I am thankful today!

∞

25 December 2014

Hello young journal!

What a day! I am so happy to have shared it with the most amazing woman! My ouma! She is such a lady!
I honoured her with all the foods that she wanted and brought back memories of my childhood where she was my ultimate heroine. Teaching me mostly of what I know today about being a woman, wife, mother and lady!
I wish I did not have to be so tough to survive and just be who I want to be, but I have been put on this path, to journey… whatever it is I need to still learn??
Today I had the honour to prepare a feast meal for my family and I prayed to God and the Universe because – I wanted to, holding my family's hands, around the table!
I have decided I need to be strong and uphold what I believe in and what is right for me! I have gained the strength within myself to no longer take what I don't believe in and know what … dear journal I believe in who I am!
And will be there for others – regardless! I love being there for my people! My family, my friends and I don't care what he says anymore! He is either going to be with me

on this or not! I have only tried to constantly please him at the detriment of myself! And quite frankly my dear! No more of that!

What made me change my mind and be so adamant?
… when I prayed at the table and both my children participated… and he laughed! What a turning point!!!

∞

27 December 2014

The journal begins right here right now!
A day of complete mixed emotions as I am here on my farm, my idea, my concept, my choice. Wonderful to feel like a stranger in your own space, as you are sharing it with someone that you have semi-lived with in name for 18 years. When you can now sit down and look back at the years that has gone by and wonder, who has kept you here?

As you are on a property which is amazing and watching your children just be children again, laughing, being dirty, teasing, playing.

And then there is this other person, that you don't know anymore, that you have absolutely nothing to say to. As you look at him and you hear your heart and soul know, he doesn't want to be anywhere near you. He is gone. Him to you and you to him. You tolerate each other for the sake of the children. There is nothing more than that. Sitting down at dinner time, may as well be with a complete stranger, who you would probably have more to say to you.
You even speak with his children and parents more than he does about things that matter, things of the heart. Being together, visiting, spending time together. There is nothing more left in this relationship, other than communal assets. How sad is it when you have reached this point?
Thank God for the tractor and a large farm with so much space that you only need to cross paths in the kitchen to get something to eat or drink.

Funny how last night fast asleep as he is wakes when I touch his cell phone.

Jip, my new best friend Mr cell phone – I do get lost in it, as I have contact with people talk to my friends and family via WhatsApp, Facebook, Email, SMS. Oh and then there is my new games, candy crush, farm heroes, pet rescue that keeps me company when I am on my ow. Keeps my mind off things and makes me fall asleep.

I have offered for him to bring his girl to come visit, because I have come to the point where I honestly can't handle this "skelm" situation and the pathetic excuses, it is making me have less and less respect. For heaven sake just let her come through and spend a day, a night! I feel so numb inside that I'd rather she just come through then have to deal with the sheepishness! Hiding the phone in the cupboard and under the pillows making excuses to go shopping!
I am waiting for a bomb to drop! Anytime now it is going to come down, just waiting patiently… I lie! I am not patient, and I am not stupid either. Wish it would just come now! So I can plant my flowers, make my garden and continue my journey!

Then my friend got shot in the stomach. My other friend found out her husband has a Thai hostess all at the same time! And I have no one to share this with, yes, I have been in comms with my Mother, but she is always full of hope that we would work out, and that he would come around!
But I don't know if I have it in me anymore to let my guard down again to get hurt again!

∞

29 December 2014

Hello you gorgeous journal

I truly had a fulfilling day – some time out and helping people!
What is it with me when it gets to helping people?
Kinda gets my juices flowing! Helped Rondo with his salary and had to deal with Mary and her very friendly self…
Why do people not just say darn; I am sorry things went wrong?

Why blame others when you have slipped up?

Anyhoo, at least I was in the vicinity to help Len get to his Mother's place and away from common people.

Had fun shopping, buying flowers and decorating. Now off to sleep!

-   Thank you for today! Was great!!

∞

7 march 2015

I am back, what a beginning. I had and introduction to more confusion which reigns supreme. Here I am sitting on my stoep again all alone, but with a candle this time! Background noise of drunk Africans, music and a nightjar whistling away! Tonight, I am flooded with emotions where I have gone from every spectrum of loneliness, energy, hatred, anger, love, compassion, tears, broken pieces to upliftment. Two little babes sleeping silently whilst I have to deal with a week where I was faced with …. Where do I begin?

A Monday fetching a baby that is so goddamn unique – that did not, oh may I interrupt myself right there, that wanted to be reincarnated into this world which needs to be with 2 people that have prayed for him, and I was chosen to be there for him to meet his parents who prayed for him. It does however introduce so many questions and insecurities to soo many lives though!

– oh might I just tell you baby journal! I have also had to endure further by not being permitted at this point in my life to be offered the opportunity right now to change the way children in South Africa is being treated! Which was a little injury to my self-esteem but was a blessing for my own children!

By the same token I was so nicely or most beautifully reminded by my angel Child that he needs his mommy. How special is that! I have also been asked more than ever for help from my baby my other Baby! How amazing at 14 years to realise that you are still important as a mom!

You do know I am married? I had one phone call and 2 nights of brief texts throughout 2 weeks from the husband by the way! What an afterthought…. Whoop whoop!

I have had a wonderful Monday night which was a bit of a distraction from everything else in my life when my Cello books where delivered – however, caught again by listening to someone else's heart story! You know I sat on this same stoep last Saturday and cried so hard and so ugly – (you know I am that ugly pulled face crier #justsaying)

As I read through a friend of mine's journals, and one after the other and felt so much pain. It made me hurt I could physically feel the darkness of every page! Yet by the same token could envisage the opportunity of an amazing story, where soo many could learn from... but reading it was painful!

Then to be approached by my son who ended up speaking his heart of pain and confusion and anger towards his father for not being around! For hurting his mother for confusion around the relationship of the possibility of separation and divorce as so many of his friends have to deal with this in their lives, and have to live the anger between their parents. The 14-year-old having to be strong for all! Then having to face the fear that his mom might be taken away by someone else and needing his friend to back him in the conversation?!

Shame my dear baby angel, I see there is still so much which you need to understand – but I don't want my little angel to be introduced to that which I was exposed to at my age of 14. I want him to still be a child, and concern himself with dealing with his being 14!

So instead of me being selfish and say accept everything and everyone in my life, I listened and am ad hearing to his requests which is making me feel like a thief, denying myself friendship which I am holding strong right now, and from which I am learning as much as giving and enjoying.

Oh wow how much have I learnt about humanity again this week? The other side – the one that I have been protected from due to my standards of living! But exposed in such a way that it is what I need to understand to ensure that if I want to save the world I have to understand how the world works… oh no! am I trying to justify my week? Am I trying to justify my human interactions right now? We all have frames of references from which we operate … our foundations and the worlds our parents introduce us to and what they profess to maintain for us!

But everyone around us have various frames, various ways in which they operate, but am I old and ugly enough to deal with it right now? I don't know? I can't tell you right now. I am however, going to make a choice and a decision and I am walking away from this!

If I need to learn something from it dear journal – please let me learn! I know it will not leave me until the lesson is learn! But for now I say good bye

Loads of love Ange

Ps when my sense of humour ever fails me – please unplug all the machines – blow out the candles – switch off the lights and donate my organs – the body can go for research!

∞

2015

When alone

Alone or lonely

In a crowd You can be lonely
When alone … You are with only one... And that is You The You that looks into your soul... The You that listens to the words that turn ...
The memories, the thoughts, the rehearsals... The decisions ...

In a crowd You can be lonely
When alone ... With your own heart You speak with your own peace, you make sense of the chaos with your own silence You hear the noise with your own quiet, you hear the music, with your own blindness You see with insight…

In a crowd ...
You can be the entertainer
You can be the clown
You can be the hero

When alone ...
Once thoughts dissipate
Decisions are made
Noise is shut down

Who are you ...

Lonely ... Or ... Alone

It is very difficult to explain always in short communication the extent of what currently has placed itself on my path...

Comms Could Be Misconstrued as demanding. However, it is the exact opposite...
Oft times when faced with existing circumstances - Narnia seems like an option - but the return is not always pleasant

Reality - cannot be avoided ... It needs to be faced

Reality required decisions which is not always met with open arms and results in masks ... It takes time, especially when mortality and the reality of immortality breaths through the passages and rooms which you had filled with love... True unconditional love... Filled empty spaces or at least tried to do so with wedding dresses and a child... Your friend is dying and you cannot give life... You can only comfort - you cannot fix, you cannot take away the pain - daily fading away and all you can do is ... Your blood type does not even match.... But your souls - look at each other and laugh whilst knowing - this could be the end .... But you both hold on to each other when all you hold - bones cover by skin... Skin Sooo thin ... When you rub in the oils you fear rubbing through its layer...

Your friend... Your confidante that shares your every second of your life... Knows every secret, every inch of your being ... Is fading in front of you ... And you can't fix it... You cannot wave that wand to change mortality into immortality - however, you remain positive! You carry, you support - your clean-up where she can't ... You carry when she can't walk, you dry the tears when your own cannot be dried...

The mask you wear when holding up the rest to believe all will be well!!

At the same time, you face the reality of everyday, a little boy ... That kisses you all over, cannot walk by without stroking your hair... Leaves your arms in the morning having the last smell to seal his day... Mom!! Loving life. Yet struggling with school... Misunderstood by teachers wanting conformity when life is more then numbers ...! excelling at all ... But being judged by numbers. So much confidence. So loving

A teen that deals with emotional, physical adjustments, confides in you that the trust in his Father is not what it should be and the bond which was meant to have been built by now is non-existent. The image of the man in his life is a phantom idiot.

A little girl... Starting her life as rejected in a packet in a veld ... Loses the only Father she knows without a word walks out ... Now an ill Mother. What do you say, I gave your life - just to take it away... Be happy, be confident?

A little boy that only knows life as criminal and laced with drugs... Steals your heart ... with nowhere to go.

Organization - built from nothing ... Closing doors, turns by your hand, expecting decisions daily, financial, humans, programs, projects, marketing, advertising, clients, public ....

Provincial .... Decisions

National .... Decisions

Ok ... Enough now!!! One day at a time!!!

85

Fingers numb .... Practicing scales in G on the neck of your Cello ... Getting lost as you love spending time learning something new... A passion in the silence of your own space ... No commentary ... No laughing ... No mocking ...

∞

15 August 2015

And today he is as friendly as can be … this morning my car key could not be found,
I asked if I could borrow the bakkie to go to a welfare meeting... He looked at me like
I asked if I can shit on his face!

We spoke yesterday upon my arrival at the farm. Let's say I gave him the time to talk
to tell me what he wants to say, after him thinking without me around for the week,
as I had to take Barbara to start oncology and find a home for "the child", as having
him in my place of safety is
 a) running out
b) my son spoke to me about not wanting "the child" around anymore
c) after my decision of getting a divorce, I cannot handle more then my 2 boys, as
there are many things to consider both emotionally, physical and finance

"the child" is a lovely boy with much potential and I will always keep contact.
Furthermore, ways are using "the child" to further put emotional pressure on me. You
see he was tolerant and understood what I was doing to help this little boy, bust
since I had told him I want to divorce, he started taking it out on "the child" by
ignoring him and say I must make a plan as he refuses to look after "the child".

∞

29 October 2017 The hurt the anger and the hate of divorce

When you have invested 20 years of your life to build and share with someone, that have a home a life. When you have struggled to have children, and have given up everything, your career your life to be there for the most amazing little angels, that you have set aside your being to give them the security of a family a home. You quietly took the lonely – the heart break, the pain of not being your man's Queen to find the lies, one after the other. To endure the jealous rages, to take the abuse, and the constant criticism and the drunk – the abuse, the verbal, psychological, sexual to the point where you quietly hide and start medicating to feel worthy of yourself and be comfortably numb to handle and cope what you are to receive upon his presence.

Now to pick up those pieces, of lost career, lost person, that you endured. The worst of all is that you are alone, no longer! Lonely as you have regained 'you' without the constant fear of worthless, when he enters the door. But the lonely as your babies, that you protected and struggled to have, and whom you lived for, are no longer with you. They are temporarily around.

You now have to watch from the outside as they grow – like a long distance lover that only gets to spend moments. You see them go through the struggles, the pain, the adjustments and you can't be there to let them fall asleep in your arms and sing them a lullaby

It is not every night, but every fortnight, every second week, every second holiday – its fucked up!

My one boy is struggling to start dealing with his change, as he enters the teens, struggles at school and I can only be there temporarily as he goes through this!

The other is strong, as he pretends to be … still needs support. I see this, as then they do see me and speak to me – I notice the pretence on the first day, but as we continue in hours – that façade fades and they become little gentle beings to the point where they don't stop loving, hugging, holding. When they return back the façade builds again to pretend to be strong.

My little girl – whom I struggle to find a close bond with god bless this strong little being – also grows from all out attention baby to strong – I am honest in saying, I struggle to bond as she was never my baby – she was my friend's baby and I deliberately stood back for them, to build their mother-child bond. There was no indication that my friend was never going to see her daughter grow up. Now I'am here, as a part-time mother, who is not only struggling to keep herself afloat, but the 2 beings I bonded with and struggled to have is my priority above all. I will of course give my everything that I have left to my daughter!! Amazing how, when all the heartbreak happens at once, and you need to find the strength within yourself to move forward, remain strong and give to your own. She has what I have left! As much as I can give and will and I do! But she also is quite the pillar of strength and powerful in her own right! Which I need to still teach her!!

So today I cry – I cry – I cry my tears are necessary as I felt them coming through for days. But they weren't ready to show themselves. But today they came and they flowed and they screamed!!!!! as they came out in abundance streams bursting through when my boys had the most amazing experience and I could not share it in person!

Instead I sit alone on my stoep in my pyjamas and all I have are photos and texts!

Being happy with them is different from being happy for them!!!! The past while has only been about sad, pain, growing, distress, failing and the moment where there could be the happy then you can't be there!!

This hurts as life is not always about being there for your children!! when they are!! in person !! but also sharing their happiness and joy!!!

Now I feel the reality of absolute alone!!!

That part of divorce that is the most fucked up. Regardless of the reasons for the breakup. It's that alone, that hurts more than the lonely – that indescribable feeling of rejection? Outcast? Outsider? What synonyms can one give to the hollow feeling?

∞

29 October 2017

It's been a while since my tears are flowing and it feels amazing – I need to re-assess and rebuild whatever it took to reach this point to let it go the warm streams that cover my cheeks as they run down lets me feel alive as they remind me of my heart and compassion I feel and have!!

Looking over my hills and valleys after the earth was scorned by fires and the rain came down to give new green pastures.

A symbol of my emotions – the earth, my earth, the internal Angelique what earth had been scorned by the compassion I have for children and humanity and the pain I felt for every being as I helped them through what I did and could, of the past while and was scorned by their words, abuse in return!

My tears flowing now as to revisit and revive to allow for new grass of hope to grow as I take on a different view and different angle, to bring for the growth through the insights and understanding and new connections that has been introduced as the earth, my earth had to go through this

To generate a new beginning of a different view of how to make the dream come true for change

The mushroom effect! You call it. You needed to go through this Ange and now the tears are flowing, the rain the wind the fire – earth wind fire water – the elements that makes for change!!

∞

29 October 2017

My dearest children

I miss you with all my power, heart and soul

When I am alone on my couch with the silence surrounding me and the only noise I hear is the wind blowing through the trees, birds whispering and the cars driving in the distance. The train blowing it horn as it passes through – my music in the background

I miss my children's laughter, their bickering, their voices. The noise of teasing, the screams the crying of seeking attention. Jumping on the trampoline and making flick flacks on the lawn. Loud music and swearing

Mom what are we eating. Dogs playing and running, the messy bathroom and kitchen and lounge and bedroom. Engines of bikes and carts roaring, stinky sweaty bodies and shoes. The noise in the foreground blaring and messy and noise and smells

I lived that and loved that every day I spend with you, I want that all the time, how I hate that it has been taken away from me

I sit here on my own and think – how can I have it back? I know if I move back to town – I will still not have it all the time as I need to share with your dad the times of you with him, you not with me, I know you enjoy coming out to the farm for sake of freedom and space. I know I can't go back to your Dad as my trust and respect is now totally gone. The empty nest has come way sooner than I expected. But it is here and I hate it. I miss you and love you.

∞

"He loves me, he loves me not"

Why the continues – you are proper missing it babe….

The letters I found that he wrote me.

2008

"Angelique I wrote this for you…
I wrote this for me …
after reading it again it seems not to even scratch the surface of what I feel.
I wrote it down because I am not sure hot say it, yet it still seems so little – I wish I could express myself better…

Over the past 9 days with clone on 4000km of the most beautiful scenery in the world and more time to thing then I have ever had. I have enough in my heart to fill books on life, love, me, you, and many other wonderful things. Emotions and feelings. What I am writing now, is but a glimpse into some one. These as I doubt that I could find ways to express what is really in my head.

But here goes…

Angelique – a beautiful woman, sexy, fund, entertaining, vivacious, outgoing, fun loving, brave, a free soul, fiercely independent, a very deep understanding of life, giving, soft, hard, complex, simple, straight forward, loving, passionate, caring.

Me – independent, resourceful, fun loving, giving, passionate, loving, caring, intense.

Together we have been friends, lovers and parents – Angelique a wonderful loving mother and me a loving father, both putting the children first in everything.

Our oldest son – a sensitive, fun, caring, giving little boy who needs to be loved and nurtured.

Our second son – a very little wonderful boy, who also is fun and carefree, loving and need to be loved and nurtured.

So what happened?

Angelique – the loss of independence, the feeling of being dependent. A caged bird that need to be set free, to experience the wonders of life. The ups and downs. Has grown cold, closed and superficially out going. The house, the business, the city, to the mundane day to day existence, with little opportunity to fulfil her own desires, and resulting in resentment, and loss of passion.

Me – similarly caught I the mundane, day to day existence. The loss of independence. Always trying to make sure everybody else is okay. Interpreting the loss of passions, as the loss of love. This giving rise to intense jealousy and resentment, that I cannot, am not good enough to share your life, our passion. This resulting in hateful outputs and harsh words borne out of frustration, Ange, fear…

Angelique – soft and compassionate, these outbursts are intense and lasting. Unforgivable and result in and even greater loss of passion, of love. Reinforcing the sense of being more caged. A desperate need to find the deeper meaning to life.

Me – as Angelique becomes more withdrawn, more remote, the frustrations result in an inability to talk to her. To have fun with her, and to just be.

The result – not just the loss of a lover, but the loss of the only real friend I have ever had.

This is a very vicious cycle that only gets worse over time. Any opportunity to break the cycle must come from radical change in thinking and behaviour. It cannot be solved by time or silence.

Angelique – a need for change and an ability to express your independence, to be yourself, to live your life, to fulfil your dreams.

Me – unhappy, fearful, at a loss as to what to do – in desperate need of a (different?) change and need to be myself again, and at peace with the world.

The boys – a need for a family. A need for a loving mom and a loving dad. For a happy home, a nurturing environment. Free of fears and nightmares, life will hold enough challenges for these two as they grow up.

Can these thins be reconciled? If so? How? And where do we start?

Angelique – needs to give herself the time and the space to do it. To find a way to lose the cage. Commitments as a mother makes it difficult. Try going away for a week or a month without the children. I am a good father and will certainly look after them. Go to a movie on your own, make new friends. Find new opportunities.

Me – give myself the time and space to get out of my own cage. See only the good and ignore the bad. Find peace in my soul. Don't suffocate Angelique with caring. Don't be jealous for it is through fear of losing our relationship, which is exactly the thing that is destroying all we have. By holding on too tight, I have lost what I wanted to hold on to.

How to be free, but be good parents?
Give time to the children, but give time to ourselves.

By being free, this will allow us to be ourselves again. The people we originally fell in love with, and maybe, just maybe, we can learn to enjoy each other again. As free souls, we can learn to be friends again, without losing our independence, for in that we would only love ourselves again. In that space we may or may not ever become lovers again.

Neither of us can live without passion, and passion can only exist when you are free and life is unpredictable. A new relationship with others allows this. But will only end up the same as soon as that relationship settles down. It becomes predictable and mundane sets in. A new home, a new town, a new job, will aloe us to feel free for a bit, but soon it too will lose its novelty and become a prison of day to day life, of work, of not achieving some higher purpose.

Somehow I think we each need to find the real core of that which is constraining our freedom. Identify those thinks which will allow us individuality. To find peace. We may blame it on each other, but it's not (although the other could make it worse)

Each of our journeys can only be determined by ourselves and we have to do this if we are to bread free of this negative spiral our relationship has got into.

My choice is that we try to do this while still providing a safe, loving home for our children. If I need to move into another room, the cottage, whatever, that is okay. I certainly understand that at this point we can't be lovers and I cannot box you in any way. We need to do more on or own. But I also know it is not for me to say what you want. If you do choose this route I must ask that you do not take the children too far from me – just the past 10 days without seeing them, or being able to call them was very, very difficult. I want to be a good father. I think that they need a father that is around and shares their developing years. I could not bear to only see them during school holidays or once a week. I know that you will understand this.

Whatever your choice is, whatever your journey is, I hope that you can talk to me about it and I can talk to you about mine.

You are a wonderful person and I promise you, you will always be my best friend forever and there never has, nor will be on the I would rather share my thoughts and feeling with, more than you. It saddens me to think, how this vicious cycle (much of it my doing) has taken away our ability to do just that.

So the first thing to do is, break the cycle. If I lose you forever through it, it will still be better than continuing the destructive path we are on. But maybe, just maybe, we can find each other again. That will be worth more than anything. I truly love you and will love you forever.

(just a little scared, but excited by what the future may hold)

PS – if it goes well, I will be happy to be your maintenance guy at your SPA.
Oh yes, maybe it's better if you stop calling me Pa.
I do love you."

And so I packed up my boys and we moved back home from my Mother.

2015

"What happened to the Man that fell in love with Angelique?

From a passionate, fun time, fun, secret, sexual affair, at a time when my days and dreams were spent filled with thoughts and anticipation of just see you again, just talking to you again…

To a mans who was filled with guilt for walking out on the two boys he loved so much. I will never forget the look of terror on their faces that day, the tears, them hanging on to me. Their fear, their anguish and their security disappearing. All they had known and I had crushed it in one blow. I did not know how to deal with it or how to express the pain I felt, by doing this to two little boys, simply for my own selfish purpose. To be with the woman I loved.

The only way I could deal with the grief, was to turn it into anger, and the person who I loved the most received the brunt of it.

For years Angelique did all she could for both me and my sons. Loving them and taking them on as her own. Still the guilt and anguish I felt still remained. So much in their little lives could have been better, happier… and it was all my doing.

Time has healed that anguish to some extent and over the first few years, they were with us more and more and more, until eventually even the guilt subsided. But for those year I had not been there for the woman I love so much. Whom has given so much. Eventually this had to take its toll. This wonderful woman had given her all, and was not receiving much in return. To make matters worse, I had not told her I had a vasectomy – to this day I don't know why? I did not try to deceive her – maybe it was pride, embarrassment, fear of losing her, or a thousand other reason, that I cannot explain. We had the most wonderful boy, after much heartache and struggle, and eventually an angel brought us our other baby boy after more anguish and struggle.

My guilt for my sons was now replaced by a guilt for what I have put the woman I love so much through. Angelique through all of this was getting further and further away from me, the loss of passion, the silence, the void between us, was seen by me as the loss of love.

I did everything I knew to try and make her happy – but it wasn't what she was looking for. Once again my guilt turned into anger and jealousy, and try as I might, it just kept breaking through. I was fearful again and experiencing a deep sadness, which made me not a nice person to be with.

Angelique longs for peace and happiness. A world where she can fulfil her own dreams.

I have come to realise over the past few day, that my thoughts and fears are a huge impediment to those things, and I need to do away with them. To do away with the past and just to love her. Be it from near of far. I need to simply appreciate the beautiful, free soul she is.

I am concerned that as Angelique is such a committed, loving, wonderful mother, that once again she will sacrifice her own personal dreams simply for our boys.

I can't, I don't want to stop her from being that Mother, but I will do my best to try and help her find the time and space she needs. By taking on more responsibility for the children. I am certain her resentment at being trapped, even by the children, will be aimed at me, but rather that, than them. After all I have put her through, this is but a drop in the ocean.

I need to find complete peach in my mind. I hope the damage I have done is not so great, it can never be forgiven.

I love Angelique more today than ever before. Even if the damage is too great, to ever be close to her again, that will never die. I hope and pray that it is not. I hope and pray that I now understand enough, not to translate fear and anguish into anger. That through this I too can find peace."

∞

"Don't fall in love with me"

2016

2016

Waking to a morning of new life with my girl giving birth to little puppies, new life on my farm was just the most amazing gift!

Sitting here in the fresh breeze with mist rolling over the hills with such joy and peace in my heart that my other son who is now at the age of his own in his own making sense of his own playing and riding with his friend, having enjoyment without a concern or worry, bring my heart such joy, that I know that as my other son grows into this, he will too realise the peace that we feel as being raised in the same.

In this time which I had called my sabbatical, was a much required time in my life to just bring all into calm and perspective. Has been the most challenging at first, to force myself to not participate in any way whatsoever in any form of - say "yes" to the world and people, but forcing the "selfish"

There were still times during this process where, let's say the 'curious' (that's me), was still participating in social media platforms. The want and need to be with or find some enjoyment in the pleasures of sexual counter parts, in this voyage. Through this, had also found peace in myself to the point that I also feel that, I have earned my space in sexual prowess. Knowing that I am not only a body to be used by others, but that I enjoy sex, as much as it should be enjoyed.

Not only for the pleasure of my partner, but also my own. That I may enjoy being satisfied without concern and worry of the other person. Realising and feeling of multiple orgasms, not only by intercourse but so too by just being… By just listening to kind words, by being adored. I too am a person that is liked and adored. That I too want to be wanted and needed, not only for the use as a sex object, but indeed because - I am just who I am.

I too am being appreciated. I have realised and accepted that - it is okay to just accept - that I too have needs, and I am allowed to be stimulated by sheer enjoyment and pleasures of the excitement of the thought, the kiss, the touch. Not only by the ideas or concepts of exposing and selling of the voyeuristic pleasures.

I too am beautiful in the eyes of many and not just a thing. I have the right to accept and to reject.

I too have the right to hold, to be held, without the force of guilt. I too have the needs of various that requires stimulation. Rather than trying to seek all in one person – which one has to end up 'training' for sake of fitting into my requirements, needs and expectations – rather to have multiple counterparts or concubines that will fulfil the various aspects, needs and requirements.
The trick is honesty, the trick is openness, the trick is acceptance and realisation. With all this it is not to be frowned upon – instead it is self-realisation and actualisation that no one owns ME but ME.

No one will box me, and no one will force me to the point where I have to not be me. Physical pleasures are just as important as mental and spiritual stimulation. Sapiosexuality is what it is called.

∞

It is late in the same day with the mist moving away.
I am surrounded by people and feel as though I can scream.
I can't have them around anymore – I want my space back - I am not ready for anyone!
I cannot cope with another person or personality permanently in my surrounds!
I cannot entertain it for so long – 24 hrs is enough then it's time to move on – its overflow, it's time to go.
Time and need for appreciation of my – me again!
Enough of same remarks – same sounds – same voices!
I am not ready for this constant human in my space.
I need my own to come in again – I can't – need my space, my silence, my breath.
Can't – see the jealousy when speaking about my outside life – that look, that change when all I want to do is to be free!

To have anyone I please in my surrounds and my space – can't – I can't – I am so not ready!

∞

1 October 2016

Starting a new journey, clearing the old mutability – change brings forth regeneration of new energies, new balance, new centres.

Loving the shrug of the journey which has brought me to this point where that which was necessary to learn from has no come to an end. For new possibilities and new paths to be tread, new doors to be opened.

You have learnt from the past that leaving yourself in the back to start and lead the lives of others – to be submissive and to assist with their journeys of the self has not only aided them in self-realisation, however, that has taught you and strengthened you to maintain a strong stance to move to a new level of self-realisation and actualisation where you are in a position to accept nothing less than respect for who you are and your journey is about. You only give love and receive little. It's time for whomever enters into this new journey of yours respect you and adores you for your strengths and not your weaknesses.

Should they wish to walk next to you and hold your hand, they are indeed welcome to do so at your level. You will remain the person you are and embrace the person you have become. You have lead a lonely life surrounded by thousands. Now you shall lead a life with true souls that will connect with you on a level that further nourishes you, in your new journey. Nothing less! Appreciate who you are and moves forward with you.

Enjoy your new journey Angelique. It is your journey – no one else's.

9 October 2016

So much has happened in this life of mine so quickly that sometimes I wonder if this is real so much excitement in the air amongst establishing new foundations in a new area new home new career involvement – ever mutable – a person in the background that makes me feel like I have something to look forward to need that to make me feel supported and wanted be certainly does that for me. A warm feeling and I do believe he will understand my quirky different outlook on life my sexual play – without judgement. He makes me feel powerful, confident. Although we have never met, it still is amazing – the interaction of the uncertainly the passion, the need to want to be makes so much difference – I love that thought of him – the feel – that there is that person that I am connect with – and the feeling I have when the mere thought of him pops through, he reacts to me and I read him, the connect is so strong its outright amazing! Another strong person! I love it!!

∞

The gates have hardly closed behind you, as you moved to what was to be your new life. The option chosen for you to start somewhere, as if you where the infidel. However, you made that decision, you took charge of your life. Enough is enough you said.

'I don't want a divorce' he said. Making you feel like you are the one that is at fault.

The gates hardly closed, the dust from the few bits of furniture, the markings of the paintings still on the walls. Children still settling….

It did not take long for the gate to open again, the best friend to move in. My old bed still warm from where my little babies snuggly slept in my arms…

Picking up the pieces to my new life, my new journey. Negotiations of assets, children's future, making some sort of arrangement for a 5th person to somewhere be included in the negotiations? I still cannot phantom the reasoning…

The losses, of divorce, of death still lingering in the air… New children introduced, new woman introduced, changes, immediate changes to the home that my children know as home. The drinking the fights, the adjustments…

Starting to find a new in establishing financial independence, a reminder of tacking the fall and being the buffer to protect others in a business that did not stood the test of times…

Alone again, sitting at the courts having to fend for yourself. Alone when having to face the prosecutor for facing the closure of your hard work to establish a business for your family. Alone when having to face the prosecutor for divorce. Alone again having to face the negotiations in releasing you from the blacklisting's to clear your name to start a new…

You cannot be employed, with bad credit, you cannot establish a business with bad credit, you cannot apply for any position that places you at the lead of any organisation, with bad credit…

You got this Angelique!! You can get through this!!

Just another hurdle – raise your self and leap across this with pride and with stride…
Just another learning curve – open your mind and allow this to erase that of
unresolved matters of the past…

Everything in life happens for a reason – don't you ever forget that my girl!!

∞

30 October 2016

This part of my journey has brought me to a point of just no strings attached, no
commitment, senseless yet, completely satisfactory sex. Arbitrary sexting to points
where multiple men are Cumming while recording themselves. Hard cock pics
coming through to me at various times on various platforms, mastering the skill of
nothing other than just unattached pictures with no emotional involvement and no
promises of any form of commitments.

Then days and weeks go by with nothing – but the same keep coming back for more
– it's never just the new. Those that I have sexted – all come back flattering as it is.
Then a week goes through so many changes work and new.
When a week starts with meeting the latest contender, as I have gone through
various meets and chats. As wonderful it is or was to meet these various people –
not one has stood out to the point that I could with confidence say – I walk the path
with you.
By the same token I am also at the point where I am tired of these new empty meets.
The last meet was intriguing and very overwhelmingly passionate – like a Casa
Blanca moment in an airport. An interlude of 2 very strong – but where will this lead?
I don't know….

In the interim I had the most satisfactory visit and cuddle, the most satisfactory night
of pure orgasms, to the point where I felt the orgasms of blacking out, and that for
such a young man – wow! There were so many variation of orgasms, to the point
where there was such euphoria of solid sleep – amazing is not the word to
describe!...
In the back of my mind this very 'Casa Blanca' meet passion – was stuck …. Holding
me… Where will 'Casa Blanca' lead me – also don't want to hold onto something
that is not of mutual interest and respect.

It works for me, to a point, however my ultimate focus is, I now need to establish
myself, my career etc. Get through this year and start afresh with new, where there
are no more loose ends. Clean up clear up every loose end that frustrates me, that
keeps lingering – the end if this is in sight.

Clear, cleanse, focus … as you need to cut all, to the point where you are in a
position to start a fresh and prioritise, that which is important.

It has been a journey this year, from such losses, confusion, meets, losses, fights,
anger, yet by the same token new beginnings.

To be taken further with confidence – Take a rest Angelique, you need a time to full recovery from what you have been through my girl.

Take your life back, and move forward with that which makes you passionate and excites you.

Priorities:

Children's schools
Studies Unisa Exams – 9 15 18 November
Event bookings
Wrap up Welfare1 – narrative report
Welfare2 – Wednesday
Welfare3 – Assist with Governance
Welfare4 – CPO registration
Mediations – Client A, Client B
Close case – rescission 14 November – lift blacklisting
Pay-out divorce settlement recon

∞

2 November 2016

I work my life in 3s….
As I have always believed in the blessings and signs of the uniqueness that 3 holds.
Like the trinity God the Father, Son and Holy ghost.
Mary, Jesus and Buddha.
Triangles of hope: Love, Peace, Touch. Body, Mind, Soul.
All this grounded by Earth – Air, Wind, Fire.

I am on this earth on this planet for a reason. I need to remain focussed on my journey and my reason for being. To date there are the love and blessings I have received by having to come this far, to get to this point, to make the choices and decision I have made, to be where I am at right now. My complete and utmost financial / materialistic bonds will be cut soon, from my previous journey of understanding and learning which is appreciated.

Strange reasons which is currently not clear – but also in hind sight a good thing, as it has allowed me to heal in my time, without adding more pressure to my healing process. For finding my feet and establishing myself. My foundation from floating with uncertainty. My children which is my key point to soul heart happiness. For us all to settle in new ways and the new lifestyle of what our new journey holds. I have established my passions this past year. My journey is now to begin with open heart and soul.

Now what is this you want:
It is a no brainer, it is for the happiness of my children, for them to settle in this new life, find the relationship, the comfort and the foundation of this new life that we are faced with. It has been a whirlwind and movement of change and uncertainty. Yet now I believe that as all settles and grows we are starting to find our feet in our

journey. My one child has found his place of schooling where he is happy and has the desire to continue with his place. My other has found his place of schooling where he is happy, has excelled and regained his confidence to continue with his place. My little baby has settled with her losses and is starting to find her heart and speak about her losses – her little path is to continue, and we still have to finalise the balance – however she started talking about her heart. The last link and loop needs to be closed for this little life, that requires still a bit of work. However, no concrete decisions have been made, as no one has been ready for this commitment as things just needed to settle. I think we are all ready for the discussion.

My passions: children, animals, art – this has been brought on my path and this is my journey to continue. I have grown from direct involvement, to being able to stand at a higher level and look at it from an objective view and perspective. To take this journey and develop what is required to make the difference from an internal direct perspective on smaller scales, to that of a global scale for the impact on a larger scale. Through my direct involvement I am now in a position where I can step back and look at it objectively. Take the steps to make that journey, to make the difference which I have prayed for. Uniting the various components to grow the planet, the people, to work together I shall plan this, I shall implement this – I shall make it work.

My personal, my me: - I have met the person that is so powerful in person that shook my world. That has taken me from questioning me and my self-worth to having the confidence to get to this day of writing this, as I am sitting here. A person that has so much confidence in his passion and journey that is not swayed by the arbitrary – THAT has just turned my world! I need not have him all the time, as I can live my journey and passions by just a simple hello – and his passion for me – is also there! Through my year I have met various characters to allow me to get to this point to know what I am prepared to settle for. With due respect to myself …. I want strong, I want passion, I want freedom, yet I want to belong… With respect, with honour and with understanding. My mind is not simple, my passions are not simple, my reasons for being is not simple…

I am in this world and this world is not simple – yet it is very straight forward with many linear synergies, similar scattered faces / vessels that twirl around on their own. "I can see the impact of unity". Having someone out there understanding that I am not simple that I have a journey, a powerful journey to complete! That is what I need and what I want! I have met this person! I know that and I feel that! It is not just a young soul that has to be mothered, it is another powerful soul as is mine! I want it in my life! I shall have it in my life! It will be in my life!

So there are my 3s:
my children: soul, love, life
my foundation: home, happiness, peace
my person: partner, journey, support

And so my journey will begin a new fresh page with all the above checks in place:

Let's take a look:

Children – Welfare, boy child girl child, boards of management
Animals – Conservation, training, domestic pets, wild animals
Arts – music, art, awareness
#UNITETHEFIGHT

HOW AND WHAT HAS BROUGHT YOU TO THIS POINT TO DEVELOP WHICH
ARE THE KEY ASPECTS TO ENSURING YOUR FUTURE GOAL?

GOVERNANCE
MEDIATION - key aspects of developing your income
COUNSELING – understanding of the human race
SOCIAL WORK – understanding the cultures = complete your degree to fall back on
in the days to come

The focus is on your knowledge of Governance!
Your mediation skill is what will be required to develop your focus!
Your knowledge of the cultures will allow you to make the inspired impact!
YOU KNOW WHAT TO DO!

∞

14 November 2016

How is it possible that the person who tried to keep things together, tried to work on
the marriage, tried to give the partner the freedom and support needed to grow. The
person that sat at home, that lived a lonely life and made a house a home. The
person that tried everything to build businesses for their dreams to become a reality.
This person has to draw the shortest straw?

That realised, that forgave, that released, now sitting here with what?

Not being with her children, not being able to work, continue having to turn every
cent, sleeping alone, living alone. Pushed aside her own career aspirations,
aspirations to travel, assets, delayed her life, and now be on her own. Trying to
rebuild her life, while the other plays around.

A day of reflection, when you feel the reality of lonely, when you are reminded of
those feelings of everything you have worked on, and here you are sitting in your
home alone, with no a child, a husband, a family member, a friend, a lover, a partner
all on your own with no one around. All the relationships that you have built in your
personal and intimate zone all gone: - just you

What makes for this I wonder… as you progress in life, where it is either; that you
have reached a point where you truly need to make more peace with yourself; or
invite people into your life; or just be with yourself for a little while to decide and
define your path from here on forward.

Where all you have done was everything to please others. And now you need to start
truly building yourself from the inner core, find your peace, and start with all the
knowledge, experience to define where to from here. Take ownership of your plans

and direction, clean up those ties that were so loose, just gather all the issues you haven't addressed, and place them in order for you to establish exactly where to from here Angelique. There are many loose ends that you need to wrap up my girl, to be truly confident in what it is that you wish to do with your future!

Clean- up, wrap up and find your feet on the new grounds. Start laying those steadfast foundations to ensure that you can move forward with confidence, that what you choose to take on, you are able to build and expand on! – that's what today's lesson is my girl!

∞

10 December 2016

How can I not want to be a part of this magnificent life I am leading right now!
My children all with me doing their thing, making omelettes, playing, talking, music…
My peace on earth having them with me, far away from any unnecessary pressures
– just being together.
My mind needs to be cleared from all and directed to making decision and future plans.
But for now it needs to erase, clear and clean up.

Deep breaths of pure exhilarating nothingness … just breathing, clearing, forgetting
– blank – a blank page is what I need to write on … without any markings, open, empty, free from any untamed thought.
That requires creativity for a fresh start and clearance of energies around.
That takes you on a new path and new journey of what you deserve.
- Go off the grid – from today
- clear – stay away – close
- be done with it

You have to escape every possible angle and though… disturbance, need, query, question, engagement of all sorts … be gone for a while…

If they want a part of you they will be around when you have found your strength. Regain your confidence and self! You can't build on not having the strongest foundation – and that is being you! Just the core of you is what you need to start and decide. Just you – you don't need the approval of others!

∞

Just a lazy day lying in bed staring at the ocean waves beating in the background. All the kids having a rest. There is Peace in the house while the rain is pouring down, drizzle then pour… Mind clearing and slowing down.
My beautiful creature is in Europe. I want him so bad - to make a decision and a choice, to be making the effort to be with me! As I think and feel I have met the person that turns my world! I can admire him and the play! – love it! And know he adores me too.

I am different to the norm and I do so believe is he! The thought of him makes my stomach turn my pulse race and my breath harder… I like this man – I really do.

∞

Here I am 44 years later…. Born in the early morning hours, in the Addington Hospital Durban KZN to the most beautiful family. Blessed I am in abundance, filled with so much appreciation for what life had brought me – lessons, friends, family. No negative karma surrounds me. Only fulfilment, love and happiness.

A soul understands the self and had endured a journey to fulfilment, to know that this is the last journey on this planet, this plane.

Blessed am I to watch my children play in the sand in the sea, laughter, songs, dance. All wanting to share their stories, their love, their hugs...
The peace the joy that fills my heart when I look at them, live with them and the most amazing is that none of them want to spend a minute away from me. Where I move, they move, where I sit they sit, where I lie they lie. No one runs away, or walks away – indeed the opposite. What more can I ask for, I have made a difference and changed the course of 5 children's lives that are currently entrusted onto me.

As I sit watching the clouds move the ocean water running by, the wind blowing and waves crashing in the silence and peace of my soul, my heart is warm with love.
I must announce in every aspect of my life – I am at peace!

∞

We introduced ourselves in September 2016

Communication flowed easily from a perspective that the interaction was brilliant. I was looking for a strong person to be with me, to also not hold me back, to explore my sexual prowess as I continued developing. Open communication in both our wants and needs, as you introduced yourself as the 40 shades character which I initially saw as a challenge, as well as wanting to understand your motivation and drive, as you were not the first one to have introduced himself as the Christian Grey of dating sites. Most of them I crushed within seconds, as they could not sustain my strength in communication, to the point that they blocked me.

You however, endured in the game to convince me that your tribes are where you wish to find me. As we continued in daily communication I am certain with both intrigue, understanding and direct communication, we furthered our journey to the point where the minutes of meeting at the airport had turned both of us on to the point, where the engagement continued to the point, where if we could fuck right there it would've happened. The energy and chemistry exchanged was so overwhelming, to the point that pheromones exchanged as we walked through the entire airport to the point of departure.

It was sealed – we will continue communication and so find a position in each other's lives.

Lying on my couch communicating through your inspiration of the Grey to which I was not enthralled by. Create your own personality and base it not on a character written by an author. For me, it was the challenge to find your inspiration and motivation to have what you would call a tribe. Your family as you later tried to explain to me, however, you played my game, by exposing your body, your every inch of your body as I requested, you played in my hands. On que, you reacted to my commands of wanting to know more, to see more and further exposure of what I wanted to learn from you – playing my game.

Driving in a car with two men completely unaware of our communication, yet wanting to experiment the nature of pheromones being detected in an enclosed environment. Where I am the driver, communicating on business, while sexting and fucking you, controlling how I reach and orgasm un-noticed and un-detected. You played along only through visual and text. To the point where you came and I reached an orgasm. Whilst picking up the senses of the two strangers to you, and business colleagues to me, both stumbled over their words, and the smell of male perspiration gave off – it was amazing to experience.

Driving to the conference, when you openly shared your business ventures and location, helping me pack my dress for the events, we drove through for 7 hours of mutual entertainment and interaction. Orgasms on the road till arrival. Continued, in conversation and sharing of minutes and hours. Still trying to find place for me in your family / tribe… sending me profiles of brainless intriguing to you, yet puppets of non-engagement to me. As I shall play with those that are at my level of intellect and not the human vibrator with flat vaginas that moan before they know why they moan, just mimicking what they have read in the 'Mills and Boon' or the pathetic TV shows. Give me something with substance …. Flabby skin and big tits with small nipples? All they do, is ride like they are on a rodeo bull and razor vulva – "no thank you!" was my response. I need something real to work with. A subject that does not brainlessly participate, and does not give me satisfaction through touching and engaging. Your search and study continued…. I loved it – again you played in my 'Master-ring'.

"You are not the average ordinary and you require your own unique jewellery box" … my response to that, was to not box me or label me, as you have never met a person that has such a strong way in ensuring a position of equality I shall Not be subservient to any… It fucked your mind to bring me to the standard that you are not used to… the Queen position that allows your freedom to engage with your toys… but when I enter – I am your Ultimate Prize and so you are my ultimate prize.

In further engagement the subject of marriage and children came through – as I have my position clearly stated, that I shall not be a subject of someone being hurt, or at any given point be exposed for my personal engagements of sexual prowess to damage a relationship of any kind. This resulted in a debate and started diminishing the sexual strength and power we hold over each other.

Although still very intrigued by your work of my understanding the need for you to engage in actions of humiliation, acts of woman in tying them up, blind folding them and making them into little girls and dogs – your stance was helping them to overcome their issues of -??? Do you keep them or do you make them understand why they are in need of that subservient humiliating position? To empower them to move towards self-empowerment or is it for your personal gratification? Of maintaining power?

Requesting photos of your times and checking when you are engaging in your games – it was indeed the times of travel rather than times of local. Your reading my texts were immediate at all times your posts on social media – did not correspond with times of having to engage with what you profess… I started wondering – how powerful you are with your tribes or families.

Your conquests where obvious on the social media posts and engagements – as if you are trying to build this empire – and all you do is a promise to ignite – yet, all you do is individually fuck woman in the hope that they would assist you in starting your tribe / family. So desperate you became that you would fuck anything to build this so-called family tribe. As when you were in my vicinity you re-listed yourself as PAUL with a new profile description – to which I enquired.

Photos sent of some person picked up in Portugal – the same person that sat on your back was the person that sucked your cock whilst driving.

The visit to you revealed more than you would think…. You arrived within seconds of my command – your persona when undressing to having me – showed no confidence in yourself – it was all about your entering me- to which at a point you were so desperate that you were close to forgetting your condom. How you played into my hands was brilliant in watching – the person that is so 'cock sure' yet sexually cannot hold – how then play your family tribe – when I am in the room your erection will not maintain the sexual games around you – an erect is what turns woman to acting more – to the point that they need to play the games you wish for them to do.

My slight tilt of my abdomen when you were inside me – made you cum in less than one count – you cannot maintain – you were done, and I did not even move… or started – the signs of someone that has not been satisfied in a while. With a pure smile and look – you could not hold back but to continue making love to me….

I cannot stay with you – my rule – I cannot take photos of me when my wife is with me – my rule

Really???

The morning dawned and there you were waking me – whispering how you wish for others to prepare me – for you – to the point I tired you that when my lips touched you, you could not hold back – while I smile …. Your member is not that big my darling, and my satisfaction was not physical in the least – as at no time did you feel or work towards me reaching an orgasm – as you couldn't – you knew not how to satisfy a woman.

The visit to your place of work – revealed more about how you would walk the street in arrogance as if I was a client – the ordering the look around – I took in every second to ascertain your position. Indeed, your woman that sat watching you, had a hold on you greater than you would believe – as we spoke in an underlying language that went over your head – the secret code of women… you touched me publicly and started relaxing only when she left the area…

When broaching the subject you retaliated in defence rather than admitting and accepting – such weakness… My subject

We met for a drink – which took us underground – in the corner – the office – not the person that holds the big seat – but the employee – the darkness of the bar – spoke more words than you would even think of your position in many ways. No – I was not going to bring some young girl that you have engaged with to play out your fantasy in my hotel room.

I walked away – with the upper hand – we are not done yet!!

To the next day to say good bye – in the cellar as if I was a business partner – she who controls your environment – walked down the stairs – to look and your reaction was that of submission rather than the king …. Spoke many words to the point that when you walked me and knowing you are watched – could not be your dark world confident self.

I left – knowing I know your weakness.

Which was later concluded as – you were done with me you said??? Yet would send me visuals as I requested it by the drop of a hat – read my every text, and then was curbed by the communication which came through from another to say – stay away

I hate you for trying to retaliate with insults to my intelligence and questioning my honesty and integrity

I love you for the experience!

∞

It has been a crazy few months of whirl wind / tornado living. Crazy entered my life and swoop up my world took me away and rapped up lifetimes into one – emotional roller coaster! WOW! Wild open winds!

What a crazy spin of events and people and total chaos and total madness!

It was necessary – very necessary to have such absolute crazy – to get me to just understand the madness out there – from a shielded life of conformity to what is going on out there and how easy it is to get lost in all the now! How quickly one can get swept up in the bullshit of personas created. The false impressions people and things create to the true reality of what is behind those masks!

So nice to breathe again!

To be me Again!

I love it!

∞

January 2017

I have been off the grid for a good reason – it was not only for the purpose of being completely outright exhausted – but also by the same token have to settle in the resolve that my purpose is bigger than just one specific organism.

My purpose is so big that I know not at times where to begin where to catch and where to release.

I drive down the road and can't read the headlines. I stop at a stop street / robot and can't look around. I drive down the road and can't drive over the road kill. I see and feel every piece of hurt as if it is my own.

My life sees and feels the hurt that is around, I anger at every pain, I feel it to the point where I want to scream!

I cannot listen to the news, read the papers and look at the photographs.

Therefore, I needed to exclude myself from it all the point where I can think and categorise and itemise and prioritise.

This is the time where what I have learnt and felt and seen be brought into reality of the magnitude to which this earth and all its being are being destroyed to the point where there is no other word but self-destruction.

I need to take my passion and knowledge to the level where I can turn over, a thinking, a pattern. To bring together the various components that are running at such disparity!

For a moment I want to be understood in my personal life by a partner, but then I want to be left alone to do that I need to do… I want to be needed and wanted and understood but I don't want to be owned, as I don't want to be set back in my journey. I want to be loved and adored, but my journey is mine, and don't want within the first meeting, be listening to how my place is going to be owned by someone other than me.

That is the fatal mistake they all make! Walk into my space and speak as if they are married to me …. And if not doing so on intro – start thinking that because they slept in my bed they have a right to my every move. Then there are those that sleep once – move on – and then come back for either advice, assistance or another place to stay. Then there are those that are just adoring from the outside.

Bottom line is, that I am not ready, or even remotely interested in having someone, anyone sharing my everyday space…

Too much to do... although with truth and respect must be said that I wish to have a free spirit around me, with the same, yet with the support and god only knows adores me, respects me and good sex please!! Continuously good, and not just once or have some sort of dysfunction of sloppy dick or fuck! Just amazing everyday every time! Has the laugh I would adore – the rhythm I would appreciate, the kiss I want to take in, the mind I want to learn from, I don't care where you are or what you do – as long as I know that you are mine and I am your Queen.

I have had brilliant sex, shit sex, have been entertained, had used, had faked. I am actually quite sexually exhausted of the mundane and not being stimulated in every aspect. I love women and love men. I have not found the right person to fill all the various aspects. I want to be entertained, stimulated, challenged, love life and share. The freedom and the belonging. The respect. Not to be taken for granted or taken advantage of… be my muse and I will be yours.

∞

What is it with the way people speak on the chatting, dating, tinder, WhatsApp platforms?

Because I am sensual doesn't mean I want to fuck. Sucking cock for a man comes natural as does pussy, have one hence knowing what we want if we don't find it in the opposite sex we look for it naturally. However, men don't like up the arse – women neither but because we know not where the vagina strength lies, we say and they want arse fuck – then they have also not learnt where the stimulus lies hence arse fucking – thank you xxx

∞

26 December 2015

A fresh morning woken to mist on the hills – rain fallen day and night.

Realisation that although the Christians celebrate the birth of their prophet, that brought to them the insight of what spiritualism and belief is. – have turned yes as symbolism of the bearing of gifts to the praise of their prophet's birth day, has become a commercialised materialistic exchange, rather than just the celebration of the origin of what was meant to have been the start of recognition of their birth and understanding of their belief system outside of their human creation.

A celebration of understanding that there is more to life than materialism has now become a celebration of materialistic needs. How did this come about other than as parents, we create this in our children? The excitement and build up with lists of wishes to a phantom character that bear gifts, trees, trinkets.

Then there is the wonder of family get together once a year to celebrate, however for the balance of the year where are we as family?

People give away their children forget they have children, loose their child in their selfish mode of drunken celebrations. Child and people disappointed at their gifts they receive. What and why has something that is meant to be so precious turned into such greed. What has the world created around celebration of their spiritual awakening and their prophet?

For the first time, I have not participated in this and I instead spent the day with my family who could enjoy this time of just relaxation and holidays and peace in their own. We could all just have inner joy rather than falsified joy. Cooking a great meal that was made with love and sharing around a table with love. The simple enjoyment of togetherness, I have realised this by have to have my younger son not with me, but rather he opted to remain with his father who celebrates this time more and the financial means to spoil in the excess purchase of lavish gifts. A person that only understands money and does not understand spirit and the essence that it brings to the material physical world. A hypocrite in every aspect when it gets to the human soul, loyalty, people, heart, relationships. Person who bathes his every being and minute in the pleasures of the physical.

My little boy being in his way at his age which I assume is approprioate in his stage still very enthralled with this joy of being showered with earthly materialistic pleasures. It dawned on me that this is in fact what we as parents teach our children. Although we as a couple had always had this clash or disagreement where to me the celebration of your own is more important and not he falsified celebration as raising our children in an agnostic, universal, holistic, spiritual, non-denominational fashion, we ought to be celebrating our own and not just the coming of a singular prophet as our lives are made up of various points of understanding and realisation. Every prophet had and has a message and a truth. It all depends on your interpretation and your realisation of what works for you and how you wish to implement that message and if you are at that point in yourself and inner growth to accept such for the sake of your own personal development.

I celebrate your life and not the commercialised life of some prophet for the sake of the masses or a holiday.

∞

Amazing how I view it all with such –
no affiliation – cold like there is
nothing to it… what have we
become? Sluts – tell me your story.
I am done, my last lifetime! I don't
want to leave any harm, hurt or
traces behind! I am done!

"no such a thing as poverty – it's
called education! Change! Reinvent
yourself, learn, read, investigate,
don't take things for granted"

"You take me the way I am"

"Lion – big fat cat – make how many
babies?
Big fat Rhino eats grass
what is the issue?
Inhumanity of killing vs trade vs
heritage vs money vs ego"
"if you can replace food with tablets
and 3D prints – then print a large 3D
Penis to stroke your ego"

Budget:
Wine R90
Cigarettes R40
Fuel R50 = R180 per day
Cucumber R20
Tomatoes R20
Cheese R45
Eggs R20

R105 per week / 7 = R15 per day
R195 x 30 = R5850 – Ange

R7500 – house
R1500 – dogs
R1500 – insurance
R700 – medical
R2000 – cell and Wi-Fi
R300 – policies = R11 700
R17 550 per month

∞

Why coming out of my sabbatical on
10 01 2017
1 1 1
3
Everything in life happens in 3s – the way I live my life

Past + present + future
God the father + God the Son + God the holy ghost
Mother + father + child
Earth + water + Air
regardless of the way you look at it
pyramids, prisms, meditation
left + right + centre

My passion lies with children as they are not only the most vulnerable, but also the future of the survival of this planet at large and education of child is what will save the survival of fauna, flora, animals, water, sea, life etc. with skill and knowledge transfer, with awareness creation through touch and feel and reality with art, performance and music, we will create the conservation of this planet for the future

The affluent cat takes their kids on safaris and camps, but what about those that can't? Again I hugged those many vulnerable little beings and it was heart-breaking to notice how many are afraid of touch, how many ducked for cover the moment I lifted my arms to hug them. This is the future generation 200 children = 200 future families. When you live in the city you only see the desperate – however when you live in the country you notice the love for nature and animals. Yet everyone flocks to the city, to become part of the severe rat race. Many go hungry, many participate in solicitations of body, mind in participation of some form of substance, to forget. When in the country you see subsistence but the human race is never satisfied – there is this constant "I want more" which is indeed another catch 22

"The village idiot vs the river" – by the same token, I am not a cub petter, but you hold a cup and feed him. I am not a whatever but you make the animal used to human contact. In nature when there is a reject it dies – all I know is that my passion lies with kids and their safety education – that how we will save the future of this planet and all that comes with it.

"have to establish my website"
"#repost"
"#endangeredvoices"
"#usewhatyouhave"

∞

6 February 2017

Magaliesburg here I am:

- Welfare4
- Counselling
- Mediation
- Children and community
- Bank – claims and invoices
- Recalculation of divorce payments
- Monthly expense calculation – without knowing your monthly expense you know NOT what to charge and what your income should be
- Training school
- Puppies
- Welfare2

∞

23 February 2017

Following the most brilliant awe inspiring reading! With all the questions answered in the most unique way when planets align and semi-questions that needed answers –

The most amazing of all - hearing a voice that once was laden with so much of the world that sounded so light

I was pivotal I am making it happen! A soul that through my doing – the result of sheer bliss – such happiness!

Praise God can we all turn every sound that falls on my ears, following my touch sound so light.
Awe inspired so gentle, once they have moved through my touch, regardless of the time spent and the moments shared!

∞

24 March 2017

What do you want Ange?

I want to feel wanted and loved unconditionally without restrictions. I want to be the Queen, Priority.
When we first started talking "J" you were very responsive and communicative, which made me feel wanted enough to pursue in a direction of super bliss, more than just infatuation. As we started, I felt honesty, truth and openness, instead you wanted, or thought of me as just another sex toy, which I am not.

Which started irritating me, as you are no one's toy or puppy – you are intelligent strong, passionate and by no means a weak character, which I have high regard for and respect for.

So here goes: whatever you present, need to entail commitment to making me your Queen, Priority, Communication. I have my friends that entertain me, and if you are my King – I will present that to the balance. If they are not prepared to accept this, then they move on that's as simple as that.

Simple, as I am as straight forward, it will be, and that is my decision – I know in my soul that this is what its meant to be, I meet connect and have people in my life for a reason, and together we communally work.

So I need to remain entertained in your absence, you will be my base to whom I wish to release my contained love – the balance to be my temporary.
You are the intellectual strength I enjoy the perfect kind for me – I want us to develop together.
If I have the assurance of that my base foundation is laid, I can move forward with confidence and surety.

∞

25 March 2017

The silence is deafening after dropping my kids off with their Dad, gone for a groom, and nervously excited about what the next few days hold.
I want to have some clarity about my future as feel in limbo right now.
Meeting this man that has turned me upside down.
Been given this opportunity to make my other dreams come true, to put a small town on the map. I am heading off tomorrow to get some answers, some decisions.
At the same time the possibility exists where the position I want has also to become available.
I will work that power position, to make a difference to focus on what I have been fighting for. Its time!
I am ready to take on this challenge to turn this organisation around into a business that fends for so many children and to make it what it is meant to be. For people to put their faith back into children and development of the organisation. I want this job!
I am ready!

That is what I want:
I want J to be with me
I want the Welfare Position

I am investing these next few days in my future and will focus on that:
1. Outsource accounting function
2. Outsource HR/IR function
3. Implement new Constitution
4. Standardise all offices
5. Standardise Government funding
6. Franchise the organisation
7. Partner with Corporates for CSI
8. Partner with Universities for skills development and service hours
9. Partner with Department of Education for ECDS and schooling

10. Partner with food suppliers and retail chain stores
11. Partner with Department of Health
12. Partner with Motor industry/Spoornet/Transnet
13. Partner with agriculture and conservation

To invest in our children and youth

∞

"I have a busy life
you have a busy life
I want to be your first and last thought
Your every dream
- so goddamn simple"

"fucking is physical
- the fear is -
what if there is a connection"

∞

23 July 2017

A brilliant day of painting and peace spent.

All is a sheer moment of not planning, a moment yet being in a position to allow and inspire. Back to the point where the clearing of the mind, was all with not holding back.
The one side of the mind came to closure, as the other adorned with opening an email of affirmation confirmation from my astrology reading, which needed to just confirm what I wish to hear or read at this time.
From whenst I am currently knowing what I want and have commenced, to what needs to find its foundation.
Brilliant!!!
Now writing this is curbing my open space which I created today, and wish not to continue this writing.
Feeling that now is not the time but will be commencing the plan in the a.m. – thank you

∞

2017

My nerves are absolutely shot! I have been chatting to a Frenchman that lives afar, for four months we have been in contact. Met him once at Lanseria airport for a few hours – where everything and everyone disappeared – it was only the two of us, like Casa Blanca the old movie. When he met me at the entrance of the airport building is was an instant connection of so much chemistry, so much passion, and a dual of sexual energy! When he took and when we kissed – strong powerful. His arms pulled me closer and that's where I stayed – close to him – kissing holding touching. His powerful grip made me want to retaliate, but also made me want to submit at the same time. Was as though we needn't have spoken but we did – he asked me not what I want, but instead told me how this will work. His concern was, my frustration, as he leads a busy life. Which I completely do myself, and understand what is meant to be busy, and don't have the time to play couple, as our focus and work. Both with what we have started establishing in our lives, our homes, our children.

Me still in the transition phase and needing to set my own grounds, my own home, my move, establishing my career and clearing my name from past debts. Not ready to engage in any form whatsoever in any relationship of sorts. I quite frankly did not have the time nor the personal capacity. I needed to get foundations laid somewhere, make a home for myself and my children. During this time there where many encounter with various amazing people whom entered my life and I needed to set boundaries.

My personal boundaries, what do I want and who do I want it with. What will I tolerate and where do I draw the line.

My first of course is for people to know and understand the passion I have for my causes and if you are not going to support me in every aspect, understand what I do - then I wish you not to be around me

I need the person to know I have young children, their happiness and stability is key and comes first. Understanding hat at the drop of a hat I shall get up and be there for them.

My other thing is that my family is important and that they too belong in my life, and I in theirs.

My animals are important and I will be there for them when they need me.

My friends are diverse and they too have their place in my life which I will not stop for anyone

Conversation – oh stimulating conversation – stories, exchange of words, not just silly, stupid derogatory jokes – no snide remarks, not just sex talk, no racism, no killing, not on the first meet start talking "we", making plans about my home, my life, my body as if they own it ... Yoh!! Not have a sense of style, funny face when they laugh – ugly when they look up.

Jokes – please no constant below the belt comments, always with reference to sex, vagina, penis.

Not wanting to travel and experience life.

Constantly speaking about their ex- and how they are hurt and damaged, but forgets it comes from both sides.

Sense of dress, class and style.
Good taste in food and wine.
Music and variation of sounds and genres.
Sense of art, the appreciation thereof.
Independence, fucking hell! live with your parents, live in backpackers, live from

adult to adult, don't have a car, don't have a life, - holy crap dudes – really!
Arrive empty handed or travel without your wallet.
Not being able to handle your drink or weed WOW.

I am so tired of this useless nonsense

Woman that want to play but too scared to do so.

Men that think women are rubbish.

I am so over it.

Silly fucken chat up lines – how are you to day…. Really … and then please god
those contractors, I am so so tired of all this shit – I can scream – OH MY then the
fucksters – sexters really – I can make you cum in 2 seconds straight over the phone
… 3-4 men at the same time!

Stupid stupid stupid

Needless to mention the fact that within one or two texts I have lost you, because
your EQ and wit can't keep up with me.

So after all this being alone and being on the various dating platforms – what is it
that you want?

Here goes:
- strong personality
- educated
- independent – financially stable
- respect
- sense of humour
- non-judgemental
- loving
- caring
- style – sense of dress
- music
- art
- manners
- love children
- love animals
- cook
- passion
- drive
- ambition
- honesty
- I must be his Queen at all times

Now: work priorities:
a) Childwelfare 1
b) mediation
c) personal divorce settlement

d) unisa enrolment – complete subjects for degree
e) Childwelfare 2
f) conservation – media and handover docs and goods
g) community development – magaliesburg
h) focus on getting interactive counselling website
i) conservation education
j) Good Governance Inc.
k) Book
l) Rates

"So it's my brainchild for the good – I don't want to become rich, I want to cover my costs and live my passion"

Good governance Inc. lady:

- Why? I have learnt what is required to implement and instil good governance in an organisation which is started for a purpose of passion.
- Non-profits are formed for this reason and the benefit of the voiceless
- People with various passion and skill from non-profits for the benefit of the voiceless and on the outset with good intentions, heart and soul
- Those that give towards the Npo do this with heart, with soul and with hard earned money
- When you work hard for what you have and give with good intention you give a part of you toward the benefit of what you have intended to save
- When this hard earned is being miss-used – miss-allocated it hurts, as you know it is a part of you, your heart, your trust that has been miss-used – you feel betrayed
- Then the opposite of the coin is real – the organisation formed for the good is again people that started this with good intention
- Just as a profitable company is formed so a non-profit is formed
- But what does it require: does and artist, musician follow his passion for the purpose of becoming a millionaire? No, they paint, sing, perform with passion
- Likewise, the non-profit is created with exactly the same
- Can a lawyer / accountant – paint sing dance – no
- Therefore, non-profits – started with passion for the voiceless can't expect to run and manage with a sense of business yet they are expected to
  Hence the good governance lady

Non-profits – children – animals – planet – elderly

Board pack:
Board training
Constitution
Financials
Minutes
Narrative reports
Report writing
Public relations

Legal
BEE
SARS
Clearances
Project management
Human resources
Affiliations
Administration
Record keeping
Community profiling

Social work
Mediation
Counselling
Courses – NLP, Astrology, Tarot = understanding humans
Register my own business
Website
Facebook page
Instagram
Twitter
LinkedIn

∞

I wonder why we always seek the approval of others to live the life we want to live. Why when you share a space with someone – which I have just done – a stranger complete stranger moving into my space I was so desperate for his approval and for seeking his approval.

Why is that? – and what happened – disapproval, changing my lifestyle, changing my haven, thought processes, daily life, tolerating, discarding, losing, allowing criticism, slaving, all for approval?

For a peck, a pen, a hug.

We had sex the first night we met, it was more a fuck – as I needed to turn my back to be fucked.

We had sex the second time where I was pushed down on him with my face so he could get hard.

We had sex the third time where it was me have to be oral to get nothing in return.

From there I was not allowed to participate in any other intimacy, unless I recruited another woman.

"Three or nothing" he said

Sex object and a means to live a fantasy

Cuddles, snuggles touching – but no verbal regard.

Bath together, share bed, snuggle cuddle touch.

But sexual arousal only on screen.

Verbal degradation, not good enough, but visits to the bathroom with the phone to wank or take dick pics.

To no touch, to no cuddle, to constant verbal disrespect, to could not give a flying continental fuck or regard for anything.

Yet, still seeking approval and thank you, a phone call, recognition, something – anything…? Why do we do this?

From my personal – I feel used

From my professional – I feel insulted

I opened my arms to you, which resulted first in sexual games, to opening my doors which turned into changing my lifestyle, turning into opening all my doors and having to hear, I am not good enough to watching you play on your devices.

I opened my doors to previous sexual partners, entertaining them at my expense, opening my doors to your friends, to opening my doors to meetings, to as far as opening my house for your drug drop offs, driving you around from pillar to post. Risking everything, while you feed your habits putting all on hold and setting all aside, to watch you while you move further away, and in the sly speak to them, when yet I am not blind. When asked, I am the one to get shouted at, called all sorts of names. You want to be pampered and intimate but yet want to wonder… Return from your business trip – all digressed from there …

Now from a professional – you think I am also stupid when I watch you try take credit for all, overstep the lines, speak with such derogatory disrespect toward women in fort of me …

- What's your ID number and full names?

Here is your one-way ticket back to where you came from … let me drop you at the airport to ensure you take that flight!

∞

26 March 2017

This amazing person so intriguing has entered into my life – for the first time I feel like I have met a challenge of not only understanding the various cultures but also the question about – can I feel safe and comfortable with someone that gets me… that in turn we can speak… with open honest sexual quest – I don't want to be tied to anyone's string but I want to be felt like I belong – and that is what I want – first I need to listen – and it is with open heart and soul without prejudice – to what the whole intrigue with me is – as I am certainly not your ordinary – and that is what I love – I thought that with what I expose – that it not be read – yet today – I heard that every word is being read – I live on social media for a reason – a for my causes and b for finding the person that will stand by my side and be strong - I am tired of babying and tired of directing – I want the person that stands by my side to hold me – yet fuck me – yet move with me as I move – because I do not want to be contained or boxed in any way – I want to have the freedom – as well as the partnership – can anyone sustain that ?? I believe in my heart of souls that I have had the part where I was the wife the mommy the sub servient that I am now at the point that I need to be with someone that not only has me sexually but also culturally, artistically, emotionally, intellectually

I am not a naive and stupid girl – I work fucking hard – I love fucking hard – I play fucking hard

I lived a life where I had a man that irritated the living shit out of me – but we needed to live our life path – to close the karma of the past – and for that I am grateful – I have the kids finally but not the husband – whoop whoop !! and my kids are brilliant !! the foundations which I was meant to have laid as a mother – I have done!! The balance I will be there – but their journey is indeed theirs

I now have this person whom I feared and treaded lightly for – that I now have in the palm of my hand – I love the fact that there is a dual – your rules – really darling – you are married and still so tied by those strings – you want to break loose and you don't know how – I want you to tell me how you plan to do this – I see the subtle put off – when you speak about the wife – convenience my ass – French society in cape town my ass – you need to tell me the truth – once that is settled we shall move forward as I am not the concubine – I am the white tiger that will choose whom I play with – you were intrigued – you where Casablanca – now you have to put the mouth where the vagina is darling – you know I don't back down and I showed you that – however in the same token I showed you a controlling part of respect – which I know we duly appreciated – as I showed you- you showed me – which I love

You are mine master – whether you like it or not – intrigued you are sir – it is now for us to find a way to make this a reality – therefore I need you to play such open cards – as I am not going to break up a marriage – I shall however – be the one that will give you the open route to make up your mind as to what the fuck you want darling

As you have a partner that enjoys life and lives life and fears nothing of this plane – so let's see what you bring to the table

I shall call this the bucket list

∞

Yes, I am outright pissed at you right now, as I know not what you think my intent is… be it as it may I shall put it to you in writing to assist you with not further engaging in this avoidance ceremony ….

There are many ways to say thank you to someone… buying flowers, gifts and sending thank you cards…. But because this is such an important thank you, for me there is nothing better than someone going through the effort to make something from the heart – a hearty meal was what came to mind… with a personal touch…

A whirlwind has taken me from where I was, where I last spoke or seen you to a most peaceful and splendific place, which I wished to have shared with you as you were there during the total mess and destruction, chaos that forced decisions and change…

Was I just a tick on your bucket list – I know not, however to me it was another sign that remaining in my circumstances was soul destroying, was rendering to self-destruction and a total world of disrespect.

Was I the new porn channel that replaced fashion tv – I know not, however it took me to a level within myself that scared me, and had to look at the reflection of myself in the mirror to say, you are not that revolting as you are made out to be.

Was I just another woman at a gig – I know not, however to me at the point of such self-loathing you thought I was worth a heartbeat.

Was I just an excuse to give you the reason to end a relationship – I know not, however to me there is someone that could be gentle with me…

Was I just a text away – I know not, however to me I had a chat when loneliness was all I knew...

Did I make the decision to take a stand to make a change to start anew, because of you, for you…? NO – I made the decision to take a stand to make a change to start anew FOR ME!!!

What you did do for me was be the catalyst – that lit the fire within me to stand up for myself and for my boys. To say no to enduring any further and more abuse! To not be the mother or the woman that continues saying – it's okay!!! When indeed it is everything other than okay!!

After 20 years I need to find Angelique Buckingham again – and I am so looking forward to that! And would like to take the hands of everyone that was there for me during this time – and say thank you in my own unique way! And introduce everyone to my new little heaven of which I am so proud …

So – I wish to thank you Brian – you mean a lot to me – as my catalyst!!

You have all of my information and most of my words…

Be Well

∞

9 July 2017

I woke this morning with a need to love and be loved in that I felt to text my person whom I thought is the strong one to be with me as I am – what am I. I am stronger than the regular woman out there for the experiences in relationships I have been through. I am scared of being with a person again that will not admire my hard work and appreciate my caring and love I have to give, I want that respect of being free yet loved and adored, someone I can look up to, that understands the way my mind and heart works without wanting to possess me, or just fuck me without understanding my mind and appreciate my knowledge and integrity.

I have the ability to separate the sexual physical from the balance of my life and can't entertain useless immature ultra-doff. I need to be stimulated mentally intellectually and physically as well as adored for my heart, my passion, my soul and yes... I am fucking lonely without that person that is just there for me, as I do appreciate being touched and affection.

To wake to an immature answer from the person I thought that would be that and understand to find another disappointment in immaturity.

I want to cry for that although knowing that, and slowly reaching that through the months of engagement that when subjects that require conversation – it lacked the body that is required to continue and receive my respect – it did diminish and wane away to the point where I was doing again the dominant mommy protector position, rather than the equal to respectful position. I did indeed push the boundary, to see how it would submit to me, and it worked to this point where now I am disappointed, at the level of immaturity.

I am – more angered and disappointed at the concept of or rather realisation that he has resulted in another weak character.

Fuck man! What the fuck – honestly?

The other one on the other hand finds me not important enough to make me in anyway a priority – but still converses as if I am. What are the chances that once the ski trip is over so would the interaction? From here on I am done!

I need to focus on my career and business which I have to complete, establish and make the necessary arrangements. What is that you hope to achieve? On a personal level you have actually crushed what you wanted to as far as the dating site scene is concerned.

I believe you should move on! – done- Many have your contact details and many can make the effort...if they don't they are not worth it...

Childwelfare – you have done what you could Angelique there are people that are getting paid to do their job. They know who you are, your abilities and capabilities and they can approach you if they need to.

Community development – same as with child welfare

AngelScouts – that is what is important right now you have to focus

Studies – complete it focus

Short term income – send mediation quotes

House – Visitor 1 and Visitor 2, pay to stay boys R1k each

AngelScouts will focus on: boy child and girl child program – studies will work on magaliesburg community development.

∞

25 October 2017

Anger, hopeless, meaningless

Yes!! I am fucken lonely and angry and sad and every bit that one could wake to feel fucking can. I just want to fuck off somewhere somehow and not participate I miss my children, I miss giving love and feeling loved

I am angry at me feeling like this

I am angry at him for taking me to this position

I am angry at the world that hurts others

I am angry at being taken advantage of

I am angry at fighting for justice when all I see is injustice

I am angry at people taking their shit out on me

I am angry at stupid people that don't think their actions have consequences

I am angry at myself for drinking and smoking so much

I am angry at myself for feeling listless

Am angry at getting to this point in my life that all I feel is anger right now

I am angry at "L" for making me feel love again and leaving

I am angry at "J" for playing me

I am angry at allowing myself to be so desperate to be loved that I allow men to take advantage

I am angry at being fucken angry

I am lonely and feel lonely and I hate feeling like this

I am angry at everyone that does not understand that I am alone, that has never bothered to ask has just fucked off and don't bother and I feel meaningless

I don't want to be with you everyday

I don't want to invade your space

Not do I want you to invade mine

I just want to know that you love me

That I am your every thought

That you see me with your closed eyes

That you read me when I write you

That you can't stop the warm feeling in your heart when you think of me or you see my notes

I want to be - that one that makes you want to be your best at everything you do

Even when you spend a moment or 2 with another that is for that momentary physical stimulus

That I have the deep seated love, warmth and thoughts that connect my soul to yours and yours to mine

The one you crave to see, to be with to share with

I want to be that Crown Queen in your every moment, that even if there is no physical contact – the contact comes from a deeper soul connection, that does not need words to be exchanged, that does not require permanence in physical space, but there is that butterfly that comes to sit on my soul – heart when your thought comes up

Someone out there loves you, and you love someone out there – my expectation is not much

∞

27 October 2017

I realise you from the pain you allow yourself to endure

I love you for who you are and what you have become. You have arrived on this plane at this time of the development of your soul journey to embrace and heal from your previous lives and journeys that you needed to live.

The change you need to bring is the changes within yourself and the love for yourself to accept yourself and to in turn learn to give yourself first before you can think of understanding the world around you!

Forgive the child inside you, birth, raise and feed the child inside you – allow it to crawl, walk, laugh and play, run and learn. Love and be loved – be resilient in not taking it all personally as you don't yet understand the world around you and don't know the heart, intentions, reality and fears of others. Look at it through the eyes of a child – look at yourself through your child's eye and say to yourself – hey that's ME! Nurture yourself through your own realisation and reality and so their eyes will open to see you as you are. Eyes, ears, now, mouth – arms legs tummy that is you – look at you through the child's eye – who are you? YOUR ARE THEIR MOTHER EARTH!!!!!

Self-love is not selfish – self-love is being able to look in the mirror and saying – I love this soul – look at you in the mirror and see yourself, not the back ground, not the vessel, not everything around you – look at you! You! You! No one else but you. And love, forgive and embrace you!

∞

27 October 2017

Amazingly I requested the guidance of my Angels

Which I have not embraced for a while and through deciding to re-invoke me in my healing of the inner aspects and inner child – there it was – Michael, Uriel, Gabriel and Raphael – hearing my prayer as I asked for guidance – the symbols as I breathed – the snakes three snakes in three weeks that crossed my path.

They need for moving, into change and higher vibrations as the requests came through from my inner soul – the cross of the layout of my cards, the Buddhism layout came through the exact emotion – motion and questions revealed as to my 'journey' now as I have been spending my day – awakening the reasons for being alone right now – with no interference and clearing my thoughts and mind

As I read the symbols coming through, I commenced with meditation, the know on my door to show me the snakes

Research now the meaning of the snake as your symbol for strength as you require this with no fail or return

∞

27 October 2017

Why should I

In all the time I have been me, I have always chased after the man! I have as Angelique, never had a man or a woman for that matter, ever had someone chase after me?

From as far back as I remember, even the person I married, no one has ever said!! "This is my person Angelique and will fight for her!"

No fucking one – "wow"

Regardless of whom, and what I have been, or done, or stood for, no one had ever stood their ground and said I am for you! And for you I fight! And understand to be! As I do for them him or her!! My fucken reality – wow wow wow!!!

The only one that has never given up on me is my Mom!! In her own nativity, in her own sometimes stupidity, her own shit, she has always… never questioned her love for me!!

 She is my brilliant mother!! The only one that has shown me unconditional love! I can be where, when, whatever, she is the most amazing heroine I know, always, love YOU Mamma!

∞

August 2018

I embrace the honour of sitting above the mountain top the highest point. Where I felt so low in my heart and soul just a few hours ago to run, but not to hide to hide, yet not to run as running is not an option. Escape from the drudgery of self-fulfilment where honour for the universe and that which is in our hearts is not seen by the other heart.

I embrace with all dignity and power that was bestowed upon me, to take on the inherent belief in the honesty and good that I know every being still has, regardless of their surroundings and their superficial requirements to be seen instead of being heard.

Every inner voice has the power to turn, yet the most externally broke, external fake beauty. It whispers in every soul till it becomes heard, even the man that quietly brushed the pillars with the paint – in his mind in his heart, the little voice keeps speaking as working through the many calibrating thoughts that go through to disseminate that which needs to be done, to reach ultimate peace in realizing how every part of his world falls into place.

The inner voice softly whispering to show him the way. We have to listen sometimes to that gentle silence. The world is never silent as you look over the rolling hills closing your eyes. The world is never silent it speaks all the time.

As that little voice, take heed as you are introduced for whatever reason to the places – the people, the animals, the nature and the sounds for the universe conspires to all, you to learn from every breath and encounter.

The message is there, it is within, oft we need to be pointed, and the conspiracy theory created the surrounding in our universe, unique to the vibrations at which our individual worlds within ourselves take every step of its journey to attain fulfilment.

∞

August 2018

Escape the space you find yourself in, open the door to different environments. Take in that which is different to what was perceived in your frame before. Bump into beautiful people that shared some form of new or older spaces. Different walks different views and to hear from others that are remote that you are acknowledged for what you bring to make that heartfelt difference – walk outside of that which you had always been in – walk outside and see experience new perceptions of others-

Walk outside and see, experience new perceptions of others – walk outside – step back and see that which you created spreads way further than your closed look the heights you have reached is way higher than what the eye can see. When you are inside – it was difficult to ascertain the impact of what you created. The journey you have started, whilst on the road all you see is what is in your periphery and in front of you. Yet when you step outside you see just how far you have travelled and what you have built. The size of the impact is often misjudged when you are standing caught in the moment.

∞

Another day – absolute bliss of an evening amongst strangers who all had one agenda and that would be to have fun, dance, get drunk and underlying competitive streaks as all had to be the best, the most charming the best dancer, sexiest being and win at their game, best person.

Amazing – to break away to being and allowing myself to be treated – to be spoiled to be just taking in what is making him also feel good – he wants to be the provider, the giver and he wants you to be the receiver. Feeling the princess. It is what is important and to have been the quiet experience and not be the strong provider you always are and just allowing. What and experience of being the recipient. What an amazing experience of bliss – subliminal bliss of just being and most amazingly allowing the experience to flow without arguing without standing up against it and without fights is – just letting be and watching experiencing and indulging in every second as every day unfolded.

What a sheer pleasure to the point that you had released yourself to enjoy and take in every moment of sexual experience to orgasms that far surpassed any expectations as you never expected you just lived and breathed from the moment you booked and allowing yourself to experience and walk into the unknown.

You need the confidence and strength within to allow yourself to walk in and arrive to – I don't know... that all just unfolds, as it should, and just be, oh my god, and you did. From arrival to departure, pure existence of people of nature of nurture. Just being – no one knowing where you are and what you do just and escape. I could escape like this always

Amazed at the fact that when you take a pen and book sit and write how the questions come to mind of people who walk by and those around – I wrote 2 x poems now on what I feel about the persons first meet.

Thabani and Nothando I could feel their spirits of anguish and love it overwhelmed me as I am sitting here so open spiritually after opening myself to achieving the most enduring orgasms that opened my realm to such closeness to a universal power of nothing– when there is nothing – I experience a being that is so real in all aspects that has just so goddamn amazing where there was nothing at all – no intro – no exit – just being

I did not even talk much, I just watched, just listened. Allowed even the smallest remarks to not take any part of upsetting of revoking of wanting to prove – to correct – to be. What a blissful experience! I feel self-indulged and spoilt by allowing things to flow which is what I need to do from now on – let it be Ange – let is flow – allow Angelique

Yes – I am sitting at the gateway in Durban the News Café – having a glass of wine Kanonkop – a bottle actually after saying goodbye – will I see him again – I don't know – will it just be a weekend of brilliance – I think – yes, as I don't want to lose this feeling of pure bliss with more! It was phenomenal – a peak of absolute stunning! If there is more it will mess it up.

Human nature want to go back and seek additional, when yet, you should just be satisfied with the experience and move on – when you reach a certain time and age, you realise that – it would be cold – but it's done – it is what it is! A slab of chocolate is great the first time you taste it – you go back to experience that taste again – what happens – it never tastes the same! Never, because the way you felt at the craving you had at that time that you first tasted will never be the same – never. So love and embrace and endure it, savour the taste, brilliant – when it's done – you are done – it will never taste the same!

∞

Getting back into reality is not every man's game but it needs to be done… flying back after being treated with such amazing unconditional humility my life has changed.

I met the most amazing soul on my journey through life, that without question took me in showered me with unconditional humility, graced me with such honour and respect, adapted my views with his presence, and surprised me with every touch… I thank you, I returned a changed person.

My journey is refreshed and my heart and mind is open to moving forward. I need decision to be made, and me to take control of my life again.

With open eyes and mind I can now focus on what it is I want again. No one will sway me right now and now one is worth more than me right now – this is me.

∞

Doctor Doctor:

From as far back as I can remember, the Doctors I have been introduced to have all made me feel most uncomfortable. From the General Practitioner that insisted on putting his cold hands on my little developing boobies, to having to put his hands down the front of my panties to check if I really have a cold or a fever. I hated those Doctor's visits.

Living in Barkston Drive, a few houses up from us was a Homeopath. We were testing remedies for finding a cure for the allergies I had. Many days he insisted that part of the therapy and research was for me to strip down completely naked, stand in front of the mirror while he took photographs of me. Back, front, sitting, walking, lying down, bending over. This was an ongoing process that according to him, he was monitoring my development and progress whilst finding a cure for my allergies.

'Mamma, I don't know how to tell you this but my urine is burning and something does not feel right. 'This was after my being raped. My first introduction to a gynaecologist. Afraid of her as she prodded this cold instrument in my vagina, under this big light. After she was done, she walked to my mom and said; 'you know your daughter had sex' …. I was so scared and so embarrassed and ashamed. I was diagnosed with having Gonorrhoea.

From age 16, every year I went for laparoscopies removing cysts from my ovaries. Cleaning and clearing my cervix and fallopian tubes. Adonomas started eating away at my right ovary. Endometriosis caused more damage to the point that my right fallopian tube needed to be removed at age 20.

There must be something wrong with me. The fault must be lying with me that I don't want to have sexual intercourse with my husband. I must have an underlying problem, because every time we do make love, I have infections. Let me go to find natural remedies and solutions. The Iridologist. You definitely have to have this solution, black ink together with these drops. You are going to feel a little drowsy, and tearful. Let me hold you, while I apply pressure to the area that you have issues with. (just to find out later that I was not the only woman that this happened to).

The damage done to my young virgin had left much destruction.
I so wished to have a child of my own.

First during our affair, I my period was late...
"I am worried, I think I am pregnant"
"no you are not, I have special intuition and can detect when someone is pregnant"
….. 'Ange do you know he had a vasectomy?'
….. 'I didn't but I don't mind, I love him, so we can adopt'
….. 'no, I will not let you adopt, you will not bring a strange child into our lives'

Every woman with a protruding belly, became my arch enemy. Shame, their poor heels as I accidently rammed my shopping cart into their heels. My feet were so clumsy, they found their way in front of many pathways…

The mission started…. Frist the Vasectomy reversal… Failed… followed by testicular biopsy… Success!

Medfem clinic became the new home away from home. Another laparoscopy to clean up any possible blockages, and cysts. Medication, anti-biotics, oestrogen creams. Then the pin-cushion party! There was no more fear of needles allowed. Then the big day arrived when my eggs where to be harvested. I was lucky, they managed to harvest 12 eggs from my one and only ovary. The healthy 4 was kept for me. A request came through for a woman that was not as fortunate, so I signed and agreed to donate the other eggs to help her. (I don't know her identity; all information I am privy to is that she birthed a healthy little girl. This little girl still appears in my dreams with her long brown curly hair).

Then I met my little baby when he was only 4 cells big on the screen before he was injected back into my womb. So blessed I am.

'Mom, I want a brother or sister, all my friends have babies, I also want a baby.'

A month before this request, I received a phone call to ask if we wish to discard of the sperm still in the freezer in the laboratories, either donate or destroy. The option was to destroy.

 Here I am back again at Medfem. Another laparoscopy to commence the process. This time the cold process of walking into a Sperm bank having to open a file with a spreadsheet. Dark hair, blue eyes, sporty, 1.8m tall, slender built, College graduate, cleared from tay-sachs. I now have to select my ideal description of my ideal father for my child.

Thought I was a pincushion before? Well this time after 4 x failed IVFs (Invetro Fertilisation) failed attempts. The process less expensive was that of Artificial inseminations. The mind started searching, as it seems like the spreadsheet-sperm is not so fit and fabulous after all. Who has successfully fathered children that I know, that would be prepared to assist? Aha!! I know someone with good looking features… A cup of coffee later, and I have my new donor. Not so cold and impersonal anymore. Seven artificial attempt later. By now my legs and bum had no more space for any more pin pricks.

One last try – then I give up…. Then that phone call…. 'do you want a baby?' – it was surreal, I immediately called Dad, 'this feels right' –

'OPEN THE BLOODY DOOR'!!!

There he was – this little tiny baby!!!

Completely overwhelmed, excited, nervous, as if I have never in my life held a baby!!!

Everything was packed in boxes, as we were moving to our new home in 2 days' time!!!

Going to fetch my other baby at school, I could not wait to tell the big news of this little angel that awaits at home!!!

Two years it took us to finalise the paper work, but there was no giving up on this little bean. From the phone call to tip me off of the transaction made by the tummy mom with the Nigerian drug lords for the exchange of R50 0000, the visitation of the tummy dad in jail, heightening of security as the extortion commenced. There was no turning back. This is my child!!

Year upon year, with Endometriosis, cysts, painful heavy periods that caught me a lot of times in the most embarrassing spaces, blood gushing down my legs, lower back pain, spastic colon, painful intercourse. There was no other option but for an early full hysterectomy.

Oh the relief – the relief of getting rid of this thing that constantly reminded me of the sick experience that destroyed my virginity!

I am blessed now with, no reminder, no more pain!

I am the happiest 'Sports model' in the world.   You see, I have always wanted to be a model, now just look at me.

Then that horrible pig in his yellow bakkie that thought he could invade me. The memories encoded in my body from the time of being raped. My body reacted to the threat again of this. The Opening of my vagina swell closed, the sick pouring down my legs. Another reconstructive surgery of my Bartholin gland and tubes.

My best doctor still is my Psychiatrist that treated me in Ward 4 after recovering from the suicide. Bless him for giving me hope and strength. Making me realise that it was not my fault. I am not to blame.

The continued search in trying to find solace during the various forms of abuse had brought me to many other healers to find answers. Marriage counsellors, psychologists, psychiatrists all telling me that I should not continue with my marriage. But I had hope, I remained optimistic and continued till I could no more.

Further journeys in seeking solace and various forms, from self-help books, (as the problem must lie with me) to studying of psychology, comparative religions, meditation, astrology, tarot. Going for regression therapy, hypnosis.

I do rejoice my healers that have worked with me on Reiki, Serio, Janine, Heiltje that have worked with me in finding answers throughout the process of healing. Finding answers to realising and understanding that what I have endured is NOT MY FAULT.

I praise and thank God, My Angels and The Universe.

I am Angelique

∞

"How do I say thank you"

January 2015

Angelique,
It is not about this this or that… it's about Ouma, we realise that your children are older and have school activities, but there are many mothers that are in the same position that cope with that. You make promises to Ouma that you do not keep. If you can't cope now, how do you expect to cope later in the year, heaven forbid there be a crisis.
You are studying psychology, you should be now, know how to cope under pressure, I can't wait for you to reach the chapter where you learn to deal with old people, seems like you are going to have to study forever. As far as her cottage is concerned that is so dirty, it is inevitable as she is old. Do you know how lucky you are to still have a Granny, and it is your duty as granddaughter to clean her place. Come on now, you are a big girl, get over yourself.

Ouma constantly craps on me because I take her underwear, stockings, face cloths and blouses to be washed. Then she would shout at me for not taking it, because when she washes it by hand it does not come clean. You can never win.
She shouts when I clean, the shouts when I don't clean. She shouts at me for not finding her stuff, about the clothes that are not ironed properly. Shouts when I phone her, when I arrive at her cottage, when I sit for too long, when I don't sit, nothing is ever right. I know how to handle her constant shouting and negativity, but that requires of me to be in the right frame of mind. I clean her cottage from side to side, wash and iron her clothes, do her shopping, count and sort her tablets, pay for the night nurse, take her to have her hair done.
I just came back from a good rest and holiday, as I had one hectic year last year which was very emotionally taxing, resulting in me near committing myself to a psychiatric clinic. Because I always smile and wave, no one ever knows what is going on in my heart. So please understand what emotional strength it requires to both talk to Ouma and to go to see her. I know I have to and know that it is my responsibility, but I do not need pressure from the family, instead I need support. I am applying for the position as National Director for Child Welfare, plus I wish to complete my studies. I do a lot for Maria Petronella. Her short term memory is no longer what it used to be, therefore she does not always remember everything. The last thing I need is to have to give daily feedback and report to the family and keep account of my every second and movement.

I have been taking care of Ouma since she had her stroke 2 years ago.

∞

19 August 2015

I am sitting at the Oncology clinic at Charlotte Maxeke hospital amongst the most amazing woman all waiting patiently to be seen by the doctor. Hours minutes go by so much fear and so uninformed and traditionally so afraid to ask questions.

To enhance their lives sitting amongst 2 Sangomas asking me to give them hope and advice on remedies for healing - Sangomas can't heal themselves they say, yet they take on the toxins of so many that come to them for healing?
It is quite amazing how many women sit here day after day…. Mothers, grandmothers, wives…. In the weeks and months, I have been exposed to the cancer wards and waiting rooms – majority of patients 90/10 are woman …. Why I ask myself?
Why so many women have to be burdened by this disease?
A permanent punishment…. Awaiting the final day of – sorry it is time – sorry we cannot heal you anymore – all waiting, yet they are still laughing and talking, sitting waiting – nurses looking at them and paging through a book, yet no one is here educating these ladies, training them or giving advice or counselling on how to deal with this traumatic experience, this trauma that they have to face daily of immortality. Giving them dietary and lifestyle advice, or motivating them to not give up hope and do self-attainment and healing in this time of lonely pain and suffering.

I just went for a smoke in the car park to meet the most beautiful old man, grey white hair, so neatly dressed with his cane sitting down to take a breath, "I am not good" he says.
"Why do you say that? Did you wake this morning to take another breath? Are you here for a check-up?" I ask.
"Yes I am."
"Well then you are blessed!"
"I am" he says, "I am 77 years old, and all my children are executives and business owners. I have put them through school and now I am proud of each one of them, and they spoil me with soo much presents."
"Well then you must tell them to rather spoil you with their presence, as where are you going to put all the presents? Can you use everything they give you?"
"No – but you have just given me the words, I need to speak to them, come and visit me and give me joy when you sing and laugh… I will not complain anymore – I am blessed."

∞

Both my two Angels passed away in December 2015.

"Breaking the Cycle"

YES – Ouma YES – Mamma

I broke the cycle No MORE – I am not waiting for my husband to leave me like you did.

∞

When you reach a point in your life. When you assess yourself. The environment you are in. You question everything in your life, in your immediate surroundings, in yourself.

I have been through this question period. Started looking at what it is that fulfils me. What is it that I have placed on hold for an unlimited period of time. To save the equilibrium. To not introduce changes, to disturb what seems to be peacefull around me. Neglected the relationship with myself to the point where you face the mirror and not recognise the person that is looking back at you.

I have reached a point where I question those that are close to me. My 2 boys for whom I will forsake the world to see them being whole!

Then through the questions, the talking, the listening. I hear and see 2 boys that only want the same for me, as I want for them. Which is to be happy. To not be lonely. To be part of something that is real.

I turned to look at my partnership I have with their father. It was like looking into a void. Looked into my heart, and stared into a bigger void. So much so, I look and ask the question to myself, I ended up in such a bundle of nervous tension, my neck turned into such a spasm. Refusing for me to turn around and look back. Because, looking back is so filled with pain, anger, resentment, distrust. I have forced to look ahead and as myself the question:

"Do you still feel like you can fix this broken plate and continue serving on it?"

My immediatie answer is … "NO"

My question is:
"If after 20 years of trying, what will change to make the next 20 years any different?"
"Could you see yourself being on your own?"

The answer is …. "I am on my own."

"Are you scared?"

"YES OF COURSE I am scared."
I have been scared for 20 years. Now I am even more scared, because I am about to make a life changing decision which will affect more than just me!

"Do I know if it is a good decision?"

"NO, I don't."
But I know for me right now, it will be the best. As I am killing myself by staying in this relationship, which I am not prepared to humour anymore!

I know I need to take this risk.
I cannot stay for the sake of others.
I need to take a stand.
I need to end this.
I need to move on – for me.
I can't proceed.
I can't go on.
I need to take a stand.
I need to move on.
I need to move forward in my life.
I need to take the risk.

∞

Much healing is required following divorce. I found this written in 2014.

"I call this – the root square of my husband's penis"

After many days and weeks of slowly taking back and building on what I have lost through the years.

The years of not being able to be yourself and living a life where you tried to keep it all together. Through unhappy day. A long time ag I should have just, when I made the decision to go – stuck to it. But in fear of the children growing up in a home of divorce, I stuck it out. Through the many countless abusive stages of this man I endured and now to the point where I want to be myself and know myself and be free from this constant pressure of survival and loneliness.

My heart had been broken and my self-esteem, demolished. I had given up so many thinks that I am now sitting here freaking out and the mere thought of having to do or think.

The Chronicles of a suburban housewife. My book I am writing, as and when I have the time to think for myself. I have built to many walls, so many layers around myself. Nowhere did I even think to leave and opening for a window or a door.

I am tired of this façade that I am projecting all the time! I am tired of pretending for the sake of everyone other than myself. I want to be free! Free from this burden of being with someone I don't love. Someone that has broken me down, little by little, sapping me emotionally from knowing love and feeling love.

No I did not kick him out of my bed because he snores. I kicked him out of my bed because of his verbal abuse, that lead to physical abuse. That lead to marital rape, the lead to selling my soul. 'Being a slut, a bitch, a whore, worthless, useless person that has no regard for anyone, that has no sense and belittling, coming from a worthless family.' – his words.

Sex is not sex unless you fuck, unless you give him anal pleasure. When you don't fuck you are a slut that gave it to everyone but him? I ask you??

Being drunk every night, hating your vagina. Lies told from the beginning about his ability to father your unborn child. Knowing how important it is to you!

First being told how pathetic you are, and then expecting you to have sex. If you walk away he stomps after you to pull you out of bed and force you to have sex. Under fear and times, you give in for the sake of keeping the peace.

Starting to have sex, him falling asleep during the act. Then being woken up and hour later, forcing you to have sex, if you don't, words of verbal abuse start flying, so again under fear you give in to fucking.

You lie in pain, with tears rolling down your cheeks while ha bangs away at you like a piece of meat.

You show him slowly how to make love to you in the way that makes you feel special. He keeps on forgetting, day after day, week after week. You end up lying there being fucked, banged with tears in your eyes.

So you drink with to hopefully numb the feeling of not being important to him, to remember how you wish to be touched, so that he can just fuck again. Sucking you like he is eating a bowl of sloth, while you are being so grossed out. The more you push away, the more persistent he becomes. The more he forces himself on you. To the point that you beg him to finish that you can just get away. The next day you have some form of venereal disease, thrush, discharge that lasts for days, sometimes weeks.

Eventually you go for all kinds of tests. Doctor to doctor in the search of answers. There must be something wrong with you. Psychologists, psychiatrists, hypnotherapists, regression therapy, kinesiology, GPs, Gynaecologists, Esoteric healer, Tarot readers, astrologists.

You end up on anti-depressants or as I call it "Happy Pills".

Now here at age 42 you are on our own. Raising children with a person, it is as though he is what you named him, the moment you started with your process of saying goodbye, to everything that does not work for you – "Minister of Finance and Recreation."

As a lover, you have said goodbye to him 5 years ago, when you had him move from your bed and into the cottage. That I must say, by his own choice. It was a blessing, as the grieving process started, together with the power of saying 'NO'. Standing up for myself, no longer standing for any abuse whatsoever. Like a dimmer switch, slowly turning the lights up to the point where I can start seeing clearer. The person I am.

The picture became clearer, as he moved away and I regained the confidence to start looking after me!

When the project came about of him not being in the country anymore. Had made it more possible for me to regain Angelique. Not Babe, not Bokkie – but Angelique!

So strange it was, that the more I became me, the more people started calling me by my full name – Angelique.

I am now at the point where I can actually say the word – Divorce!

How did I get here?

Well in addition to the abuse directed at me, verbally, physically and sexually, there was another side to it.

In the beginning of our marriage I had to leave my position in corporate which I was happy to do, as I started my own business working from home. Later I started another business with family that moved and grew. During this time, I was out of home and became more and more out bound, then in house. Slowly this became a problem, in as far as remarks of jealousy, arrive at my workplace unannounced with certain aggression, verbal abuse and boisterousness. I cannot recall all the words said, because I had shut it out. It got to a point where I had a physical breakdown. It was necessary for me to go for a hysterectomy. I just recall living in fear. Him using the children, sleeping in my bed, he would go and sleep next to them, so I am forced to sleep elsewhere. He started drinking more heavily. When drunk would become aggressively abusive and forcing himself in my intimate space.

Well then came the hysterectomy. I gave up on all the businesses of which I was to blame for it failing according to him.

His favourite is of course, 'you are just like your Father, always wanting the limelight, flirting and drama.' 'You are just like your Father; you have no sense of business. Everything is always your way, and the only one that is right is you.'

Yes, I have wonderful parents and they have their own personalities. However, when it gets thrown in your face in an abusive manner, with a derogatory tone, it is not funny! It is outright abuse.

Then I started studying. One of the subject modules – Survivors of rape. I was raped at age 14 years; I was molested as a little girl. So please understand that I do have an underlying issue with abusive sex.

I asked him to please read through the module. I wanted him to understand what I have dealt with, and still dealing with. The book remained where I had placed it on the table with a special marking to know when he reads it. All remained exactly where I put it, collecting dust…

Then … I bumped into the person that raped me!

On both these topics:
The module – he said he read it.
The rapist – years before he assured me that he took care of it. That this guy is no longer around. He assured me, it's been taken care of. Here in my face, is this man!

Last year after watching him carefully, as he starts after 50 years looking after himself. Shopping for his own clothes, dressing like a young man, losing weight. Me supporting him in his quest. Standing in the kitchen night after night, preparing for his special new diet. I noticed he waxed his back, shaved his chest hairs and scrotum hairs. Being more and more disgusted with me and put off by my physique.

He was in the car the whole weekend, shopping for all kinds of odds and ends. His I-pad and phone became is obsession. I found him texting a girl from Kenya. Which I stopped immediately. Oh yes, I contacted her, and asked her if he was promising her a life in South Africa, that she must not believe his crap.

Then this shopping, I-pad and phone obsession continued. Until one night, when I plucked up the energy and guts together. I made him ultra-drunk and said to him, 'come, lets role play in having an affair.' Down in the cottage, displayed myself on the bed. He kept on having to fetch something, with his phone in his hand. I asked to see the phone. He kicked the phone under the bed in shock. He insisted it is just a friend that needs advice. I kept turning him on, to the point that he was so hard he could not stop… it was at the peak of his near climax that I asked him to tell me exactly how long his affair has been going on, and who she is…

It had been going on for 3 years. He confessed. Approximately at the time that he started the major weight loss and fitness program.

The waxing and shaving was, according to him, for me. He had read an article in the Men's health that said that pubic hair, causes infections and STDs. He knows I love body hair…

Well it was that night, I sad it is okay for the affair to continue, but we need to start sorting out contracts as well as the Will and Testament, to ensure that everything we own goes to the children. To which he agreed. I left the cottage and went back to my bed in the house.

The next day, I asked that we need to draw up the necessary contracts, which he was happy to do.

As time went on, he started denying the fact that there was someone else. His habits of shopping and cell phone obsession continued.

I then constructed another encounter to see how he would behave. A friend of mine came over, we had wine and started dancing. He started coming onto her, as he does with all my friends, so much so that I have lost a lot of girlfriend refusing to come over to the house, as this is what he does. Only a hand full had stuck with me, as we are mothers together.

So when the two of them started moving closer to each other. I put myself out to pretend that this was part of a threesome. He fell for this, continued choosing her over me. I left the two of them, and went to bed in the house. They exchanged numbers and kept contact.

I shared my disappointment in him, as he never even looked in my direction, or even stood up to say. 'I love my wife, and won't participate." No, he went on merrily fucking her…

I thought to myself, okay, perhaps this is my fault… She came over again, skinny dipping. Who was ready for action again? None other than him… he took her to the cottage and fucked her the whole night, as I went to bed in the house.

Confirmation, affirmation… in front of me…

Not too long after that, I received an anonymous SMS, that your husband is having an affair with a married woman.

But, just to get back to my semi-friend…
He turned the whole sexual affair onto me, said it was all my fault! Seriously? Where are you shaved balls?? If you are soo very innocent, and love me soo much, why are you turning to fucking other women and not turning to me???

Okay, I know and realise I could have expected that, but still, it was hurtful as I was somewhere deep inside me, hoping that he would somehow, somewhere stand up and turn to me. Say NO. Say this is my woman. But, hell no – look at him just pouncing on the other woman. Where does that leave me now, after round number 2? After I had explained to him that it would be different if I was the one for him?

So on we still go with the shopping and the haircuts, the phone obsession…. Till that SMS.

I received this on the Wednesday, amongst all my other drama, of my friend being diagnosed with cancer the day before. Writing 3rd year exams. Attending meetings as Chairperson. Flying to Cape Town for Trustee meetings. Sorting out the household and children. My little boy whom I have tried to help, has to go to rehab as his mother gave him dagga and CAT. Here we are, THE SMS, as I walk out of the Children's Court. Oh, just before I left for Cape Town, my son started chatting to me. Yes, I wanted to get as much background information on this as possible –

My 14-year-old son, starts talking to me, about his emotions and feelings. He asks me "is Dad having an affair?" I just said that he needs to speak to his father about that. I cannot answer that question, as I don't know. He started telling me how he has not bond with his dad, how he has no respect for his father…. This was the beginning of many more conversations to come, regarding his father and relationships.

So I kept this new SMS information to myself…

Trying to deal with this, in between the rehab for children, having to be a mother, sitting at the oncology clinic at Charlotte Maxheke hospital, being faced with the vulgar images stuck to the walls of STDs. Running up and down passages in this Hospital dealing with the public system. Urgently trying to find a slot at one of my Tarot card readers, in the search for answers…

A-anonymous is nowhere to be traced, it's a Namibian number. No information from my inside connection at the work place, that could come up with information…

I prepare myself for the home coming… I called a lawyer to seek advice and do research to be done on releasing him from his fiduciary duties of me as his spouse. I had done research on that, because I don't want to be every second weekend and holiday mom. The easiest would be to contractually release him from being my husband. It makes sense as we can still continue co-habiting, seeing he is hardly at home.

Husband never being at home… That is another story all together. Since we got married, he started travelling to other countries for work. Initially it was to London. I trusted the whole thing, until he became adamant about buying a house of his one mistress he had, according to him, it was before me? But, I know better. He forgets that we all worked together, and I suspected that he was seeing her at the same time he was seeing me, even after we moved in together. She moved to the UK and he was very set on us buying their house, till I said NO! Very often he flew to the UK for a project. But that faded away in due time.

So then when working back here at Head Office. He had this secretary, who tried very hard to make me her best friend. Everything soon became about this secretary. At a colleague's wedding on the way there and as we got out of the car, he forgets all about me. Everything was all about her. I nipped that in the butt quickly, as I made no secret that I was not condoning this encounter at all.

During this inspection of the "THE SMS", my internal inspector personality 'CSI Miami investigator', tested the subject…
The response was "oh the person in Zurich"
Now, he was in Zurich for about 2-3 years on a contract. I suspected something, but I was too focused at that stage on my business, my step sons, my own son and IVF. (Then as I recall I will have to check my letters and notes I wrote; sure I was not very happy then.) Anyway, be it as it may. I have learnt through the years to file in file 13 and move on, for the purposes of remaining strong.

So back to "THE SMS" … I kept my cool. Preparing myself for the big words…
"I am releasing you contractually from your fiduciary duties of being my spouse, in other words, spousal responsibilities."

During my research I found that there are indeed spousal responsibilities, especially pertaining to bedroom activities.

I don't want him to not be a friend, a father. To not feel welcome on the farm or in the house that he has worked hard for! I am happy with the living arrangements, but don't want to feel burdened with this – we have to share bedrooms, beds and sexual activities. To feel guilty if and when you need to be with other people. I thought that was a very amicable arrangement. No you don't have to call me your wife and I don't have to call you my husband.

That is a major progress in today's norm of so many other couples, probably going through the same. No division of assets, parental rights and responsibilities. I thought this would be an amazing agreement.

So I had it all worked out. I was indeed nervous as hell. As if I was about to address the Nation. We were going to discuss this, as he had just landed from his business trip. Would probably only be 3-4 whiskey's strong. I would have to catch him at the right moment before he gets too sloshed and tired. We had guests unannounced.

After making them feel comfortable, I asked if I could have a minute or two… Hell no! I have been preparing this speech and did my homework for long enough not the make the statement.

I took him aside, outside the cottage on the veranda.

"I have released you before from having sex with me, as I told you that you are welcome to find it elsewhere. The moment it gets to the 3rd time with the same person, as everything happens in 3s, you need to come clear and move on. As there is more between you, other than just the odd, casual sexual encounter. Which I refuse to give you, as I know we are not sexually compatible. I took you in my arms in December 2014 on New Year's Eve, I told you that I emotionally and sexually completely release you. I am now contractually releasing you."

"Divorce?" he asked.

"No, I don't like that term. I feel that I am not a second weekend and second holiday mom. My children are my life, hence, contractually releasing you, means that everything remains exactly as it is, except I am no longer your wife and you are no longer my husband, for want of a better word."

"you are crazy, what brought this along?"

I showed him the SMS, and left it at that...

We did not broach the subject again, until Sunday. He came with a whole long story of how he has made friends with this lady that works with him. He has gone for suppers at their home. He said it is either divorce or nothing. Her husband had also received the same message. He said he had fired someone, and this person is disgruntled.

The next weekend I get told that he had invited her, her husband and their kids to come stay with us. The reason was to go to Xfighters in September, and they were also to come to the farm in April. Yes, I did entertain her and her husband at the time. Whilst the two love birds where flirting, dry humping each other in the kitchen. Calming the husband down, as this was really happening infront of us, no regard.

My son and I had more chats in the meantime. One night, oh I had a few too many glasses of wine, when pushing all the right buttons, I opened up, and told him the truth about his father. So my heart melted when he came out with all his beans being spilt. He told me he knew it. He remembers clearly all the abuse. Pushing me out of the bed. Running to Barbara because they were so afraid of their dad. Dad getting into the bed trying to have sex with mom while they were awake. How he feels he was raped by enduring this. How he tried to protect his little brother from being exposed to this.

God Damnit! I thought I was protecting my kids. Thought I was giving them a home with a mom and a dad. Here my son feels like this!!! Oh hell no!! Having no respect for his dad!!! All this time I thought that it is important for them to know their Dad's good side and protect them from seeing his bad side!!

What have I DONE???

So my son decides, being disappointed and angry at his father… Again my bloody mistake and big mouth… But on the other hand he knew about this nonsense, as he asked me outright…

He decided that, he was going to say something. His dad had told him some superfluous shit about work, to make small talk, and him throwing the cold shoulder, was then accused of not caring about his dad's work. In turn, he told his dad to stop treating his mother like shit!

Dad came home and all of a sardine, tried to have and open conversation with me. Saying that his son had talked to him. We need to resolve our issues and relationship. He would like us to be friends again. That is all I want, is replied. We can work on an amicable arrangement. Many couples don't work out and still have a good friendship and remain good friends, but not be married. We need to be mature about this.

Well that went from: "Okay, 100% is yours and the kids" to "What if your projects pull off, let's make it 50/50" to "I don't want a divorce" … all in one night.

The next day was the other personality again… I am stupid. I am a piece of shit.

Monday comes… I am now treated as the goddess and the queen. "wow, you look so nice…"

The following weekend… no shopping sprees, no phone, no I-pad. I received and SMS to let me know he is safely at the airport, and safely at his home.

Last weekend … shopping sprees again, phone, I-pad. Big arrangements for the September visit and bookings. No SMS to let me know he is safely at the airport, and safely at home.

My routine – remains unchanged.
Friday – friends come over
Saturday – activities with the Children
Sunday – couch and movies.
Monday – 3 cups of coffee and the Children

Monday night, my red wine, cigarettes and writing!

I just want to know, are you leaving me? Or Am I leaving you?
My book with you!! Is DONE!!
After trying to come onto my friends again on Saturday!! REALLY!!
I AM SO SOOO SOOOO DONE!!!

Oh I do need to say that he has this retaliation fair, that he always throws in my direction to make me feel guilty… Truth be told.

Approximately 9 years ago, I received a vIsIt from a very old flame of minc, from when I was 20 years old. Nothing ever happened physically but spiritually, emotionally, Wow! It was probably during my time of some form of abuse… actually Goddamnit it was… As I remember being dragged by bed out of my four poster, king size bed, both my boys in bed sleeping …
This person came to visit, it was at though, I don't know, it was just so nice to see him again, we talked as if there was no lapse of 10 odd years. He phoned me even after returning back to the UK. Then I through Ange, you are being appreciated and noticed out there. You are worth this abuse. We wrote to each other, and I through to myself, Wow… what if? What if I leave right now and take my boys? What if there is someone that won't hurt me anymore…? This was all on email. It was soon after I busted him jerking off to Asian porn on my PC.

So that was called off as my friend said that I need to divorce before anything happens… he found the email… sheepishly I returned to the marriage and continuous abuse.

Then incident Nr 2 was friends with gays, musicians and artists, which turned into a total barney. The person came for a glass of wine, as I turned my head kissed me out of the blue. In my opinion he was gay. In my opinion I was convinced gay, perhaps still in the closet. Going on a mission to expose him, as he was dating a girl, which I wanted to help prevent from making a wrong decision in her life… then being accused of having sex with this guy in the public toilets? Seriously!! Needless to say all blew up and out of proportion. But the girl was saved and she is now with a lovely man, supporting her career and had a beautiful baby.

Then incident Nr 3, again and old flame who came to have a meeting for business. Yes, we had a bottle of wine, chatted about life, wife, kids. Me about my life, husband, kids. When he blocked me and kissed me. This again pulled out of context. As nothing happened but a kiss. Which I had told my man about the very next day.

This all happened sporadically years ago. But never was it anything to write home about.

I was ready to leave the marriage… but thought let me just get away and sort out my own head, so I went to KKNK. Oh such fun I had. Meeting people from every walk of life. Watching different forms of art, performances, music, eating, drinking, dancing like there was no tomorrow! At the same time, I was testing myself to see if I could do this, every second weekend and holiday this with my kids… One night, I got so drunk, that the one artist offered to walk me home. The I slept in my bed, him on the couch. This was again pulled completely out of proportion!

So the justifications I have for all the infidelity every time is the stories above!

What is not at all understood, is that because of my sexual history! I know what enters my vagina! I will not participate in such crap unless I am convinced that is will be a lasting relationship!!

I am no one's sex object! I will not allow anyone to enter my secret space, unless there is gentle love involved. I have been fucked too many times in my life, to not want any more of that, without being made passionate love to, with a promise of gentleness.

Anyone can fuck… but no one can make love and mean it!

I don't want anyone to use me as another fuck! I want to be made lover to. Heart, mind, Soul first! Then you can have the balance of me!

I am in a 20 odd year relationship. Where I thought I would get that… but still, I am just another fuck…

Learn to make love to me, and you can have me!

I need to somehow, somewhere say! That my current husband, although he is a wanderer, is my best friend. He is a very good person. In my view and eyes a very good father!
Husband … not really for me… but the rest – he is Fantastic!!

So on a scale, what has made me swallow my tears… Just that… He is a great person! So many good qualities! That is what has made my decision so goddamn difficult!

Because of the other qualities he possesses of being a good person, hard worker, great provided, stunning father!!

But Angelique, what is a good husband and a great partner?

- Shares the same interests
- Supports everything you do without criticism
- Has conversations with you face to face
- Understands your needs, both emotionally and physically
- Partners with you on every level
- Listens when you need to speak, speaks when you need to listen
- Has you as his one and only
- Loves your children
- Supports your every cause. Participates with your everything.

- Listens to music with you, reads with you, has meals with you, walks with you, walks with you
- Holds you in his arms, and thinks you are amazing
- Adores your every moment
- Does not loudly ridicule you
- Only has eyes for you
- Will cook with you
- Will accept your friends
- Will accept your family
- Picks that flower for you
- Will laugh with you
- Will know when you are feeling sad
- Will be in love with you
- Will make love to you
- !! YOU WON'T BE ALONE!!

So I don't have any of the above and would love to have that. Hence…

I have requested for a release. I am not about to go out seeking for the above, hell no!! Having to go through failed relationship, after relationship, going onto the Web to see if someone is going to participate… Can't see myself go through that.

I will just go on as I am and if someone crosses my path, good luck to him, that is all I say!

I just don't want to feel guilty, or have an axe over my head if someone does want to participate in my already existent life. I also don't want my current husband to feel like ha has an axe over his head, should he wish to have a life of whatever makes him happy.

That is also the whole stigma of infidelity, jealousy and all that crap people are fed with… it is part of life! I am happy for him to meet someone that serves his needs, but by the same token, so should I be able to do the same, without judgement or questioning or jealousy!

Hence, I release you from your contractual duties toward me as your spouse!

'Shit happens, life goes on!'

'Every hurdle is a learning curve!'

Thank God I a stronger for it!

Luv my work!!

∞

12 June 2015

Hello my journal

What in incredibly interesting time I have had – a journey having to face any life questions and now at a cross path my friend, where I need to work up the courage to actually put myself first.

I am faced with mortality or immortality right now and wondering what am I doing? How am I? wow what a big question that is? I am always fabulous! I am always the life of everything! And for once – I am so not!

I have 2 most beautiful kids which I have honestly given my everything to, I am in a relationship which I have honestly given my most everything to! And now I am asking myself… where am I?

I am the loneliest person on this earth right now! I am on my own! The person whom I have been with for 20 years of my life, who I know backwards is making me destroy me! Slowly but surely I have endured jealousy, physical abuse, substance abuse, verbal abuse, emotional abuse to sexual abuse, now to the point where I am realising that I am nothing anymore. I question my every thought, my every feeling, my every action. And in the end, I am unhappy!

I am lonely and I am broken/hurt… I have no trust, I have no voice, I have no feeling and no love. I am just on everyday cope mode! I ask myself – what the fuck?? What the fuck are you doing Ange?? This is not you my friend? This is not Ange, so empty?? You are not this person that you have become!! You are lifeless, you are dying inside my darling! That when anyone remotely give you attention or praise you question their truth, you have been lied to and betrayed my friend in so many ways that you had even forgotten what honesty actually is! All you do is question everyone's intentions in such a way that you have more walls then life left in you! where are you my girl??? Where???

∞

23 July 2015

I am very angry today – caught up in the emotion of feeling betrayed. I am not a person who enjoys fighting and lives with that thought of being selfish in any form. I am not a person that has to think constantly about self-gain. But now I am faced with this situation that broke the camel's back, right here, right now and I cannot continue living like this but by the same token I have to ensure that my children are looked after at least till they graduate!

 a) I am at divorce doorstep
 b) I am possibly facing being widowed

Who knows which comes first? Either way I have to closely assess what needs to be in place!

I am also not a bitch and not unfair in any way as even though he has brought things to this point, has also worked hard to gain the assets which has built up and I cannot take it all away should the divorce come first. That is just outright Nasty!

All I know is that I am done! I am Done! I need to finish it – and need to trust that my kids are going to be fine with my decision!

How wonderful it is to wake up in the morning to peace and quiet and tranquillity fresh air and cold breeze. With my little doggies so happy to be with people. My boys seeking for clues on who or what caused the strange death of baby Dino.

Inhaling fresh mountain air filling my lungs and exhaling negativity and anger which I had been harbouring. Which had filled my body and soul with such pain. But being here with no one but my little boys – just me – has been amazing! To wake up without having to be nice or looking into that face or dealing with that energy of 'you owe me' what a pleasure what a relief. How free!

I am listening to the stories of little Mike the 13-year-old boy that I have as my new project to making a difference ... how at the age of 13 you have had to endure near death experiences of drowning and jumping in quarries, seeing people stabbed, bleeding to death and watching babies drown. Surrounded by drugs, murder, sex, abuse, death, so much to deal with. Where no focus was placed on education instead, he reads like a 7-year-old, spells like a 6-year-old, emotional intelligence of a 9-year-old, and exposed to so much cruelty.

But what we see as being normal, waking in a warm bed, eating a good meal, having a warm shower, children playing – the innocence of a child that was taken away from this boy and now having to be reversed into – you are a child, behave like a child, play like a child, learn like a child, speak like a child, all needs to be introduced at the age of 13 years. My heart goes out…

I am learning through this project to find the solution for these kids, as he is not the only child that has been exposed to this and how many lives remain destroyed because of their childhood. My project my case study to find and answer or a direction to heal this ill! I need to make it my mission to find a solution build a case study to help these children. My focus has changed or is changing and I will make it my goal, to reach and combine the various laws to assist these children to change and reach their full potential!   - my new goal!!

"Mom I admire you for your strength if I was you I would cry day and night. How he abused you, I remember clearly"

I hosted my little boys in my bed which was a way to protect myself and have my boys with me to shield them from the abuse that they could not wake and be forced to face or walk into a drunkard display of their father. I protected myself from the idea of having to share a bed with a person that will be abusing me and cursing me through some part of the night. Sometimes I could not stop him from it, and had to allow him for the sake of keeping the peace and there were times that the more I avoided him and did not allow him sex, the more abusive he's become, so I had to give in. The worst was that the kids would wake up during the act – now it comes out that they were witnessing this and felt raped! How do I deal with this now?

What pisses me off most is the deceit. I don't know if the know and confirming was worse than the suspecting. Maybe when I was suspecting I did not feel like being double betrayed and double lied to … because now having to deal with being made out to look like a fool …. To be patronised by this man say I am dreaming up things… like I am stupid.

After he had explicitly told me, after doing this inform of me after seeing photographs after other people including my 14-year-old son confirmed his suspicions and now I have to deal with this knowing! And being made out to be psychotic, dreaming up, thinking up shit. All my friends telling me now, that you know this is the reason we stopped coming to your house.

We had breakfasts discussing how he comes onto us! I am now not sure if the suspicion is better than the knowing. All my card readings confirming it! Oh my god the anger and anxiety the feeling of gall building up in my stomach right under my heart! Feel like I can't breathe!

YES "0" I hate you! You have not gradually abused me, but you have finally let me down and I am hurt, disappointed and I want you to go away! I want you to disappear without me having to tell you to go! Without having to make me feel that it's my fault, that I am kicking you out, that I am breaking! up that I am telling you to leave! Just go! just get out of my life! Just disappear! Go Go Go far away! I don't want to face you! or see you! or be around you anymore! No explanation required! Fuckoff!!

∞

On 31 July 2015

I sat him down and told him that I can no longer continue being his spouse. I cannot handle the constant abuse of
a) being lonely
b) sexual abuse
c) the alcohol abuse
d) the financial economic abuse
e) verbal and emotional abuse
f) the infidelity
g) total lack of trust
h) constant walking on eggs because you don't know when he is going to explode
I) constant feeling of being worthless
j) always hitting on my friends.

The biggest deciding factor was when my son started opening up to me and told me that he can see how unhappy I am, and how his father treats me. How he can see his father spending 10s of thousands of rands, how he suspects his father having affairs. How scared he is of his dad and how he as my son has no respect for his father and does not give a shit. Asking me to do something before his siblings get old enough to realise what he is now realising.

Oh shit Ange – you thought you were keeping the family together, that you were the only one to experience this abuse?? Sorry my girl!!!!

So do I teach my boys it's okay to treat your wife one day like this? That she will stay with you come hell or high water or visa versa, if their wives are the abusers that it is okay? No it is not!! It's time to stand up and say NO MORE!!

So I have been reasonable in my request as I am not after his money I just wish for my sons to be looked after.

Then he spoke to me:

' I want to start by saying I don't want a divorce, but understand that you need to go for whatever reason, which is fine. As you want to divorce me, I don't want to look after you. You said to look after the boys till they are 24 years but I will look after them till they are 80 years. The farm is in your name so you can keep it which is fair and I will keep the house. I love both the farm and the house considering what I owe on the bond it works out the same in value if we were to sell either farm or house. I cannot maintain both. Mckenzie and happy costs R5k and gas R1k so that's R6k. Barbara and girly's school R5k and Freddie 3K plus extra help R1,5k all works out to R18k. Dog food is costing R6k per month before anything. The farm electricity R7,5k and rates R1,5K. house R6k – R7k on Eskom that's before anything then your car. I cannot use my bonus to pay off anything anymore as I now need to think of retirement as I only have 4years 9months to work. The plan was that when I retire you look after us which will no longer be the case. I don't thing we can move the boys at the same time as divorce as it will be too much for them. I will no longer be able to afford university for the boys. Living on the farm woman alone with 2 kids is not secure and after four years will only be you and the youngest son. This family needs to cut back on spending as my salary does not cover our monthly overheads. When I no longer work in Namibia my salary will be cut back by 12 k per month. You need to tell me what you want"

My answer: I am working on it and looking at it all, I have a spreadsheet. Thank you for talking to me.

Then when I sit with the boys he starts texting me from the bathroom how I need to make a plan with Mike (the little 13-year-old boy that I took in off the streets) the next morning when I go to my board meeting which starts at 7:30 and ends at 8:30 and started using my social life as a means to try get to me!

My social life?? I ask you ??? my friend had her birthday and he took the boys to the farm.... Needless to say kept texting me about Mike the whole weekend play on my emotions. I had my son and his teenage friends at home having their ending exam weekend – my social life??? It was 4 little boys my children on a 28-hectare farm.

Then I had Rita's 40th – was away Friday night after sorting boys on the farm, sorting Rita's birth day, 25mins away from the farm at Peacanwood, 4 women, I was back on the farm Sunday morning to prepare for his boys and friends for his birthday party.

He kept on sending me texts while gone, about Mike, he would drop him at the cop station if he is on the farm – what a tense time!!

When I arrived on the farm he gave me such a cold shoulder and dirty looks, like I was a piece of shit. I just went on preparing the meal and the table for all to enjoy and celebrate his birthday. Through the night he kept trying to pull my arm and pull me the neck, to tell me what a fucking bitch I am and I am worse than his first wife. He kept on standing behind me, and repeatedly said those word in my ear, whilst I was cooking.

Paula had taken Mike with her on Sunday. I left early Tuesday morning and slept the whole of Monday

And today – coming back from the meeting I slept until 15:00 – I am exhausted!

I had found a home for Mike – its breaking my heart but hope and pray it will be a good thing for him.

When I spoke with him, I expected him to react intensely, but he got up and the only thing he said was I must return all the credit cards. The very next morning he took the AmEx card from my purse and the Sunday morning 8 am I received a formal email from him. He wanted all the bank cards back and I had asked if I could get some leeway to sort out my bank. First thing he asked for the Tuesday morning after his birthday was the bank card. Transferred 5k into my account. So now I must account for every cent I spend. While he spends money just as he pleases!

∞

02 August 2015

Dear Angelique,

To begin with I would like to confirm I do not want a divorce. I think the past year has been particularly stressful on both of us - for different reasons - and do not think the time is right for such a life changing decision which seriously impacts both us and the children. I would really like us to give it another go and am happy to sit down and reach agreement as to the terms of this. I know we both will always put the children first whatever may happen.

I understand that your mind may be made up as per your What's App profile "And then she started living the life she'd imagined". I don't want to hold you back from being who you want to be.

My initial email I drafted was a far more emotive response to you but after some thought I deleted it and decided to try and keep it practical. To that end, if you really do want to go ahead with this we need to address a few things in the short term:

- As we have often discussed I agreed to support you being at home and looking after the boys as well studying and doing welfare work as you would take over as primary bread winner when I retire in 5 years as I only have my pension and in all likelihood of university and completion of schooling. You being bread winner at that point will clearly no longer be the case and I need to start trying to make provision for the above as I have no other investments. To that end I need to seriously focus on reducing our level of debt.

- I do not want to move out of my home and at this point am financially going into a negative position on a monthly basis trying to maintain both the home and the farm. Affording a third dwelling for you is out of the question. We would at least need to sell the farm for you to do this. As per the previous bullet I would also need to ensure that we are not spending more than I earn on a monthly basis in order that I provide for retirement period which may require us to sell both the house and the farm to afford two smaller residences and at the same time reduce debt.

- In the meantime I would request that you provide me with a budget breakdown and your account details so that I can transfer money into it which can be used to support the household as we need to understand your monetary requirements and do not think it is right for you to continue using my account. I would request that you return the bank card linked to my account to me. I will continue to support you personally as long as we are living together and you are not in a position to support yourself, but would request that you provide me with receipts supporting your expenditure and that you limit such expenditure to essential items that we have agreed upon prior to incurring such expenditure. I will no longer be in a position to support full time staff (and related expenses), expenses relating to others living in our house, high cell phone bills, costs you incur in your welfare related endeavours as well as entertainment and similar non-essential expenditure.

I am sure you will understand that I just have to get monthly expenditure under control as our future plans will no longer take care of any of that. I only have 60 months to do this together with the prospect of children being at university during my retirement.

Happy to discuss further.

Thank you for u for understanding
I shall indeed sit down with a proper budget

Please understand that all I wish to do is ensure that we remain civil throughout the whole time and that our children come first and their interests remain the most important item in the world

House	Amount (Rands)	Shared Kids	Amount (Rands)	Farm	Amount (Rands)

I have started taking record as from 1 August 2015 of all my expenses and keeping slips and invoices as supporting documentation.

I think the only immediate option is to sell the farm and to reduce other monthly expenditure.

I would appreciate your explanation as I have not been privy to our financial matters for years.

Ok. You have not wanted to share in the finance position over the past few years. You should have your vehicle statement? Happy to share bond actual an as well as CC actuals. Your summary is missing quite a lot.

As per your request I only summarized and focused on my spend which would be debit card transactions as previously stated is the only access I have to financials

After much deliberation I have come to the following proposal, which of course is up for discussion/negotiation:

With the best interest of the children at heart and a way forward with the least impact and easiest transition.

First and foremost, I wish to thank you that you are willing to honour our agreement:

Division of Assets/property:

House - will be your primary residence

Farm – will be my primary residence

Considering the above properties:

a) House is registered in your name
b) Farm is registered in my name
c) House has highest market value and for this reason I feel it only fair considering that you have been the primary bread winner since 2012 that you keep the property that will give you the best returns on your investment.
d) All contents of both above homes remain intact, however, I just wish to have the art, and my office content, books and Buddha collection and personal belongings such as clothes and jewellery.
e) We have made homes with familiar items at both residences for the children and they are happy and familiar in both places. Which would make any form of transition for them easy with the least impact. This would also eliminate the need for a 3rd residence which will be a costly exercise. Furthermore, both residences are close to all amenities and close to either or both parents. The children are also familiar with the staff at both residences and we both trust our staff with our assets, safety, animals and children.
f) I would like to suggest the we enrol the boys at Bekker School, which is a good school both sports and academically as from 2016.
g) As far as my welfare work is concerned, this is also in driving distance from the farm. I have also been involved with the forums in Magalies and know and understand the social welfare requirements of the area, which is lacking my current and future skills, that when I do qualify/graduate in my degree of studies, that I will be able to commence with my career, this being said, the farm is not to remote that I will be able to practice in other areas nearby, should the need arise and it be financially viable. As you know that I wish not to be a financial burden on you for much longer, and that it is important to me to be financially independent.
h) The overheads of the farm are also less than the house, as far as Eskom, etc. which will assist you in the long run.

Children's Costs:

(I wish not to insult you by listing this, but will be a requirement to be documented for parenting plan, as I know that you will not at any given point in time take care of every financial need of the children, as you are and will always be an amazing dad)

a) All school fees and extra mural activities as well as books, stationery and school clothes, sports clothes be paid in full until they graduate from school.
b) All personal items such as toiletries, clothes be paid in full till they leave home or turn 24 years' old
c) All food, and entertainment be paid in full till they leave home or turn 24 years' old
d) All medical costs and medical aid be paid in full till the leave home or turn 24 years' old
e) The children be made sole beneficiaries of all assets, policies, shares etc. which may not at any given point be over ridden by any other party, contract, will and testament or spouse at any given point in time.
f) Monthly allowance be paid directly into the children's accounts until they are self-sufficient or turn 24 years' old
g) All Tertiary education costs be covered in full till they graduate

My costs: (until I earn a reasonable income, I hope I am reasonable in my request)
a) Farm homeowner's insurance
b) Farm household and vehicle insurance
c) Eskom
d) Staff
e) Unisa until I graduate
f) Fuel
g) Allowance for clothes, personal items, entertainment, sundries
h) Medical aid until I can afford my own
i) Cell contract which is currently shared with the children
j) Vehicle
k) Multichoice M-net on the farm
l) Internet / Telkom on the farm
m) Animal food

A) I would like to propose that we are Co-holders of parental responsibilities and rights which implies that we are according to the Children's Act 38 -2005 as amended (ss30-32) – holds reference. In summary that no decision that will impact the children's lives i.e. education, health, primary residence be made in isolation but by both biological parents.
B) That I will be the primary caregiver of the children and that their permanent place of residence will be with me
C) That they have open access to you as their dad and there will always be and open communication channel with you at any point in time should they wish to speak with you or visit you.
D) I would like to propose considering the above and the age of the children that they spend every second weekend with you from Friday till Monday morning.
E) Considering your work and leave requirements, we agree on either ½ of every school holiday is spent with you or should your leave not allow for this, or should you wish to take a long period of leave that you are welcome to take the boys with you on vacation.
F) As the farm is the place where they need a dad's hand and skill to ride bikes and make tracks, that you are welcome to spend the time with them on the farm, should that be their wish.

G) That we enter into a parenting plan as is the requirement by law according to the Children's Act 38 -2005 as amended as the children are still minors, this also needs to be done by a social worker/mediator/legally registered person and then be submitted after mediation to the family advocate.
H) Based on the above that the children's needs be placed first at all times
I) That neither parent coerce the children at any given point in time to take sides against the other parent and that any discussions regarding the children be done in open forum or in consultation with each other and be agreed upon in writing.

Legal fees: (if I was in any financial position, I would have gladly shared the costs)

a) Mediation costs R2k per 2,5 hours should we not reach agreement as to our terms
b) Psychologist R700 per hour, which I had 2 appointments with to date, to assist in the decision process, also would like to propose that she has a session or more with the children and if you wish to go as well? Just to alleviate any form of unspoken words during this process. She can also draw up the parenting plan
c) Family advocate needs to submit and signoff parenting plan etc. as legally required.

In closing:

I would like to again re-iterate the fact that I do know that you are a good person and a wonderful father. Which I cannot deny you and will never deny you.

After approximately 20 years of being together and with various efforts of trying to make our marriage work I have had to make the decision for our marital relationship to come to an end. It was not an easy decision; however, this partnership needs to come to an end.

What had drawn me to this final decision was

a) The photos and text messages between you and the lady from Kenya in 2014. (you have denied this as a friendship only)
b) Your confession of the 3-year relationship with another woman whom you have been working with. (you have subsequently denied this as a friendship only)
c) The SMS message received from an anonymous source on 20 May 2015. 'YOUR HUSBAND IS HAVING AN AFFAIR WITH A MARRIED WOMAN WORKING FOR ….' (you have denied this as a friendship only)
d) Your continuous daily use of alcohol which results in verbal and emotional abuse when inebriated.
e) Your Suggestive and Sexual advances made on my personal, female friends, whom has confessed your behaviour to me.

Please understand that I wish not for the children to know about the reasons for my reaching the decision and would rather we keep it to irreconcilable differences. I know that we will be and remain good friends.

I trust that you understand and that the children and their best interests be first and foremost concern at all times, and that we will reach an amicable agreement.

Kind Regards

Dear

I thank you first and foremost for being frank with me on 14 August 2015 Your words to me

I do not want to divorce, but if you want to divorce for whatever reasons I, we can I feel that a divorce and moving the kids at the same time will be too much for them to handle I understand that there are good reasons for them moving, however for our children being a self-proclaimed city kids will not be easy, I cannot uphold both properties on my salary as our current expenses are more than what I earn.
Full time staff R5k + gas 1 k The Eskom rates and taxes 7.5k you get the bills

I love both the house and the farm

We are in the red every month

You can keep the farm it's in your name and it's an even split on assets which is fair then there is your car

I only have 4year and 9 months to earn an income and what I owe on the bond and what I can get on the house to what u can get on the farm works out even.

I can't afford the kids to go to varsity

You need to tell me what you want

No, not at all and will not unless you and I agree!!!
As parents we need to be on the same page before we talk to the children!!
You know that it's important for us to make decisions in unison at all times!
Prior to involving our children!! It's very important to me!!
I think you have seen and noticed a difference in the children this week just being children!!

In all honesty we need to look at every possibility and opportunity

Dear

The points I made in our conversation on 14 August were as follows:

1. I do not want a divorce – I do however understand that you do
2. I cannot support your proposal regarding you and the children moving to the farm as I believe this would impact the children very negatively. They are at an impressionable / sensitive age and forcing compounded change on them would be very detrimental to their well-being:
   a. Parents getting divorced
   b. Forced to relocate to a school where:
      i. they lose the security of the good school they have attended for years
      ii. they have no friends at the new school
      iii. the school is culturally very different from what they are used to (farm school, quite Afrikaans, isolated)
   c. Forced to move out of their current home which we have been in for almost 11 years:
      i. which provides them with the security of a good home
      ii. where the children have their own comfortable space
      iii. while the farm is great over weekend and holidays, especially when they have friends there, it will be very lonely and leave them feeling isolated if they are there on their own for an extended time
      iv. the farm house is not exactly conducive to the space and privacy for the children's needs
      v. a woman alone with children on a farm is not great from a physical security perspective, this will put further pressure on children to try and be the 'man' responsible for protecting the family. This will in turn fall on the other children's shoulders when the eldest goes to university in four years as they already told me their wish is to study overseas
3. I do love the house and the farm, but understand your proposal that you keep the farm as it is already in your name and given that it was funded from the home bond. I keep the house and the associated debt. That, together with you keeping your car and the furniture on the farm.
4. From a financial perspective I am not in a position to support the house and the farm going forward. I know you said I could as I am doing it today, but as we have discussed previously I retire in 4 years and 11 months and currently spend my full income, including bonus, to support our current lifestyle, as it was always the plan that you would become the primary bread-winner once I retire. I need to make sure we are living within my monthly salary and using any remaining as well as any future bonus to settle all debt and make provision for the children to go to university after I have retired. Expenses which cannot be maintained at current levels include amongst others:
   a. 5 staff (currently 2 on the farm and 3 at home) and additional costs they incur, including school
   b. Rates and taxes as well as Eskom fees on the farm
   c. Maintenance on the farm as well as dog food, vet's bills etc.
   d. Maintaining other children
5. As agreed I would appreciate if you could give me a breakdown of your spend as well as confirm with me before incurring extraordinary spend as we have agreed. I have excluded this from the points above regarding monthly expenditure until such time I get the breakdown from you.

Regards

Dear

I wish to thank you for having a meeting with me on Thursday to discuss the next step.

I do realize that you wish not for a divorce however, I hope you understand the reasons for the decision that I have made to reach this point in our relationship.

As per your request:
A) I will submit my monthly expenditure soonest
B) I will endeavour for my financial independence to not take a year or more as per your request
C) I understand that due to your previous divorce you do not want to engage in maintaining me as your spouse and would maintain our children and therefore would prefer to pay the children's expenses directly and no alimony to me
D) I understand your concerns regarding me and the children living in the farm from a security and isolation perspective
E) thank you for explaining the expenditures on the credit cards both Gold and Amex to which I have no access
F) thank you for explaining the balance of the debit orders on the bank account
G) thank you for agreeing that I am allowed to keep the farm and my car
H) thank you for not apposing that I be the primary care for the children
G) thank you for allowing me to be financially independent before signing of the divorce agreement, although this not being dragged out to a year as per my request, but it be sooner rather than later, to which I ensured you that I do not want your money and that I am attempting to find the best suited option for financial independence as the mere fact that I am not earning an income as we speak is not the position I wish to be in, but it was a decision made in the best interest of our children.
I) I also understand that the children are of the age that they are in a position to make decisions regarding their schooling and living circumstances, and will therefore allow them to make informed decisions, and that you wish not to be there on the initial introduction of the idea of perhaps relocating to the farm or changing of schools. However, we both agree that as parents we still have the right to make the necessary decisions for them, as we do not want to repeat history of the children from your previous marriage, who made decisions, as children and the parents followed the children's call, instead of parents making a uniform decision for their children.
J) thank you for agreeing to not influence the children to choose sides

Given the above, thank you for being understanding, and thank you for treating me with respect this weekend.

I shall ensure that you receive all the requested expenditures and that the house will be in order to receive your guests this coming weekend.

Agreed

∞

As I am going through negotiations with my partner / husband of 20 years, it takes me by surprise that after all this time, I am a business transaction, of 'tell me what you want'.
I cannot understand which is what hurts me most of going through this process…
Let me put this to you in words…
As I have started capturing all the various pieces from the heart that I have written through my life, I now look back and think to myself.
My dearest love, Angelique, selflessly you gave everything to this relationship, you have not a cent to your name, you have clothes in your cupboard, you have a house and furniture. Whatever monies you had or earned throughout these years you invested right back into the hope and dreams of happily ever after.
Even following the many people's advice to keep a little nest egg on the side for that one day – when something might happen, you still did not believe that materialistic needs or capital gains, is more important than having your family.
Now you are dealt with like a business transaction which needs to live on rations and ask for money to live your life, look after the household and the children.

However, look at you - your ultimate optimist, this is the chance, you have to recreate yourself…
As this economic abuse that you now have to face is just another control tactic that you need to not allow, to get you down.
You have it in you to recreate yourself, and to move those mountains to ensure that you are okay and to make another plan to look after the welfare of your children...

Very few know about the life you have lived:

The constant uncertainty that of unfaithfulness and infidelity of your husband.
The alcohol abuse that you have been subjected to that you needed to put certain measures in place to ensure your safety and in turn the safety of your children.
The temper that rages when you least expect it.
The constant comments that makes you feel worthless.
The pacing and stomping around.
The standing around and not sitting when you are at the table for a meal.
The standing or snoring when you want to watch a film together.
The falling asleep when you start with sexual foreplay, just to be woken in the middle of the night, and if you don't perform you are a slut or a fuckup or a whore that fucked other men but won't participate.
When sleep apnoea kicks in – he stops breathing in the night, you wake him to be told to fuck off and starts lashing out at you physically and words that are hurtful.
When he is drunk you have a choice of two, either you are being told how pathetic and useless and what a bitch you are, or you are being forced to have sex… at times the latter has to follow the first and if you do not participate in either…. You fear are being grabbed and with evil forcing being shoved around.
I remember the day, when my little boy was about 2 years old, and the drunken rage of wanting sex after falling asleep during foreplay, I turned to fall asleep myself, as I

felt that, shame he is tired, let him sleep. Waking in the middle of the night with being forced into sex and I said no…. resulted into being pulled by my feet out of bed and I went to lie with my little boy in his bed as he woke up crying… the stomping up and down the passage and in the bedroom with words being forcefully whispered in my ears of what a bitch I am… whilst lying next to my boy…. Yes, the next morning standing in the kitchen with my little boy, making cereal, he came in and turned the kitchen table and started shouting, I grabbed my son and ran down the garden to hide from him while he was chasing after us screaming and shouting and my nanny came out of her room trying to help us….

The amount of anger rages and abuse that happened in that house was terrible – boot marks down the passage walls, being pulled out of bed by my hair or feet night after night… days and nights being on my own while he was always at work, or traveling to different destinations.
Looking after my step children and their friends, hosting parties, cooking, and going through IVF treatments….
If it was not for my sister, who was my dearest and closest friend and confidante and my house executive…. I really don't know….
Home-schooling my step child…
my brother going through his bursts of psychotic schizophrenic attacks, my sister in law having her bipolar attacks….
Having to start my own business as I needed to move from my position of employment……
I tried to help him myself through the process of dealing with his decision from divorcing his wife, dealing with a man that constantly needed to be raced to the ER as he stopped breathing and getting severe asthma attacks that he turned purple and blue….
He travelled to London regularly, the woman he had had an affair with before during and after he had been having an affair with me, had moved to London with her family…. He wanted us to buy her house in Emmerentia …. Trying to convince me that it will be ideal and close to my son's school….
Luckily I was not going to fall for this.

Oh and then the contract in Zurich commenced - I had a suspicion, but I kept sending all the messages of love and devoted wife, making house a home, welcoming every return with special treatment.
Never going anywhere with my friends – staying at home like the dedicated mother and wife. I still had a suspicion as he was very secretive when he returned, till the gifts of the KTM arrived from a complete stranger?

So going to IVF treatments on my own, I saw the house we are living in now, and fell in love with the house…. I was convinced that change in scenery would stop the abusive behaviour and perhaps when we are surrounded by new environment that the abuse would stop. Hello – so not!!! Countless efforts of making time and seeing psychologists, marriage counsellors, psychiatrists, and even leaving him to move to my mother in the previous house.
Still that did not change the abuse. Not allowed to discuss money matters, not

allowed to discuss children, not allowed to talk too much about my day.
I worked from home, I did not earn a cent as I would rather build the business so that he could have something to fall back on would he resign or retire from Corporate. Every cent I put back into the business.
My little pocket that I had built through the years, my pension pays out bought our step child's first car, my tax pay-outs, was paid into the second child's deposit for an apartment.
The policy pay out was paid into the business to pay the children's salaries.
The profit pays out on the separate business was paid into the family holiday in Mauritius. Every cent I had to my name was paid to the above, with the promise, "as soon as I receive my bonus, I will give you the money back", to just be told, "it receives better earnings in the bond" so after all this, I am left with absolutely not one cent to my name.

I have set aside my studies and my passion for psychology during the time of starting and running the businesses and household and raising my children for the sake of having something for him to fall back on. I have done this because I believed in the magic of happily ever after….
The friends that I have had visiting my house, as it was just less abusive then to go out anywhere. He would stalk me, with calls and or just pitching up wherever I was, if I ever went to a restaurant with my friends for a cup of coffee.
With my friends visiting at home, he would harass them, my friends being too afraid to tell me would just stay away and not want to visit again. I cannot expect my friends to always just visit me, so everyone has faded away through the years.
If the friends where male, he would be so jealous and protectively obsessed with me that he would go out of his way to make them feel uncomfortable including my own brothers.
Having to entertain or host in such circumstances of always fearing for some fight to break out, I would rather just be without friends

Yes, I have been accused of:

a) A gay boy that was part of a production with midgets from America putting up the stage show. Although he was dating a girl, one day he decided to kiss me… but I knew in my heart of souls the boy is gay, as I have a fantastic gaydar that never fails me (Growing up with a gay uncle and having to cover up for him all my life). This boy was going to hurt this girl, and I could not let this happen. He was an outright asshole, for the empty promises that he was to give this girl. She was in love and was hoping that they would live that happily ever after! Mother Theresa, I was, out to save this girl from hurt.
Why come into my house and kiss me, why flirt with boys and be totally gay, when you are living with a girl and have not one good word to say about her, and she adores you! Pig you are!
– because I know he is gay – I had no concern about him going to the same public toilet as me, and because he was just a so called friend/acquaintance I saw no wrong with inviting my husband to join us for drinks on the Sandton square – but yap, I was and still is accused of fucking this boy in the public toilet...seriously?

b) After a spate of serious abuse and then busting him, jerking himself off to porn in my office, then jerking himself off on the couch in the communal lounge of my house where my boys at any time could walk in. (Oh the Asian porn started after my friend from Columbus came to visit and we hosted their friends, the wife is Asian and he tried to harass her) The Asian, fantasy began.

An old friend of mine came to visit from the UK. He was so caring, and complementary, concerned and damn good looking. We only had tea at my house, but we had regular phone calls and emails talking about our lives to date, catching up.

When receiving all these nice words, complements and attention, I thought to myself, why am I standing for this abuse?

I had always wanted to take the children to the UK. Why not just pack up and run away with my children - far far away!!!

He found the email communications and that was the end of that fantasy, history!

– but trust me not of the accusations and the regular – 'oh you tried to throw yourself at another man, that clearly did not want you!!'

This was approximately 9 years ago when this happened – but he loves throwing it, the favourite accusation and reminder, telling me how no one would want me, whenever he is pissed like in drunk, or pissed like in angry with me.

c) My sister had moved to Oudtshoorn, I wanted to get out of the relationship after another spate of abuse.

My biggest and most concerning issue is – having to face the possibility of not seeing my children, every second weekend and every second school holiday.

I was emotionally and physically finished. Broken, exhausted, and I had to get away.

I went to my sister at the time that the KKNK was on.

I bumped into an old acquaintance of mine, and we painted the town red! Getting inebriated in a beer tent, met some painting artist. The one night we went to a pub 'Die ou Kliphuis' to listen to a live performance. I got soooo drunk. The artist offered to walk me home, as it was early in the morning hours and the streets were quiet, concerned for my safety.

Everyone knew I was married and have children, as I made no secret of that. Trust me many know my sister and my brothers amongst the Afrikaans artist community. He walked me home, made sure I was in bed and he took the couch, as I passed out on the bed, too drunk to speak.

When back in Joburg they came to visit and the artist said, that he had walked me home and apologised for being alone with me, oh my …. I still do not hear the end of that.

d) Now for really being caught with my hand in the 'cookie jar'!

(also blown completely outa proportion and being accused for more then what really actually went down.)

In the business that I owned, an old acquaintance being a supplier of products came to see me to advertise their products in my showroom. We went for

lunch, and one bottle of wine lead to the next. We laughed and talked, until we realised…. Shit, its dark!
I better get home, we walked and laughed and chatted all the way back to my office. I needed to pee, but all the doors were locked so I sneaked behind the building to pee in a plant pot. Coming back around the corner, there my friend was slap bang as I looked up from scratching for my keys in my bag, his lips touched mine, and needless to say, there was a little open mouth kissing.
I heard footsteps… looked around the corner... it's my oldest son... oh shit!!!!
What the fuck to do … I threw my handbag … told my friend to pretend to make a pee and ran…. Fuck!! I got the fright of my life!! Then thought – fuck Ange, why are you running? Go talk to your son and face the music my girl… which I did.
 – except for my friend, coming strolling through, trying to pull up his fokkin zip as he was soo pissed, said "hey pel, your mother and I are old friends and there is nothing wrong with a kiss and a cuddle"
– I could have fokking murdered him right there!!
Men – I swear!!!!!!!!!!!!
Anyway, arrived home I told him that I had done something wrong and told him the whole story. ALL hell broke loose, phone calls to the wife of my friend…
This happened, was it 6/7 years ago – but still – "you fuck pissed married men" is what I deal with all the time….

I wonder if men actually understand that as a woman you kinda know who enters your vagina with their penis, for fuck sakes...

I have made attempts to leave this man:

a) When I just moved in with him and he started abusing me, throwing me around, I ran off to my friend one day… I stayed with her for a couple of days, and he begged me to come back, and that he would not do that again and he is sorry
b) When my son was about 2 years old and I left him, stayed with my Mom for a few days, my baby cried when he visited with his dad and wanted to go home to his dogs and toys… I was promised that we would go for counselling and that it would never happen again
c) When we moved into this house I took my children and moved to my mom, I was begged to come back and it will never happen again
d) When he found the letter, I was promised he would go for therapy and begged me to stay and it would never happen again
e) When I returned from Oudtshoorn, I was promised that he is in therapy (and that I also will benefit from this lady, which I had gone to see as well) things will change and it will never happen again

I started standing up for myself.
Made him move out of my space, into the cottage. Changed patterns to avoid being

around him, especially when the whiskey is poured.
Started separating myself from him or the possibility of abuse.
Motivated him to go away as much as possible.
Started leading separate lives.

Then – tell-tale signs that he has furthered his horizons – the hair, the clothes, the slimming, the hidden cell phone – the excuses to not be around.

The bust – naked pics on the form this girl in Kenya.
Then the phone being kicked under the bed, too drunk to think of excuses, the confession of the 3-year relationship

Then – the SMS – your husband his having an affair with a married woman at work.

I had spoken to him and said, I understand that there will be times when you meet someone, intrigued by the first flirtation, perhaps you bump into them again. However, you go back a third time, there is more to it than just a flirtation. That is when you need to tell me, it will then be my choice to allow it, or to end us.

You know – I was still trying to keep it all together even after the first two incidents. However, I had brought a friend around, we had gone out and had a few too many, came home and continued having another few, he put on the music and we started dancing.
I thought to myself, your asshole, I am going to see how far you will take this.
I started kissing the girl, and said let's take it down in the cottage. He started honing in on the girl as if I was not there, I got up and left while they continued. I went to my bed in the house.
The next morning was quite awkward, I was upset:
'How could you, in front of me take another woman, as if I don't exist?'
'Well, you got up and left, and next time please bring a better looking woman'
I checked his phone a few days later. They had been texting.
I thought you shit! Again, I brought her back to my stoep, curious as to what is going on.
Again they went for each other, while I went to bed.
Yes, I started it – but fuck hell no I was not going to sit back and be told that I am mad, that he does not fuck other woman! He just did that in front of me – in my face!! To a woman that he thinks is not attractive and that is supposed to be my friend and he knows her boyfriend!!

After his confession of his 3-year relationship, the topic of The Will and Testament came up, I wanted to ensure that all the children's names are updated and that everything is equally divided amongst them.

The next day I had asked him to invite his new lady over for a braai so she can meet me and my kids. If she is going to be a part of our lives, he still had the audacity to tell me that she will probably be more into me then him. You know he now tells me, I made it all up, that there is not anyone else, and there was never anyone else, that he never said there was a 3-year relationship!!

> 1 September 2015
>
> I wish to do the attached and was hoping that you would assist me in
> financing upfront, I will repay you once I am qualified and earn the
> necessary income
>
Hi,

I have the following proposal for your consideration, which I would like you to think about with purely the best interest of the children at heart, which I know you will do.

Further consideration needs to be given to your current and future employment and contracts which currently requires weekly travel and with the possibility of future travel.

My work options will be based on the following decisions as primary caregiver:

Option A:
The children remain at their current school and remain living at home.
This would require for you to find alternative accommodation for when you are in Johannesburg. This would also require the possibility of driver assistance as backup for me, if and when I am not available to drive the children to and from school activities.

Option B:
The children remain in their current school and alternative accommodation for me and the children.
There is currently a 3-bedroom townhouse for sale opposite the school in a very secure complex.
The townhouse is in the market for 2mil which will be bought in the name of the children. They will be able to walk to and from school if I am not able to collect them for whatever reason after school activities.

Option C:
Myself and the children relocate to the farm The children relocate to schools The school is smaller, financially more affordable, and has different options to explore, and will be less distracted by current peer group to focus on academics. Initially this will be a big change, however it would still be a permanent change which would enable them to settle once used to it

Please let me know what option you feel about the various options and which you would prefer taking the children's future into consideration

Hi

Apologies for the cryptic response – in back to back incident workshops so typing while I am in one of them!
My response in red text below. Please let me know what you think.
Regards

- I do not want to move out of my home and at this point am financially going into a negative position on a monthly basis trying to maintain both the home and the farm. Affording a third dwelling for you is out of the question. We would at least need to sell the farm for you to do this. As per the previous bullet I would also need to ensure that we are not spending more than I earn on a monthly basis in order that I provide for retirement period which may require us to sell both the house and the farm to afford two smaller residences.

I really cannot afford to continue maintaining the house and the farm given the changing circumstances, particularly if you require a new residence.

Regards

Why should the farm be sold...? It was bought for the kids and they enjoy being there riding their bikes etc.

I have decided that selling the farm will be the option, therefore had spoken to agents who will get back to me, as first option placing it back on the Market.

After much deliberation and asking the children how they enjoy the farm and looking at the reasons for investing in the farm ....

This was bought for the children to live out their love of riding and for them to break away from city living, everything that has been constructed and built was for the benefit of the children! As their interests are in riding and therefore I have an additional option:

House remains your asset

Farm remains my asset

Rental of a cluster / townhouse within walking distance of school where myself and the children will move to

This way there will be no additional bond, maintenance of the property is dealt with by estate owner and no long term financial burden of bond repayments, allowing for flexibility for both you and me as far as ongoing financial commitments are.

Let me know what you think?

I have drafted a divorce agreement together with a parenting plan for your perusal.

I am trying to save us unnecessary costs with lawyers and mediators etc.

Please take a look at it and tell if you agree with the terms.

As soon as you are happy with this we can then continue to submit to reach finalisation.

Just to give you background as to how I got to the lump sum:

Over the past few months that we have been doing the budget and looking at the monthly expenses it averages on approximately R40k per month which covers most of the living costs which is incurred

40k x 12 = R480 living expenses

19K x 12 = R228 rental accommodation

20k = mediation course (invest or pay another)

35k = complete Unisa degree

237k = vehicle settlement

As we agreed that ongoing maintenance and support for me is not an option and that I wish not for ME as Angelique to be a burden to you of any kind that we would rather work on a figure in full and final settlement. This way we would both be released as spouses and our focus remain on the wellbeing of the children, and that we can remain friends without having to concern ourselves with money matters. I wish nothing more than for us to remain in good friendship, as you have been my best friend since 1993 and never want to lose that.

I assure you that it is of utmost importance to me to regain my independence with URGENCY!

To put light to the subject:

Your favourite saying – Its cheap at the price

Looking forward to your feedback

Luv

Angelique

I would like to highlight that should you not wish to continue with the 20 x 4 split I would like to add a clause that states that you pay me an additional R1million to invest at my own discretion for the benefit of the current known children.

Angelique

Looks fine. As already agreed in WhatsApp conversation the other night there are no other kids so you can revert to 100% to the four children.

Thanks

Under Financial responsibility, could you please add the breakdown of the R1 million as per your original email? As well as that I can settle the cash amount I must give you in two parts which excludes for example the vehicle which I must settle with the

Bank and the rent which I must pay the agent monthly?

∞

13/10/2015

Dear Mom and Dad,

I don't really know how to begin this but to just go ahead and say...

We have gone our separate ways. I have moved into a cluster home which is walking distance from the kids school your child is still working on Namibia and has home to come home to on the weekends.

We have parted our ways as good friends and have very amicable agreement whereby home is kept, which makes sense as to the higher returns on investment. I keep the farm and the kids including as dad they have time to spend building tracks and being boys! As that was the initial reason behind the investment.

The children still see their dad on weekends as and when work enables him to do so. We have co-parenting rights which means that we share custody over the children.

Myself and the children have settled into our new home and the older children are in support of our new arrangements! As a matter of fact, they both phone to check in if all is okay!

We are still going to Austria together for the wedding in December/ January!!

I want to take this opportunity to say that...although after many years (20 years to be exact) we have attempted to make our relationship work. It has come to a point where we needed to make a call... And we did!!

We are good friends and the kids are (although divorce is not easy on any child, for which we have seeked Counselling) well adjudged to the new living arrangements.

Please know that because we are now in separate homes does not make you separate grandparents nor does it make is separate marital daughter/ parents!! You are always and will always be welcome in my house and welcome to give that naughty car phone Sunday outing or Saturday outing call to jay chat!!

Your son is an amazing man and dad and will always be!!!!!
We did not work as a couple!!

I love you as my own and will do forever and my four children are yours forever!!!

I hope you understand and love you!!!

Angelique

Great letter - give them a couple of days to get over the jet lag before u send ...

∞

Response from mom and dad!!

Was my biggest fear ever to let them know as they are my absolute ...

But - would rather they hear it from me then some person in at work

∞

Hi Ange

We are lost for words!

We are absolutely stunned & surprised to get this news out of the blue.

But we know how you are both devoted to the children and that you will make sure that they get the best of everything and all the love & attention that they need.

Sorry that we did not respond last night, but we just felt blown away.

Our thoughts and prayers are with you all

Love

Mom & Dad

∞

Hi

Please peruse through all the documentation that is required for submission in respect of uncontested divorce where minor children are involved.

Please confirm that you are satisfied with the content contained herein and should there be any amendments made to please send this to me in email to ensure that all relevant information is contained herein.

Should there be no changes we will then submit to Sheriff's office on Tuesday morning

Made the changes as discussed:

- Another child (deleted)
- Financial responsibilities (updated to reflect minimum payment schedule)
- I am doing my recon now on all expenses outside normal with regards to study fees, extras etc. We are now settled, so there will be no extra-ordinary expenses from what needed to be incurred during the move so I will be able to project and budget accordingly.
- I have not paid this yet as I do not have the cash flow right now.

- If you would be so kind as to pay to prevent any queries, I will really appreciate it
- Angelique

- Dear Angelique,
-
- I have done a recon of the settlement figure due to you below, taking into account that I need to settle the vehicle by end April (and sign transfer forms) as well as me paying the rent until the end of October 2016 (as the contract is in my name).

- Please have a look at the numbers below and let me know if you agree as I am doing my best to try and work out how to settle in full as per your request.

RECON OF SETTLEMENT FIGURE

- Insurance – should vehicle have been settled this would not have been a necessary cost to incur (please note I am not being petty, but have been indeed very understanding to date)
-
- TOTAL PAYMENT RECEIVED

- BALANCE DUE

- I would really appreciate it if you would be so kind as to settle the vehicle and ensure the necessary transfer to my name be done, as I need to arrange for insurance
- I would also appreciate the settlement figure of the divorce be transferred to me before end of March 2016
- I would like for us to finalise this before end March 2016 to enable both of us to move forward with the rest of our lives. Please know that I have been extremely understanding and accommodating to date, and would like to close this chapter.
- Kind Regards
- Angelique
- I am being understanding and my calculations are correct in terms of the agreement. I will settle in terms of the agreement.

29 Mar 2016
- I am trying to be understanding and nice and patient –
- why should I be the one waiting to move on with my life while you are spending on the renovations of the home which was not urgent
- I wish to have my independence I have been very accommodating and would not like this to become personal
- I wish to have full control of my life and finances

- So with due respect – please settle according to my calculation – so we do not drag this out any longer

Dear
-

- Please note the rent is in my name through to October so I am liable for the debt so need to pay it myself and as per the agreement it comes off the settlement value (Dec'15 to Oct '16) as per my email below. Should you manage to get out of the obligation in full by finding another tenant I am happy to pay the balance to you instead of to the landlord.

-

- Also note that the settlement of the vehicle is quoted as at end of this month, so you need to add on payments made post 30 Nov '15 to get back to settlement value as at 30 Nov '15 as per my original email and as per the divorce agreement. The calcs in my original email take this into account and are correct.

-

- I was not being petty about the insurance as it is a cost incurred on your behalf, but will waive this as I did the overseas trip.

-

- I really am trying to settle you in full as soon as possible. I will be able to settle the car but will only be able to settle you once I have the money which I am hoping to secure through sale of shares / facility which at best will be by end May. I will do as much as I can in the interim.

-

- Given the above the outstanding settlement figure remains at my original email plus insurance.

-

- Please check again

-

- Just do what u need to do - I am over it

Angelique

∞

FINAL DECREE OF DIVORCE

IN THE REGIONAL COUR FOR THE REGIONAL DIVISION OF GAUTENG HELD AT RANDBURG

ON: 30 NOVEMBER 2015

Alone I stand – facing the Magistrate.

A whastapp to say you are formally released.

Off to fetch my children from school.

Stay strong Ange.

30 August 2018

I want to tell you how much I hurt, I want to face you as my perpetrator!!

To tell you how I fucken suffer your pain you have inflicted on me – you shit! I hate you! I hate, I hurt, I am sore!

Again the man that I thought would be there to stand up and assist in fending, fighting, supporting me on this day when again I was violently invaded, to watch him be too tired to fucking care! To give a fucking shit for 2 seconds. Oh no, I am on a telecom, so sorry that you had to go through this… When he knows he has to fucking face his own shit he has done to me!

The denial of every fucker that fucking hurts you! That uses you as a sex object – fuck fuck! Jesus Christ who gives anyone the right to fucking try and invade your humanity, your personality, you being fucking human/nice/innocent – no fucking one!

Your heaven, your space has been disturbed by some evil fucking cock! That does not know how to control himself. You lost yourself, you lost your kids, your home, and now your peace haven! Because of fucking sex, cock, fuck year after year, you have to remain strong – fuck you all!

I was fucking abused! Sexually being made to subject myself to a man, who could not respect the fact that I am not going to have sex with him, turned evil, and strapped me and threw me onto the back of his bakkie! In my own place in my home! In my heaven!

I trusted my neighbour. Me, the person to have good intent, to make the land work for all! I gave him the benefit, to have to turn around and to hurt me! To take away my dignity, to take a way my home!
Is that not how a child feels! I am an adult! And I am shitting myself, imagine what a child feels when such indignity is done!

And the perpetrator gets away with some bullshit story that he saw the demon?? I gave you water to feed your family, your animals, your crops. You came to my home and you assaulted me!

Mr President I know if I take this through the system it will end my life! I therefore ask you to assist me in this time. This man is a so-called candidate in your team of officials. If I report this, I live on my own on my farm, will I see the light tomorrow if I continue to report this man that walked into my house, my home, my heaven, my peace? Do I stand a chance? Single white female in a rural predominantly black community, standing up against what? I fear my life will be ended, quietly.

It amazes me the reactions my body has given to this. I have sick running from my vagina – I have a body that is so sore and stiff, I have bruises and scratches. My heart and head doesn't know when to cry, when to scream! I kept it all amazingly for my children, as they are with me, and I need to be a mom, yet inside I am dying! Yet I am strong!

I have to live here, facing you driving past my home, fear the possibility of bumping into you in town. Your canary yellow bakkie!! You Pig!!

Thank you Liz and Sam for saving my life, for hearing my screams, for releasing me from the straps that tied me to the bakkie. I shall be forever grateful and indebted to you.

Bless you!!

Being attacked in my own house, in my own space, in my peace haven, AngelsFarm.

∞

22 October 2018

My liewe Madelie

You touched so many hearts so many souls – your beauty your humanity changed lives.

When you entered my life as I would probably speak for many – there was only one thing I can with absolute honour tell you my love – you are an angel that came through and worked in our hearts the path that only contributed to the amazing world of being a social worker and believing through your eyes through your heart and your passion the truth behind what we do. Oft no one knew your heart and what went on beyond that smile and that laughter and passion as you continued to fight for the good in every person. My amazing human I shall never forget your words 'ag nee jirre Angie hul is simple man"

You believed so much in every person you only looked for their strong pointes and tried your level best to uplift that and gave everyone the endless support – although it was in times that you needed some – yet your little twinkle in those eyes and your laugh – one always knew when you were in the room or on the other side of the line.

We had a special time my friend outside the work where I had the honour of your children and your parents which was so important to you. They were your life!

I cannot remember one word you could every say wrong about anyone regardless of who and what they were, you never judged a single soul or a single person. It is your fault that many of us never gave up and never turned away and still till today fight for what we intrinsically believe in and that was your passion and belief in social work and child welfare.

You are and inspiration to many and your heart will always be a blessing to everyone, you are angel as it is on earth so it shall be in heaven.

I thank you Madelie for blessing us with you, in every aspect, in every being, in every word. Amazingly you graced us with you and how sweet your soul will remain for now and ever more

Love Ange

∞

'Am I ready yet?"

The universe is amazing!

Mining and eviction, selling of my land – community development

I want at least 5million zar to invest to have my kids schooled and travel and give my children opportunities. That's what I want.

The past is old and done – he did what he could – he did what I wanted and now it is up to me to establish me and I shall travel – with my kids.

∞

Every night and every day I try to find a cure. For the rights I feel the world deserves. For the wrongs the world has endured.
Conflicting emotions when you wake and say this will be, yet another day versus, wow this will be a blissful day.

When you go by your every moment experiencing not only what you read?
You breathe?
You eat?
You see?

Channelling what you feel the moment you wake to say this is me!!!

How do we cure as we go through our every second and moment in our lives as we meet the next...?

They say breath in ... Breath out ...

But what if you feel the pain of every person, what if you give joy and all they seek is the joy you give in return? You keep on giving and giving and giving ... You end up being sapped ...
Building walls all around to prevent you from being broken.

Faces, smiles, masks ... How many are walking around with - but I know, you feel and you see beyond what is portrayed...

For long - I have blocked the channel of feeling the ill of what is around me... To such an extent that forgetting who and what this plane is here to teach...

In vulnerability- the crack has slowly become a glacier... And the ills are sapping the pool of strength which needs to be replenished for the sake of the soul!!!

In moments ... The relapse of weakness brought upon - what??? Vulnerability... Lack of control ...?

Bullshit!!!

Find the cure!!! That will heal the broken!!!

Amazingly bring in a new work of art that many will admire ... And many won't understand - the backdrop but you do! As you cast the production as you go through your life, knowing the end result will be...

The cure

"Standing on the beach with the gun in my hand Staring at the sea, staring at the sand, staring down the barrel with the Arab on the ground, I'm alive ... I'm dead .... I'm a stranger ... " The cure

Angelique

∞

Words we speak, read, hear, speak
What do they mean?

Could be interpreted in many ways ...
Dependent on the recipient

The recipient has its own motion of being, in its own space, in its own time

The speaker, writer again in its own motion, space, time

For a moment the two are on equal plane - Be it as it may ...

Can either take and move on?
Give and move on?

Or are the more words unheard, unread, unspoken, unwritten?

Or is there just silence ....

Oft this is misinterpreted by both giver and receiver ...

Is it?? ...

Words are never left unspoken ... Never ... For they return ... As words need to be spoken as they will return in some form or another until they are heard or read....

∞

When you lie in bed and thoughts pass through your mind, what do you hold that makes everything, everyday worth the while.

Is it me ... Is it what I have shared, is it what I have done?

We are surrounded by a world of so many variations of some familiar vibrations of movement, thoughts, sights, sound, energies that either saps or turns nothing into something. Motivates, births, breaks or kills...

Yet magical moments could be 2 minutes, contact... Thought...

Touch is the most intense way of knowing what thoughts are ... As a conduit of soul ... A mere touch can bring forth a birth or a death.

U cannot birth if there is still a death hovering.

I surrender ...

∞

Having the most honest communications with the star child which you thought would be of lesser understanding.

Opens realities way beyond what you ever could have anticipated. The moment you thought you are protecting ... They turn around to say .... I know.

The provocation brought about when least expected... And the heart most open at the pint of sharing.

Could souls be so caring to say .... Move on??
Souls touch through many portals.
In ways of seconds, minutes and sometimes hours.

A journey is created far beyond that of what we realize in our human state of being bound to this realm of what only humans known to exist... As humans/earth/body/flesh

When reincarnated to be a part of the earth, Souls are bound to meet ... They carry messages ... Through various forms

They answer questions, they need to know, they need to question...

Souls meet ... They need to pass ... They need to maintain ... They need to be a part of the journey created by various shapes, sizes, ages ...

Oft times ... Bound by the physical space the soul has taken on to project itself as the vehicle which somehow prevents its current journey... With time ... Souls will meet regardless of its current vehicle's state - souls are destined to meet

∞

28 October 2018

I spent time with my people this weekend. Listening to the stories of women with passion, that have given their lives and souls, dedicating every inch of strength they have for children, life protection and social work. I do know that my life path and passion will not wane away, as I continue, I to strive for the protection of children at a larger scale. For the profession and acknowledgement of the profession. The people that are dedicated to protection of little voiceless beings that enter onto this plane for reasons only their souls will understand.

It has been a human ill to cause damage and hurt, and I wonder if the births of so many is not the way that shouts out more by the universe to say STOP hurting and start protecting.

As life and humans evolve and with the growth as we experience how, with the awareness and immediate exposure is a means to the universe, soul and planet to say Enough is Enough.

I take in my time, during my exposure to the wrongs of adults whom I trusted to protect me or to just love me. Who was there for me? Where did, or where could I go to be safe and heard? I did not know where to turn, and even if I turned to others, would they hear me, or would they judge me? Would I be further abused and hurt by their judgement? Would I be in trouble for opening my mouth?

As I grew up and was subjected to abuse, I would confide in my, what I saw as support, yet – they looked at me, as if I was talking nonsense they would not believe me- which as a result made me feel as if I should introspect, that the fault lies with me – leading to believe that the psychosis is from me and not from my daily experiences of abuse and rape in every way.

My exterior should not be my punishment, it should be my pride.
My vehicle must be honoured and not abused.
My, me, everything should be respected, I respect me.

You also have to do the same.

∞

2018 – numerology reading – notes:

Put away 12 % of income

Rules and conversation – till December introspection, I feel – air on runway give it 6 months – on 12 June you will turn that corner to become that pilot and have destination, direction, introspection, investigation. Synergy and repeats are reminders of patterns. December holds joint injury and failed health.

Career about where you are going: - September – put thought into action, year of fortune or misfortune, me and my business, other opportunities of income, need to value me, win opportunities – 2,5 years every 9 years, steel phone and gift phone = win, value yourself. Age 48,49,50 dodgy regarding business, 50 – 53 = home and house. Do money, don't compromise yourself. As you want to step away people want to partner – don't employ = project to project. Official legal documents on 19 December – invest – as receiving – signing up for.

1 1 1 8 8 9 6 6 – family, voice, 6th sense, listen, look, homeopathy, responsibility, angel number =6

3 3 collective growth development

2 2 us – we

7 investigate and research

9 years old – life path year, home free of responsibility, move into personal, introspection not out there to find you, being and accepting and okay, I do what I want to do, children expanding, I need myself and move forward, massive changes 63 – 27 age – owning and doing. Upbringing intense emotion inside the help by helping. Creative, not marketing or selling, focus on all or nothing. Introspection 33/34 about career change. Life path year in personal space, cruise, coast, knowledge, wisdom, understanding, teaching. Emotional romantic, caretaker. Discussion of money, need to make rules for self and value self. Set rules. Create associations, by 47 websites up for a year, may only, coaching and teaching in research before motivate and insight. Resonate and connect. Married at 25 no pressure till June and start turning –

∞

30 November 2018

When do you say this – do you express your emotions with immediate effect or do you wait the perfect moment to express! Is that what a perfect leader does! You wait for the perfect moment!

The world was not ready! We should make that difference!

The launch!

Child trafficking, the virtual office, training, skills development, arts and nature conservation.

#training #Education #women and #gay #rape #rapeculture #music … combined!!! #unitethefight

I am coming for you – either way, the world will be shocked, to make everyone realise that the hurt cannot continue.

∞

Music – a song

The concept of don't! It lasts between 3 – 5 minutes!
Because it doesn't work for you!
It doesn't mean you can't wait it out for someone else!
How long does a song last?
We don't have the patience to just allow the song that works for the one person to

play from beginning to end.
Let them listen, as it means something to them, the rhythm, the tune, the lyrics.
It only lasts for 3 – 5 minutes…

∞

11 November 2018

What happens to a mothers' heart when her kids depart...?

Before they leave, you make sure they have that hearty meal that is cooked with all the love poured into it, to remind yourself of the purpose and reason that you are here for them. When they have that last meal with you, the joy displayed on their faces as they devour the tastes. With full plates, they are fed with every part that you can give to them.

A plate of food made with such care, planning and love, that you know you can provide – it is not much in quantity or not much in material value, but what you give is from your heart.

The senses that come through creates a memory – far deep seated than any superficial can ever create.

Nothing replaces that smell, that taste, that memory created by one simple plate of food. It lasts a lifetime.

Around the table, you have a story, a lesson, a memory created forever.

A simple act of love that creates more than one could ever replace.

My baby could not share our time this time as he has to focus on his studies – but Mama made that extra plate of love that I could cover and send home to him, that he could also share in the tastes, the smells, the memories – that with that plate of love – he knows that even if Mama is not there in person, Mama is there in thought, heart and love. I wrap it to you in love, while I miss you. While you are not with Mama, know that you are in every possible way a part of my soul.

Eat well my children, eat well my babies' forever

- Moms plate of food

∞

1 December 2018

I was asked today to give a talk to people at the Methodist Church on abuse and rape.

How do you prepare a talk if you are yourself a survivor?

There are no statistics that can justify or quantify the experiences that you have had to deal with in your life.
Where you are today and fighting this with passion – when you are a statistic

yourself. When justice as you know it, will fail you and will it incarcerate you for coming forward.
How do you speak up in this day, where you still to protect the identities of the people who had done this to you?

∞

'All I ever wanted all I ever needed is here in my arms – words are very unnecessary...' – Depeche Mode

I went to sleep last night as I wanted to be held and embraced by this new person, whom has made me feel special. Being his first and last thought, while I was proving my strength and independence in my way of self-protection, to say I can actually look after myself. I can actually sort out my ways, while you are also just being everywhere.

Yet, in my own way I created an expectation in me to have him with me – dismissing many. To have a moment of just being close, and sharing whatever I need to share with him. Be it his space or my space. I just wanted this everyday work up, that so far has only actually been 2 weeks, to come to a closeness of what I would want in my life.
Yes, I did protect my heart and person from the possible disappointment of not being with him – it was my little world I created in my perception of protection – of me – however, when it all came to the point when all failed, I wanted more. I was disappointed in whom?

He communicated his changes in schedules, and work all day every day. Yet, you in your world of expectations, as you wish that everyone can be as spontaneous as you are, their world cannot change at the drop of a hat.

You don't want the boy that just does what you say when you say jump. Now you are disappointed when you are turned down by the boy that has actually given you that attention, and can't jump at your beck and call.
The battle you have my dear = is the protection and the walls you have built.
This is a new man Ange. Yet I know your fear, you don't want to just be another pornstar / sex object – you want those words to be real. You don't want to just be another lodger – you want those words to be real.
Which actually Dear Lady is not that much to ask for.

∞

8 December 2018

The magic surrounds me as I have the most amazing position!

A - Being so much of exactly who I am – awaiting traveling, spontaneous, sporadic as it comes along! My dream and wish when my children are to go, being an attentive parent and leaving when they can handle it and go away! away! and live the dream – not tied down, traveling, experiencing yet feeling the need for some admiration and the emptiness of sharing hence you clutch onto this one that is semi-anchor to feel that sometimes there is comfort...

Why we always seek for comfort as that is what a parent is! I am 45 years and still go to my Mom's kitchen and open the cupboards and the fridge – through sheer habit and she is fine with it. She always asks me first thing, have you eaten? are you hungry? are you warm enough? Now, that is all what we all yearn for, and if you don't find that in your partner, you start all methods and motions of rejection, you test, you wonder, you see – but no one asks those basic questions!

Have you eaten
are you hungry
are you warm enough
are you comfortable
do you have anything to drink
good night, sweet dreams
don't let the bed bugs bite

I have just realised how we send our kids to sleep …. With bed bugs or sweet dreams…

∞

My brilliance right now is that I am encapsulated by 2 x Geminis what I am to learn from them as this is my life and I need to take something from them? What is it? I am totally intrigued and so are they!

What are we to learn – they are both in travel extensively, both in the beverage industry

…. We all need to drink and eat – respect what we drink and eat

….. biggest social ill – if we could teach all respect and grow

…. It all boils down to basics of eat and drink, we need to find the balance to gluttony – reproduction – feeding + replenish – rest the cycle – so simple

So what if you take sommeliers – into the 18 – 24-year gap – growing wheat – growing vines to address alcohol abuse – they are all waiters – study – they all drink – restorative justice.

They have to grow wheat
they have to grow grapes
they have to bottle it
they have to pair it
they have to sell it
they have to design the bottle
the brand, the market
regulate the principles around it
the family being lost
the children being made
by not teaching from a young age not to abuse the substance
what a rhetorical circle
but that is not always the case -

when you respect the grape, the wheat – you tend to care less about the after effect

I am so fabulously physically and psychologically and emotionally tired right now – good night

∞

I am worth more than serving you while you disregard anyone

I will always remember you for being your angel and your slut

I will always remember you for say no one knows love, till you have a child – and then your left

I will always remember you for teaching me to stand on my own two feet – through the abuse I have learnt

You came into this world alone – you are going to leave alone

The only master of your life – is you

You are the master of your own destiny

When you were 5 – the book titles

I was you at 14

Cornicles of the suburban house wife

Tainted love – listen to the lyrics

One last thing – Ange I love you as no one knows you like me

∞

12/12/2018

Really so amazing from my past as it is to my new realizations

I have been used and abused because I am nice – but in the process learnt as I go along that being nice versus being the critique is great but it exposes you – then what do you do?

It remains 'a question of lust and a question of trust' – Depeche Mode

∞

17 December 2018

Who says men can't multi-task

This is outright nonsense – their makeup is just different to that of the mother nature nurture.

He indeed works, while ensuring bills are paid – his contribution, however it may be at the life span and evolution of the marriage, age and stage.

He indeed contributes: when engaging, have to play the role of worker, bread winner, good dad, broken shoulder/wing man to get that nature/nurture from another, while being the bread winner of the house, while being the fun father and the boss of the work place and the pitiful lover boy.

I believe in men, they want to return to nature/nurture phase, same as women wanting the same. So if we all see the unique role that each need to play in their setting at the appropriate age – one would look past that – just lost my train of thought

> The name peridot has come up a
> few times – research.... It has some
> significance

The home – the wall – in the kitchen – take it in any way you wish from a point of labour – regardless of there will always, and in every part of the world remain a class difference, and no matter what language you speak or how small your kingdom grows there will always be 3 classes – upper, middle, lower

∞

19 December 2018

So I met this person on a dating site – right, we had our first date… totally in public – my gut said… when he stood in the parking lot then came to my house.

When I ask – he travels all the time, you ask for a pic and he gives you a standard. He gives you a local number – then loses it soon. So every other time I wish to meet, he happens to be busy, the phones are broken, the vehicle is in exchange, he never books in to what you have arranged… sends already tested texts. Tried hard to tell you his son …. Blah blah…

I unfortunately cannot always understand nor participate based on my frame of reference – yet if you are real – show me… if you are – abduct me now – I have never experienced that – maybe it is cool – let me experience that maybe it is cool - I can come back and tell the story…

Who are you – new man?

∞

21 December 2018

The worst thing anyone the second person could ever do is be the parent. You are not the Mother; you are not the Father.

They have a dad, they have a Mom, no one will ever fill that space – regardless. You are there for my Mother; you are there for my Father – you are not there for me!

So stop trying to fill that space – it is not a gap. It is not your space.

Mom – Dad! stop trying to sell your person to me. I will find the time and space where I want them to be part of me. You rub them off on me, you sell them to me – I will reject them.

Don't be different – just be my parent.

You keep teaching me to be myself stand up for who I am, be what I want to be.

Yet when you are with someone new – you show me not to be like that.
You treat My Mother/Father like a piece of rubbish.
Then you tell me I need to not do it – when I do it, you chastise me.
So treat my Mother/Father with respect, but you don't do it?

∞

21 December 2018

I do have to go through my emotions and interactions of my own children, as they move through their emotions. As much as I wish to go through forms of denial – I do – thinking I have given you what you do not understand – a life that would have been horrible, disgusting and terrible – but that is 'my' frame of reference.

So now I want that recognition and want that acknowledgment. Selfish bitch, no! It is about that little being even if born unto you or self-birthed.

The first one you have all the time. The 2nd, 3rd, 4th they don't ever have 'your' first love and attention. Regardless the others have to just make do. Whereas the first has it all, however, you make the first the caregiver and parent when you are not around. The first becomes the parent, yet the first years for all the attention. The 2n 3rd 4th becomes the shadow of the first always.

Then there is the last – the baby that remains the baby until the parents decide it is the last. Once the parents decide it the last, because their money/relationship is depleted – then it's the baby – the baby remains the baby forever. No one will replace the first nor the last born.

Is what it is – beginning and the end – what happens in between is peripheral… reality of life – therefore have 2 children, 1st born and last born – they can carry through – Mama and Papa…

"One day when I am big - will be someone … please transcribe all my epiphanies as I write them everywhere …. On pages, on books, on walls… they just happen – as I happen!"

"I have people that try to participate with me – yet they cannot keep up. Bless them for trying as I chew them and spit them out along the way while I have my journey in life!"

"My every night I go to sleep in my knowing I did what I could do if it was not part of me knowing, it was not part of me, therefore I cannot be held accountable for it."

"Your ransom is not mine, your anger is not mine, if I could diffuse that – brilliant if I can't – it is what it is."

"I have what I have, I love giving. I am what I and who I am, and I love it. Enter into my realm and you will have what you thought, you can handle. If I cannot show you, the little bit about you as I show you a little bit about me when you enter my world – then we are not ready for each other."

"The know and the realisation and the maturity needs to be there. Don't enter if you cannot handle – I am me. Happy – such a light word – let me seek the true word – I am at peace with me."

∞

Have to put my baby to sleep 14 years old – had to deal with his father screwing a 23-year-old, his bio mother dying, went from smoking cigarettes to sniffing petrol and now cutting to not passing his years at school – fuck fuck fuck

What to know what else he knows – does he know?

His mother was nearly raped, does he know, his other mother, is getting fired – what all is in his mind who does he talk to what is in his being??

This is a different world, I need to have to enter, need to be attentive, something is happening and Mama has to be attentive, what is he missing, what is he seeking and where do I need to fill the gap – my new challenge awaits.

I look forward to that as the journey my child is about to take me on – is the one that all need to learn something from. I look forward – I welcome this my child – Mama is ready – love you, angel pie – I love you – I embrace our journey as we take it on.

I have just decided – we are going to make this all about You my child! We are going to tell the truth, his whole truth and nothing but the truth and we shall celebrate this together.

Dad on Sunday when you come through and we shall celebrate

Had a tummy dad and a tummy mom

And he is questioning himself

So let's celebrate – we are going to celebrate everything!

"if her mind doesn't speak – why would there be a verbal word that utters a sound"

05-12-2005 =5 – balance

09-02-2001 = 5 balance

01 – 02-2011 = 7

12-12-1972 = 7

10-08-1960 = 7

∞

I can pull it off – launch – new vision and mission

Magalies mardigras in may

23 December 2018

Oh my God, I wake up this morning feeling absolutely blessed and amazing! Spending dedicated lone time with my babies uninterrupted and no peripheral human around.

Just being us close and peaceful.
Children made supper and when the storm came with thunderbolts taking out the electricity it was silent – no man made lights nor sound only candles and our peaceful hearts and voices.
Where closeness love and togetherness was so noisy that the embrace of sheer happiness was deafening.

With fulfilment goodnight hugs and kisses we all excused ourselves to our pillows and early night falling away in our dreams, each having their own as we all fell asleep in the peace that was only us.

Waking this morning with new refreshed love and kindness that every little face shows for one another, we ready ourselves for another day of just us. For the love and togetherness that only this Mother can wish for.

My time with my children is so unique and ultimately so special. Every second I can have with my babies fills my emotional tank, to the point where I would rather increase the height and depth of my feelings that allow myself to say "the cup runneth over" – as none of it will be spilt, shed nor lost as I capture every drop. I am selfish that way, with pleasure I shall admit, that I am selfish that way.

My children my love my life. When I can physically feel the warmth in my heart, the burn in my stomach and the full in every cell as it holds not space for anything but my babies, my children, my love.
You know not love until you birth, until you hold your children in your arms – you know not love!

This is no explanation for feeling of wholeness till you have a child, and in my case 3 x over.
Dynamic and unique – you are not different.

Love mom

∞

26 December 2018

I thank you Paulo, Osho, Ramtha – my peace and silence have come at the time when I needed to be reminded of my time here on this plane. For what I have set out to be and remind myself of my journey to enlightenment and the forever lasting life.

I chose to be here with my surroundings. I have earned every pebble, stone, grass blade, sand particle to attain what I have come to learn and to embrace. I own it.

The aspirations the dreams creating a haven for my children, my brothers, my sisters I have done just that – a home filled with love, peace, tranquillity which is felt in every corner!

Spaces and places where security, freedom and thought in nature can be felt, experienced and embraced! Nature, nurture, love, peace!

This is what every soul and heart needs to be at one, to remind itself of the purpose of this plane to which we have returned. As reminder and an escape.

The love that comes from every movement as it happens is the reality of this time. I shall never grow old of creating love corners for every soul to feel embraced and empowered, to continue their journey as they set out to be.

Spread my wings to bring more to realisation that there is a new beginning for everyone to realise and embrace. My studies my journey will inspire more to acknowledge this, as their own truth and their reality to feel safe on this plane. To find their feet again, so that they can soar on their own – or with me, or ascend before me.

I am that rebirthed child that will start another journey as I ascend again, to the new as I open this chapter that stands before me from this day forward.

I died the other night – I died in every aspect when I lay on the floor and defecated and vomited and passed away the emotions the content – the realisation – I died. Alone I was laying on the floor going into another shock to make me wake to a new transition – which is the awakened soul that had to rebirth.

The sick that poured out was necessary. Without death there cannot be life and without life there cannot be death. I thank you for my life as I can continue my journey in fulfilling the reality of ascending.

I own this… I own this… I own this!

∞

26 December 2018

My children I have given you a part of my life to be the mother that gave you that initial nurture, and love, and protection. I have shown you the path of love and the trust that you require, to give you the confidence that you need in yourself.

To know that you have the self-worth, the strength and the self-understanding that you have come into this world alone and you will die alone.

I have not introduced you to a false religion or hope that there is something else other than yourself that will carry you through this life – what happened yesterday, you can only learn from, what happens now is what is important to dream and plan, for the future is only a dream – this can change.

The only certainty is, that of now how we face the now, and how we deal with the now is what shapes you.

Take chances – risk your experiences, live your life.

Make decision, have choices – suffer or embrace the consequences – know that you have made a decision and learn from every step you take.

This is the only lesson I can give you, is to believe in your own abilities and trust the choices and decisions you make.

Be adaptable to change as we never know what tomorrow holds – as we have not lived it yet, we can plan it – we can dream it – we can envisage it.

Thank you for every day I have you in my life, as even when you are not with me, you are with me in soul, spirit and mind and deeply in my heart.

In every unique way – my heart is yours always

Love mom

∞

28 December 2018

My journey

Michael Uriel Raphael Gabriel

Ariel – protecting angel

Ace of pentacles – stability prosperity growth rewards

Ace of wands – new beginnings of projects and creativity, optimism and energy

Lovers – union of mind body and south ideal partnership where everything feels right unspoken unison – twins of Gemini

North – fire / intuition – 4 of cups

East – thought / air – 2 of swords

South – faith/sensation – knight of cups

West – water/ feelings – 8 of wands

28 12 2018
1   3   2 = 6

Are we ready for each other?
knight of pentacles – yes
sic of cups = yes
2 of swords = yes
Hermit = maybe
Five of cups = maybe
Queen of swords = yes
Six of wands = yes
8 swords
Queen of pentacles
Ace of cups
Knight of cups
The world

Magician
7 of wands
The empress
Devil
2 wands
10 of swords
4 of wands
Pythagorean
Freedom seeker
8 is the life path
Chaldean
numbers 5 and 9   His name is Adam
∞

2019

1 January 2019

– I manifest my 3s –
Sex Travel Freedom
Freedom Travel Sex
Travel Freedom Sex

The No 3 year

The year - that the prism in your life will bring a Rainbow of colour.

Everything happens in 3s!
This is the start of a new journey and new beginning!
What does that mean to you Angelique?

Love, self-love:
 – you have meditated about this-
Your year was ended off in blessing yourself. To open up for that journey of Self-discovery.
Left love, where you will be learning to trust first and foremost in yourself. Trust your instincts, trust your heart, trust your soul, trust your ability to trust your heart.
The light that enter now is the light of self-discovery!
Owning yourself, your home, your world.
Only that which brings in the light will enter into your life.
Your mantra has been Travel, Sexuality and Freedom.
Those that enter your journey will allow you to Live this Mantra.
This Prism that you are now to start in all aspects.

∞

The Blessing of reality on this plane, that as much as you wish to be – when just that decision to embrace the concept of Sex, Freedom, Travel –
You take the time, to have the freedom, to get into your vehicle, to travel to town, to hug the first person you see, and the joy that you brought by giving that person the words, and the closeness that they never thought possible!

 – the journey need not be miles away – the journey and the realisation is just here, in you to make that happen.

– you need not seek on the other side of the ocean, you merely need to seek within. You have it all right here, in your own, the freedom to live, to love, to travel, to have love/sex wow!!

We all seek for that journey outside ourselves yet – it is right here.
When I close my eyes I can go into the world I wish to have – I can dream about it all – yet we need to open our eyes, see that which is just around you!

If you don't acknowledge yourself – from there you acknowledge yourself – from there you acknowledge your immediate surroundings, and from there you can go further outside and that is the quiet that makes your soul journey a reality.

Bringing your dreams, which is that world that you escape to when you close your eyes!
Now open your eyes and realise, that you can implement those dreams in your everyday!

Your immediate surroundings, by merely traveling with your given body, your immediate mechanism of transport, and have the freedom to express.
The sexual love making process, by merely interacting with the environment. To receive that orgasmic bliss of the sounds, your body, the immediacy of your system as it is – wow!
The orgasm just had my soul pair with my reproduction system, internal g-spot – mother fuck!!
Oh the freedom I feel right now is that of such wholly and holy subliminal bliss.

Gestation / freedom/ life / love / live
Orgasm
Departure

Freedom
Sex
Travel

Respect
Honesty
Truth

∞

16 March 2019

Another possible set for rejection.

My insecurity, in this possible, what I thought and been emotionally preparing myself for possible commitment. With a person that have been part of my move away from being in the dating phase, or what I thought was dating. Finding that partner, that would be that A-another. To accept me, appreciate and love me, or even just like me for that matter. Someone that will not just be that breeze through your life, that you have to mother, but someone that keeps a caring eye out for you, that is your "go-to" person.

Yes, being a strong outer layer, with much ambition and strength, to hold face and project complete independence - but even with such self-control.
What is behind that mask, is the amount of love that you wish to share with a peer, that you have respect for. Emotional, intellectual, economic.
The trust that you have, that you will not end up having to mother another, but in every aspect, is that person that you feel can be trusted. To grow with, as you grow.

That one you know you can come home to. That sees you for who and what you are. Accepts that you are not perfect in every aspect, yet you are perfect for them.
That sees you as their absolute Queen and adores you regardless.

Makes you feel secure in the partnership of life in every aspect. That trusts implicitly what you do and who you are – the growth to find that path that leads to greatness.

Not for any other than to build together. That allows for development space, in every emotional, growth, and aspect of life. With trust and respect, that there is no reason for you to feel any form of unsupported insecurities in life itself. That you are there for them, them for you. Without a doubt nor question at any given point in time.

I thought I had found that person? I think there is a possibility that the person has not found that in me – I am about to be let down in my quest? That is what my gut is currently telling me, and it is very disturbing, yet again! I am to be completely alone, in my journey to finding and being with that person?

How the body and the mind works together, and the affects they exchange, is extremely disabling. Going through all these emotions is disturbing in every aspect. The wait for nothing! The wait is an empty sickening feeling – when you know there will be a let-down and disappointment soon! With that uncertainty, the body is completely affected by this inner turmoil.
That is what being in any form of relationship does.
Especially when there is distance between, commitments to others or work related.

Open communication and understanding is of utmost importance during such times. To address such feelings of empty turmoil, as you sit, you wait, you are setting yourself up – you are creating space. You are closing up to other possibilities of engagement with others. You have that hope to be with, that person, building towards a sense of security.

So now I am sitting here in uncertainty, as I know I want to be committed to making this work. However, there is no certainty that this is requited from his side. It is extremely disorientating to say the least.

And so it is confirmed – you knew this was to happen and it did – a WhatsApp to tell you this is not working! Your intuition has not failed you! Even though it was all in the cards. You woke this morning with that 'omen' feelings – this then being confirmed – a WhatsApp to tell you that not coming through – a WhatsApp telling you it's ending! Refusing to walk away and take your call!

You have been diminished to that?
No, you have not been diminished!
He has diminished himself to the point where he is not deserving of you! Your standards will not be dropped to the point where you are to grovel for love and attention!

The person that will do that will not deserve your time, heart and effort!

You are worth more Angelique

∞

17 March 2019

Why Adam, why did you decide to have me fall and feel, just to have to give me that let down of hurting – I am so goddamn sore it is burning inside – it is hurting so fucking bad! All the build up to start feeling again. To open my heart to look forward to being someone's a-another.
Being understanding being open to so much. To view the world again from a point of feeling – to just be dishonoured, to just be broken inside – it is so goddamn painful to have to go through this!

After years of preserving my heart, and allow it to open again to build on something. That gave me hope for perhaps a new relationship – it hurts – and has taken away my hopes that someone out there is feeling the same.
That someone out there, fucking likes me enough! To make me want to be a part of their lives.

No more my girl – no more

It hurts too much!

∞

22 March 2019

I am so fucking frustrated with me today it is fucking hectic!

I felt this feeling coming on and it is hella disturbing I was actually so comfortable with Adam in the background just liking me and being there – and now it's gone – it feels friggen empty – as even though not physically in my face – space and life, it was perhaps that fantasy or hope or something that kept me dreaming, wishing, and keeping me going that was enchanting.

Now that's gone and I miss it, I really miss that.

I don't want someone permanently in my physical space – I want to know that somewhere out there I mean something to someone. I am surrounded by people in my every day that wants me in their everyday – but I can't.

It's just too much to have to deal with. I can't as I end up giving everything of me to them. Instead of being selfishly moving and doing my thing as I do...
To have my space filled with a constant body, presence and being freaks me out.

To have my children with me is so fulfilling – but now I have this person, again in my space – a semi-constant and I can't cope with that.

I really enjoy the long distance hope and build.

∞

23 April 2019

It is not always clear at the moment where your life journey may lead.

Often we have time to sit and reflect, however we hold back the fear of exploring, does not necessarily require the revisit of the past.
It is merely taking the current moment as you wake to allow you to embrace just the joy as you feel at that waking moment.

I cocooned my beautiful being today as the energy of joy of fun, love and laughter still echoes between the wall from the pleasure of my children being with me.

Having to be in the kitchen preparing meals that are cooked with absolute heart.
Sitting at the long kitchen table just laughing, sharing, eating away at the love prepared for them.
Still having the chaos walk through the rooms, down the passage, dishes stacked, the smell of food the experiences and memories created in a safe haven called Mama's home.

I was not to disturb this joyous energy that still remains. The love that surround every particle of it that still floats through this home.
I bathed in the current moment and took in every second of the joy still lingering.
∞
My children, my absolute universe has been filled by the bright smiles, the running the teasing, dancing and music surround.
God has walked through my home and blessed every corner and every space. I was not to disturb this today!

Instead I bathed my heart and soul in the pleasure of feeling whole.
I still smell the cinnamon of the pancakes as they were standing around and not wanting to leave – eating every crumb that came from my hands.

Taking in every second they could of Mama.
With such love as they could receive with such love as they could give, there was no goodbye – there was only a temporary wave to say – see you soon…

"I dropped a tear"

∞

DONE!!
Sponsor ME as the Next President of Welfare!
I AM THE NEXT PRESIDENT OF WELFARE of CHILDREN!
MY PROPERTY WILL SELL
AND
I AS ANGELIQUE WILL SAVE THE CHILDREN!!!!

∞

25 April 2019

With absolute disappointment and anger I went to sleep!
To the point where my whole night was disrupted by dreams and visions of urinary infections, bacteria and filth….

Yes – I felt that yesterday when dealing with more children being raped.
I feel like I am failing them, because I don't know how to stop this from happening before it happens.
I feel right now as if I want to just go so far away and not being part of this society of humans that hurt children from running and never coming back!

Then yes, I have had a day of not smelling brilliant myself when I was last with a person I really like. He constantly reminds me of the one day I stank, I even stank to myself … never mind him. But god knows why that one day, now has to prescribe my life?
Has to predict my future of being with someone!
Is that what my life has boiled down to?

You are fucking ruled by your vagina!
Your life is predicted by your vagina!
Your future depends on your vagina!
Your happiness depends on your vagina …
Relationships = vagina??
What the fuck?

If my vagina doesn't look, smell, feel good – I am not to have the person I like?

Sex – does that really rule life, relationships, minds, future, happiness?

I lost my husband, my home because of sex.
People I meet just want sex.
Relationships are made and destroyed around sex.

Vagina and penis = that's all!

The balance in life = what happens to the other components that make a person? That make relationships? That builds trust? Everything falls apart! Everything is based on sex!

I am sick of this constant thing that just gets thrown around!

You don't hear from people unless they want sex!
Trust me – my phone is silent – my phone does not receive a text – but wait – let them want sex then all of a sudden – I get a "hey!"

Conversations all lead to sex – daily chats at some stage boil down to some sordid sex!

No one can just be any more!

It hurts really – nothing gets done till you have to resort to reporting and fighting!

No one listens till there is violence attached or any form of abuse = death, hurt, pain!

No more respect for life, for people, for earth, for anything!

This is what hurts me MOST!

There is just zero regard anymore! One must revert to death threats before people behave!

Shock – horror – pain! Is that what makes people think before they do or act??

ENOUGH REALY I CAN'T!!

TORTURE!!!

I SHALL BEGIN MY TALK WITH – 'LET HER FUCKING DIE'

Yes, those are the words my Father said!
Those are the words that I last heard when my life was at the end – I was the one that had to apologise to my father for being raped, for watching him go off with my friend, for being told by him I am a slut!

And you know what? I still do that!

I still am the one saying 'I am sorry for being hurt!'

Taking the blame for other people's infidelity, for other people's incompetence, for other people's ignorance, for other people's wrong doings!!

! I AM GOING TO TELL MY STORY!

! I AM A SURVIVOR!

Why am I allowing myself to grovel for this man that is outright abusive? What the fuck?

Why am I grovelling for you?? why???

I did this for my Father's love!
I did this for my husband love!
That after all these years gave me what??
Fuck all!!

You are doing exactly the same!!!

!!!HELLO ANGE!!! HELLOOO!!!

27 April 2019

Waking this morning with feeling more content:

Magaliesburg Angels farm
you give me the quiet peace to allow me to embrace my surroundings
you give me the quiet peace to allow me to embrace my inner soul
the autumn sun that covers the hills my eyes are bestowed upon
the autumn sun that gives me the warmth on my skin
a light breeze that makes the chimes, the leaves, the grass speak to me about their love of mother earth
in the distance I hear the sound of people racing from one end to the other – in their man made vehicles
you give me the options, the choice to remain in my autumn sun and listen to the wind, the birds or chase after the man made life

Magaliesburg Angels farm with the view of little Tuscany the hills set behind and the yellow sun flowers in front
your dreams of travel and your love of home
you give me the best of those worlds
serenity that gives bound of self-realisation, self-peace and self-knowledge
to convalesce so you need to hide from the world and create your own reality
creativity flows through your veins as you have the time to heal, to think to be

Recalculate as your veins work through the ink of your pen
self-acceptance and realisation that: charity does begin at home, heaven is within
and love is within! Healing start with you, the world – is your world, your world is your reality

Self-nurture, self-love, self-acceptance
embrace your power to heal who you are and protect your being
Magaliesburg angels farm – your healing power is what makes you unique
surround yourself with love and attract love and you will receive love
when you accept your own you will be accepted
your power lies within
your strength is your own – your knowledge is your own
Magaliesburg angels farm – love, nurture, nature, peace, acceptance, healing, power

∞

When the mother sits at your gate.
Want to have 2 minutes with her children – let her in, she is still their Mother. She desires to see her children regardless of the nonsense that he told you about her!
She is not that wicked witch, she just didn't work for him.
She still works for her children – she is still the mom – she is still the one that will kill for her children – NEVER mess with that!

∞

I wonder what had happened? Where did my marriage go wrong? I am sure I must have loved him at some stage?

I kept a journal – I did….

09 may 1997

'Friends always"

Busy, busy, busy
Always with that of your own
with that of others
living in day light compartments
often forgetting those whom will always be your friends
the one person whom always make the time for those who she bore
those whom she raised to the best she knew how
should one then strew her with gifts only once, twice
maybe three times a year
she deserves more
she deserves that which no materials could ever bring to the fore
she deserves all the love that world could give
more than she has to give
from the womb, to adolescence to adulthood
through all these stages I still have you as a friend
we laugh together, we cry together
we hate together, we love together
we do everything that friends do
she is my best friend,
she is my only friend
she is my mother

Anne

∞

From me to you:

From the day of birth, one gets taught what you know by two people whom had cared much for one another, and turned that into a human being. They take that being and develop it into a creation after their own image.

That little being develops and grows, but most of all it grows within from not only what it was taught by these two people, but from those external influences which has crossed its path. This particular being created had experienced that which they had taught her, and found it not to be sufficient to her expectations of life, she expected more, she found more and through her walk she had learnt from not only these two but also from others and their walks of life and what they had to teach.

She had gone and done and hurt and learnt. But what she knows, and what she learnt she had kept treasured and that seeped deep within. So deep, that only she could understand and only she would dig out and know exactly where to find it and where it was placed. Through these lessons she had learnt a recipe to organise, and to reveal on that which is necessary to those crossing her path.

How disappointing it is when those who she idolised cannot trust her judgment, and can only see the negative in the decisions she decided to make and make it apparent to them. Is it because they do not understand her that they can turn around and condemn her decisions? She had been a loner for a lengthy time, do they know why, have they ever bothered to ask, or do they just take it for granted that she is too busy? Have they never wondered why she never talks? Why they never see her, why is she always running?

They much rather roam on her achievements for they are far greater, apparent and easier to reach, then that which is deeper than the eye can see.

She turns around one day to ask them questions, to confront them on their hypocrisy and all they do is even further flair up and only confirming the confrontations by hypocrisy.

Furthermore, hypocritically condemns her world and her decision and contradicts her statement of supporting her and using that which they claim to be their belief and condemns even more, is this then a way in which they support?
She is a loner, to avoid such. She never speaks to avoid such. She never opens to avoid such. When she does come out in the open, this is what she gets – she retreats and she is a loner again.
A world of her own filled with peace, quiet, love and truth.

I love you – from me

∞

What is wrong and what is right, no two worlds are the same. One world can never condemn or judge another world, for no one world can pre-empt another. How white is white? How black is black?

∞

I did – I did love him:

25/01/97

I just walked back into the house from saying goodbye to my most amazing man. Feeling completely satisfied and content with the love I have received. Being able to have shared with him another 3 hours of pure bliss. Making love, talking, laughing.

Upon arrival he was very pre-occupied, a very successful man he is and all around has a very high regard for his intelligence. He has been roped in to what we call a BJH pet project. A project that, and as I know him, is a major challenge to him and as he says – 'I can't lose' very true sometimes taking on more then he can handle at once, yet, I know he will make it through to make yet another mark in life. Very prone to biting off more then he can chew at once, but whether it means, perhaps spitting out a couple of crunches he will do it. Another two weeks of this, but in that time, as things stressfully go at the moment I will just have to love him more.

I on the other hand was spending my morning in one of my uncertain phases again and all thanks to me. Last night I yet again went a little too far in expressing myself tactlessly blabbing in all out, without prior thought or consideration, I started talking about the way I feel and turning an evening into what started off filled with aggressive love making, or rather sex into a pitiful 'you must divorce' leaving a very dead feeling in the air. One apology after another, paging, phoning paging still left me feeling like and absolute selfish cow. And forcing him to say the words, 'I will think, I can't promise you anything'. When yet, in the beginning of the evening he said: 'if you should move to cape town, I will not survive without you, can't not see you, should that happen I can find a job in Cape Town, or even become a beach bum, as long as I am with you.'

I turned it so sour, that for the rest of the evening I was living in that uncertain world till today. I cannot force him to think of me the whole time and divorce and marry me. Although that is how I feel, I need to understand how difficult it must be for him to make that decision for the sake of the two boys. The once son is 10 years and The one son is 13 years old just started with standard 6 and as I know from my own experience and a well-known fact that this is a rather crucial stage in any child's life. A transition period from being a child and now going into the adolescent stage, with more strain then being a child, what if we now have to go through the divorce? True that divorce is traumatic for any child, at the stage of going through that but also another fact that with the correct treatment, it will be overcome and they learn to accept it. But that all depends on the parents and how they handle the divorce, will determine how traumatic an experience it is for the children.

I am talking divorce, because this is how for the relationship has progressed, that at this stage, I want to be with him always. For the first time I have honestly considered marriage as part and partial of my future. I have always said, and maintained that I will have two illegitimate children and never marry. Mainly due to the fact that I don't need to be with a man, I have never been understood by any man I have been with, I will rather just be on my own before I get married. Children I definitely want, but man – no way!

This man can I say now, I shall marry any day. He fulfils every wish and characteristic I have always wanted in a man.

Physical and mental strength, power, masculine, good looking, presentable, funny, sense of humour, intelligent, wise, sensitive, loving, caring etc. Never have I felt this way about anyone before and although I am 24 years old, I have been around, I have been in love before and have been loved before but like this, never. The best of all is the way I feel about him; I know he feels about me too. Fair enough I sometimes doubt it, but that I believe is very much due to the fact that, he is so afraid of divorcing and not living with me.

But for today, I am happy, I am fulfilled, I saw him again, made love, talked, laughed and very much in love with him. Said goodbye so that he could go to work. He left here in a more content state of mind, eyes sparkling and very much in love. Now all I can hope for is to see him for a while before he goes home tonight to entertain the wife's family, and I go to a braai on my own. And the way things go, unless I see him or speak to him before I go out, I know I never enjoy my evening, so let's hold thumbs.

∞

26/01/1997

I did see him – much to my surprise, and we were able to spend 2 hours together. Having fun, being in a playful mood. Then I went to the braai and he went home. I drove past his house on my way, hoping he would either be outside or on his way somewhere or something, but everything was quiet. The whole night, hoping he would page with a meeting place and time. Nothing, so I drank too much again. Ended up being thrown in the pool and not allowed to leave, arrived home early in the morning hours.

Had little sleep as the builder was to come around to take measurements. I went to do washing at my Moms. Paged him in the morning. No reply. Phoned and only got voice mail. I really wanted to speak to him, just to hear his voice, and the reassurance the he loved me. For what a horrid nightmare I had, dreaming I walked into my room, found cards on my dressing table. The first reading he loves me, the second read 'Dear Lucy, I am sorry to have put you through this, but I hope you forgive me, I love you', the third was a card with a date and time with a meeting place addressed to her, as I read the cards he walked in, and I asked him what about me/us, he merely laughed and said, 'do you really think I was going to give you more, you fool you just another fuck and that was all I ever wanted from you I will never leave my wife'. I started crying, and he just sat there laughing at me… what a nightmare never to repeat itself please!!

29/01/1997

Don't try him – don't test him, you, silly little fool! I understand it is difficult – when you are cleaning up sorting out – you want to do that in all areas, but this is one area you should not touch!

Why are you doing this? I ask you?

I know you want it all to yourself – but off now - get off your high horse – this is not just another little aspect, another little issue, this is long lasting love you are fucking with! Down with the defence mechanism – all knows the fear of getting hurt is taking charge again of your sensibility – the words whirling through your mind – ' I have been thinking about it since we last spoke, I will never make that decision', combined with the dream devoting love to another, 'you are just a fuck, I can't promise you more' – then that of today – ' I can't take you on Friday' – the words of last night – 'we will find a way for us to see each other' – the agreement – 'for as long as we work together, we will never be able to live together'

This now all has to tie back to:

'I can't not see you.' 'my thoughts all consist of you.' 'I love you more than the universe' 'eternity'. 'wherever you go, I'll come fetch you.' 'I want to spend the whole time with you.' 'you are the only one I think of, sleep with, talk to.' 'what would you like to do, live together? Live together, then get married? or get married?' 'I want to see you in that white dress.' – 'I am working on a plan, to sort this all out,' 'let me go back and start talking.'

How fucken promising, and as soon as you build up some hope – SLAP BANG scenario number one.

Hit with a baseball bat! – I Beg your pardon – first you get thrown with rose petals, and as soon as you get the sweet smell of roses, you get fucken darted with solid marbles! On the one hand you know you should not push the issue, you are always understanding, patient, accepting, considerate, feeling sorry for the wife and the children, not wanting to hurt them.

But – on the other hand what about you? You continue like this you actually fucking up your life, their lives and his life even more.

Wife – she has no friend, no husband, no lover

The children – they have an occasional father, weekends, some week evenings, for perhaps 15 minutes, some Fridays. Even when time is spent with them, it is half hearted because his mind is with you, always trying to find a means of contacting or seeing you. All effort is being made to rid of them to see and contact you.

Him – time shared between the kids, work, you and wife. Work is very demanding – no excuse accepted – pressure. Kids are very demanding – no excuse accepted – pressure. Wife fairly demanding – excuses are running out – pressure. You that is all life revolves around – demanding yet patient and understanding – pressure, because all he wants to see, talk to and make love to is you – you then put pressure on him by making him feel guilty for not spending more time with you – but yet flexible. You want answers.

You – all the possible spare time, you get, all the affection you get, all the love you get. Yet the way you feel is all alone, you always have to understand, live in a constant fear of the day when you get told 'this is the end'. Never knowing what the future holds. Scrambled eggs? You love someone so deeply, but cannot show or tell the world. Always have to hide from who might see you, who might find out. Feeling like a thief in the night. Wanting to share so much – but can't. Hoping you still have a tomorrow. Making love – just to say goodbye. Have to live a whole day's love, affection, advice, talking, laughing, sharing, giving, taking in two/three hours.

When basically there is a very easy solution to the whole problem.

Imagine what life would be, if you could spend all the time together?

At the moment everyone involved is getting the short end of the stick, everyone is unhappy, should this continue in the way it is now: - then:

Wife – she gets less and less of her husband she gets frustrated, she is being withheld from finding someone to love, to start a new life with, someone else, being unhappier being denied more by her husband. Trying to win him back, failing every time. Being satisfied with 33%. What is a relationship worth without someone to talk to, make love to? Having to find out – hurt, trust, insult!!

The kids – they always need to track Dad down, never get to see their Father, always have to be happy with 33% of him. Should they find out – their respect, trust and confidence, crushed in their Father, relationships betrayed, hurt, disappointed, hate!

Him – continue in this pressured, confused state, filled with guilt towards his children, me, wife. Uncommitted on al ends, feeling like a bastard, losing self-respect. Getting frustrated with the children, wife, me. Living a life that goes against his grains!

Me – continue never knowing what tomorrow holds. Loving and never be allowed to give. Getting frustrated with having to say goodbye. No trust in yourself, him or the relationship. Feeling guilty for denying the other three people a life. Never knowing. Paranoid of being caught. Being satisfied with 33% and sometimes 0%!

('Just a little interruption of today's happenings – 30/01/1997 - So happy again, had a wonderfully devoted time again this him. Time spent this morning for smokes on the big balcony full of smiles, love, laugh – talk. He moved and scheduled time to be able to take me to the airport tomorrow, spoke to me for ages on the phone. Saw him this afternoon when I stopped to buy cigarettes and an overwhelming burst of butterflies, sweaty palms – just wanted to jump out of my car and jump him. But phone call from the child – major guilt both of us – him because he is with me rather than with the kid helping with homework, me because he is with me rather than with his child helping with homework. But still made arrangements to meet him at home before and after meetings. Departing very much in love.)

Now there are two solutions – this one I don't want but still worth mentioning – after all these are my feelings:

Myself and him going our separate ways: …. NO!!!

Him – have to go back to his wife and revive what they had, as he says now – NO Way

Me – I just don't want to love someone else! Why must I let go of someone that I desperately love? Why must I go out again to meet up with a bunch of dickheads – that see me as some form of pillar, sex symbol, continuously trying to change me to the weak female species, and with probably only one characteristic of my ideal man, and the rest of the characteristics I have to improvise on. Bullshit – I don't want to go my own way! SHOULD IT SO HAPPEN – I definitely have to move away, I will never be able to be around him and be happy! We'll end up getting together again anyway.

The other solution: – Much more viable proposition – the reasons – self justifiable:

He gets divorced, and we will be together!!

This will be the outcome and the way to work toward it with as little as possible affect and impact on the children, wife, him and me. This is normally how things fuck out if one does not work through something like this with logic and a plan.

Fair enough, there is always some pain involved, I know I have been through this myself both grandparents and parents, both in my family resulting in a complete fuckup! Because we will stay together initially for the sake of protecting the kids from getting hurt and in the end the kids find out the truth. Found out that they have been living in a false world, feeling betrayed by both the parents, have no respect because Dad was never at home, not because he was working, he was with someone else. Then to top It all both Mom and Grandma roped the kids in to spy on Oupa and Dad. Both of them did not have a good word to say about our Oupa or Dad, bad mouthed them. Ending in disliking Dad and Oupa and the women they are with. All of this – because neither Dad nor Oupa spoke to Mom or Ouma, they just wacked them with divorce. And within 2 days for Oupa and month for Dad left. Mom sleeping in her room and Dad in his room, under the same roof arguing day in and day out! Wrong Wrong Wrong. If only they spoke to us from the beginning, and explained what was happening, was honest about the whole situation, we would all have accepted it! Don't hide things – they will always come out! Don't pretend everything is cool, when we live in a real world. They all tried again for the sake of the kids and in the end it resulted in a prolonged disaster.

(Another little interruption with major implications: I just came back from a weekend in Cape Town where I was propositioned by a friend to go into business with them. The property market, this is an opportunity of a lifetime, as the property market is booming, but this means moving down to Cape Town. I am scared, though very excited, as this could be my big break in life. However, just spending two days without him was absolutely horrific. I was supposed to enjoy the weekend just as much as sussing out what the proposition implies, I missed him so much it was miserable. I was miserable. Coming back, I all of a sudden I had a personality again – could not wait …. What a wonderful homecoming! I introduced the prospect and possibility of me accepting and moving to Cape Town – it was not taken lightly. Now and this is the new issue – major implications as this could mean that should I go, am standing a chance bigger then now of losing him. However, now for the very first time I actually really hear him speaking of divorce. Something he never really mentioned before. But the truth is, I however don't think it would surface. What I fear is, when I go or should I go it will be a matter of time before I hear the words – you must go on with your life. What the heck do I do then? Hope they call and offer me the position).

Yip so a lot had happened till now, the wife had kinda found out that there might be someone else. All headlights are on. What does that do for us? A major fuck up – now I can't see him anymore, no more phone calls, no more visits. I miss him, I miss him so – sitting here all alone, all I have is a little picture, snapshot – I miss him. How come love has to be so painfully difficult? Why can people not just understand? When that flame between two people are so dim, there is really nothing to hold on to but the convenience and the habit the only thing to break? Why hold on, to what – I ask you. I love this man, like I have never loved before I can't wait till it is all over. If it so be, which I very much hope it will – that we could be together, the way it is supposed to be.

∞

01/03

Babe

My first night here, thought I'd write you a little letter. Roads were okay, bloody hot, but made it.

The place is absolutely amazing, I think this is just what I need, nature, tranquillity, no phones, no rush, but I miss you. The first day, and we saw 4 hippos playing right in front of our chalet. (by the way – I did take the main bedroom as requested, but somehow although the room and bathroom is big enough to play in – the bed is a little small and room is sound proof) never mind a whole entourage of little monkeys sitting with us, on the stoep sipping gin and tonic. The only unfortunate thing is, that we look right in this humongous tree, nevertheless, it is beautiful – just wish I could share this with you in person, you'd dig it.

I had a little snooze this afternoon waking very disorientated – because you were sleeping right behind me. All the way down/up here, you were right there, I could feel and see you the whole way and even now - I miss you. I have never been so stupid about anyone before, all soppy and love sick. Always used to keep myself very well together and now this girl – all wobbly. I hope all works out the way we want it to, we just have to be strong I suppose. We spoke – enough of that – going to sleep now and yes with your arms wrapped around me.

I love you speak to you soon.

∞

02/03

Hello babe

Another day of mere sleeping, eating, reading sleeping eating talking shit and ready to go to bed.

I was woken this morning by the loud laughter of a hippo family, the view from my bedroom right into the river, just lying watching them lazing in the water. Waiting until the monkey clang moved past, so I could sit on the veranda with a cup of coffee, and speak to you a bit in my innermost, before the other two woke. But as I opened the door, from all directions these monkeys just jumped up next to me and we ended up sitting all together on the stoep, till they realised I don't have any nibbles and moved on.

Em and myself went for a short walk this morning, and the hallelujah people that was here for the weekend started setting-up for their congregational meeting at one of the chalets – no joke - having a full on Great Trek together, hymns and Bible and the whole 'gedoentes'. The only thing missing was clapping hands and throwing it up in the air, with their solemn faces.

Steve made breakfast and supper, Em trotting around pouring gin and tonic and I just sat – missing and thinking of you. Oh, I did make the marinade but I had more important things on my mind. Basically starting at you, working its way around you, and ending at you. I hope all is okay at home – still wish you could be here it would be rather nice to have you slip inside me right now – missing you - love you more.

∞

03/03

Hello babe;

What a wonderful sound to have hear you voice again. Although not too ecstatic from your side, but suppose understandable, you still having to work, whilst my whole day consisted of lazing at the pool and thinking when the right time would be to call you. I really would give anything to have you here with me, you should not concern yourself about me relaxing and taking it easy, because that is all I am doing, but all I am thinking of is you. Not stressing though, just thinking. I am not even doing the weighing up scenes, considering whether this is what I want, or any such black and white shit. Just purely by knowing this is what I want – I need not stress about it. I just would love to have you here with me at this stage. Especially after speaking to you today, I must say all I am picturing is your arms around me and making love to you in the bush. Right now skinny dip would have been ideal – swimming alone is not much fun. It was about 29 today, therefore caught the first layer of tan and tomorrow, don't know if you saw the weather report +/- 31, hope you will like your little Aboriginal girl? But got to doe doe now – love you miss you

∞

04/03

Babe

How wonderful it was to speak to you again, although I know we should not, but one has to make a decision in life. You either go for that which makes you happy, or that which make you unhappy – so basically – we speak many times about these things, and I have come to the conclusion, that between the two of us, we will just continue living on the edge until it completely breaks as I am convinced that neither enjoy playing games for formality sake – it either is or it is not. So basically we will just continue till all hell breaks loose – if it ever really does. Although we both also realise the consequences – it will be difficult, but somehow we know we will survive. As every time we talk about these issues, we make these decisions, and what do we do about it – continue the way we always have been.

But about my day, woke, suntanned, read, swam, drank beer – ran to the phone – got back, had a bath, read – went back to the phone – waited – read – spoke to you – got back, made mieliepap and shebo, ate and now ready to go to bed again – nice life! knowing you have to handle all the 'kak' back home, I wish that I could just grab you away. Not only do I feel your arms around me now, I could actually feel you hand between my thighs, tightly gripping in only the way you know how. Still hope you get enough rest for when I come home. Goodnight. Love you.

∞

05/03

My babe

I spoke to you a bit harsh today, I know that! I know also you need not be reminded of such things at a time when things are rather stressful at work, but I gathered, seeing you had time to take Lilly to lunch, things are not that bad, that I cannot tell you my feelings.

It is so that at that time, I for some unforeseen reason replayed you and Lilly, and your reason for not continue trying with her? But then it made no sense, as I was involved with my boyfriend at that time, and you are and were married, which was your reason for being with her, – that did not put you off from pursuing me, how come this would stand ground with her?

But then I remembered the promise you had made me before I had left, and that was 'no special attention when I am gone', only a 'howzit', then why should I bother if I cannot trust your word? As trust is what one builds on – not so? also trust is what you earn – not so? In anyway – you can answer your breaking of your word later! As I am rather hurt by this right now. I am not going to write any further to you shall speak to you tomorrow 14:55.

No – I cannot go to sleep feeling like this. So here goes … I was lying thinking today of all that is going on – taking the one side, say if we do continue living on the edge all explodes, your wife has to find out about me, sue me? I shall be strong – because I really love you and would take the flack. Should she want me in court, I stand a chance to try prove her wrong – but I think at that stage I will be so 'gatvol' of hiding my true feelings, that I will just pay her off and tell her that no million and would ever be worth all the love you have to offer. I shall gladly pay her off if she can put a value to what you have to offer, it is worth more than all he riches in this world. Should the kids rise up against me, is shall just handle them with care, and allow them to express themselves in whatever from, till they have let out everything. Then explain to them that I shall never take their Mother's place, and their Father is there whenever they need him.

Should you tell me you are getting a divorce, I shall patiently wait till it's over. During this time, should you need me I'll be there and even afterwards. Should you tell me you divorce, and later change your mind, I shall have to accept it and perhaps even accept Cape Town or somewhere far away.

Should you tell me you are not divorcing, I shall have to see if I can handle it, which I doubt, as I am not good handling rejection, then I will go to Cape Town. As my friend will always welcome me, or at least some other company. But facing you every day I don't know. Should you tell me you are not divorcing but you love me for ever, I will not be able to face it either, for I shall feel betrayed for 8/9 months as there I was believing you loved me and you will still – you ending in an absolute hypocrite, I shall never be able to trust! Harsh but a fact.

I need to sort out my life! I need direction and where to from here! This rut of pure disillusioned thought processes, and trap I have fallen into till now is not me. It is important to me that my love for someone is not being wasted and played with.

Another honest confession though is: should this not be – is shall find it very difficult in future to let my heart go, as initially in the beginning I feared letting go, and falling so deeply in love like never before – my trust and confidence will have to be so strong in any other, before they will be able to come close. Not to make you feel bad, I am just being truthful as who else could I talk to, as all the others don't and won't understand! Everyone will turn and say – 'told you so' - just another statistic – other woman.

But I had the nicest dream about you, out underneath this tree outside my windows – I was walking down to you naked, everyone just starring at us as we embarrassed, your clothes disappeared. You lifted me off the ground AND WE TURNED AND TURNED AND TURNED, YOU PUSHED ME UP AGAINST THE TREE AND Fucked me so hard – monkeys scattered and I could feel you cum so hard, I could taste it in my mouth – then my bother arrived in the Mini, to fetch me to go to work.

You just don't realise how much I love you and what you truly mean to me. Although I feel this way I know my luck, therefore I am preparing myself for 'those words' everyday …

But still makes me crazy if I hear you say – 'you know what? I really love you!!'

Goodnight

∞

After I spoke to you this morning – I still continued as I walked down to the river and sat on the bench watching the rapids, the clear sound of water, soothing sounds rushing past after the heavy rains. Even that which comes down, as water is normally associated with cleansing, has some debris from further up, washing down, it made me realise that by avoiding thinking about that which fills your thoughts, one cannot let yourself go completely, as that which resides in your subconscious will always come to the surface at the most unexpected times.

Therefore, to face and clear the sub-conscious, is the most crucial part before allowing yourself to cleanse the conscious of it thoughts – avoiding such will eventually create turmoil.

I still continued my conversation with you as I know you listen – the only friend – and after all that is you, that I'd much rather speak with. So this is it – no 'what if', scenarios 'just me'.

I had never been able to trust, never been able to confide, never been able to really talk, never been able to love, never been able to think of only me.

But now I am able to do all this for once. I had always claimed that no one will be able to enter into my room. I shall allow no one access, and for thirst time I had unlocked these doors.

What do I want – I want to be able to share with someone, my everyday thoughts and every day's doings. Even the thought of pure relevance and irrelevance. Be able to wake in the morning, leap out of bed into a pants and shirt go to a coffee shop, and order coffee for two. Make breakfast for two and cook up a lasagne and turn the kitchen upside down. Maybe burn the food, get dressed and go out for supper instead. Be able to be the belly dancing queen for only him to see. Have his burnt toast for lunch and not mine. Read a book with my head on his lap.
Even when- I feel like arguing, I have someone to argue with and make up afterwards.
When I am being silly, I can hear someone else say it for a change.
At the end of the day I am tired of being alone.

For first time I can say that I have met the person with whom I see myself sharing all this with.

I had always said that should there be an interested party somewhere along the line, I would have to test it first by living this this person and probably never marry, for even though I have not much faith in marriage, I still want to believe that he who weds me weds me for life. So I have to be 100% or at least close to sure that he would be my ideal.

Now what I have here, I will not even contemplate or doubt my decision – for this man I shall walk down the aisle with any day. A karmic feel as though I have known you all my life.

Now I stand at the point of not wanting to hide this feeling any longer – not wanting to fear who knows or finds out that I have met my perfect match.
Sense of humour, ideals, wishes, nature, lust, zest, thoughts, needs all correspond.
Do I think I will lose this 90% NO – 10% maybe. I have a good gut feel that my loneliness is about to end.

I want to stop being prejudice when it gets to myself. I always want to make the world a better place for others – I come last. Now the wheel has to turn. And whatever comes with it – I am willing and prepared to face. No one will deny me my happiness again.

Strew away those negative thoughts and the feel that 'the world and everything in it has it in' for you.

The rapids still flowing strong over the rocks more debris washing away…

Work: – that which I have fought for will be paying off soon, and should it not by entrusting the turn in the hands of others, I shall take upon myself to ensure that I receive what I deserved and what I have earned.
Taking myself and looking back – this battle I fought alone, and I shall ensure I come out the victor.
I did bounce off problems every now and again, but never received words of advice, but sorted it out myself, still fighting the battle against pessimism, feminism, daft humans, age, grades and to absolute amazement, or shall I say amusement, when I spoke with you this morning, I realised I am up against nothing.
For even though I bounce issues off you, and I speak my anger and frustrations, I still worked out the solutions myself and never look at you to solve my problems outside your area of concern.
I never helplessly looked at you for anything.
So really even though I fear some form of threat, but still I need to tell myself regain to halt and think. For at the age of 24 compared to those of 27 – I still come out the victor.
So basically what should stop, is being so critical on myself.
I still fear doing a presentation though and running workshops as I have never done this before. And standing in front of all those people feels like placing myself in the centre of a public square, to be ridiculed and laughed at when I make a mistake.
The impression I have of myself – self-critical. But we'll see – maybe I master that too then what?

I anyway – just played a quick game of scrabble – I lost, but its holiday so I can lose.

So basically I have been panning out all this stuff.
Conclusion: I should stop competing with myself and the world, chill a bit and not get tangled in such a ball of depressing – stressing snot.
After all, if I feel I have achieved what I set out to achieve then who can complain?
Now this is the way things will be – Fuck the People, I am the People!
Fuck knows what I will do if I should lose my ideal man? Work harder or resign to another company or move to Cape Town or another country.
But I know I can't lose him ever, I also know that what work is concerned, I can give up now – I am nearly there. What I am concerned, I just want to be loved in the same way I always give love and what better way then to receive it from someone you really love, to receive it in return.
I shall speak to you soon again … 14:55

∞

06/03

Hello – me again

Well since I last spoke to you had a snooze woke up went on a game drive – saw a whole Waterbuck, 4 Zebra, 3 Giraffe and the view from the top of the hill, was entertained by some young game ranger dude that tried very hard to be our friend, but in the end I think we spoke English too fast for him, so gave it up as a lost cause. Then we went for a swim till after dark, saved a lizard from drowning in the kiddy's pool, came back, smoked a spliff and played scrabble – and won by 85 points – so whenever I am at loss for words I shall just have a spliff.
Steve did all the cooking and carrying around and now after supper, doe doe time. So actually for a day that started off quite shit I must say it is ending rather pleasant. I am ever more in love with you – hope you know that even though I don't think, you'll have the balls to get divorced, I still think you are the best and I love you to absolute bits.

How long do I think we will stay away from each other? Not long maybe a month at the very most, all depends on how well you control yourself. As for me – make myself irresistible – oh yess!

Allow you to fall out of love with me – no way – unless you insist, and really want to – other then that I am going to close my eyes now, and think of all the various positions you put me in and how you always make me cum in all different ways …

Lekker slaap and hopefully if I concentrate hard enough you can feel my lips right now.

07/03

Babe

All packed and rearing to go – I feel much happier now that I have made myself a darker shade of pale today, I feel far more confident about everything since I spoke to you today. You sounded much more reassuring today of your love and how much I mean to you and how much you miss me than ever before. I had a smile from here all the way to Munster, very chuffed with the fact that I am being loved by such and amazing man. Do you realise how happy you make me? Note: I need to hear all about your dream – explicitly!!

Well this was a very relaxing hot lazy week and now for the coast and the sea water. I so much wish you were here – and deep down inside I hope that some magic will happen that when I arrive at the coat you would be there waiting

Fuck I love you young man!!!

Till munster

Hope you have a good night on the farm

Ps: very glad the other parties aren't joining you and when you fall asleep tonight that my head is lying on your groin where it belongs.

08/03

Babes

Fucking tired – drove for 10 long hours not stopping. You know the premonition I had? – well I killed a wild animal on the road this morning at +/- 5:00 which smashed my indicator light I have never killed anything other than the odd insect before in my life, and then I nearly hit a dog too, thank God I slowed down for a truck so ending in only chafing him slightly with my tyre. When driving through Volksrust the Nedcredit Vintage Harley race stopped to fill up with petrol, which brought some light to the day. But what a fucking long road. Got here, and guess who has to fill the surrounding flats? A whole wad of Indian families! You know how noisy they can be, with loud boom boxes and music blaring, and the more they drink the louder they speak! The direct neighbour must have confused the baby's milk formula with extra hot curry powder, for the child has not stopped screaming the whole day. Inexperienced mothers!!!

So went to the beach had a lovely dip in the sea had a shower and went for supper at this restaurant in Glenmore. Where were you? Had 20 of the most succcuuulllent prawns – thinking of you with every suck

Now I am so tired – hating the fact that you aren't here but sleeping in your t-shirt

 Seriously missing you wish you would just decide to surprise me

Love you goodnight

09/03

Honeybun

I have now had enough of not being with you. You know holiday is pleasant – being at the sea is really very relaxing but it is not the same without you. Little miss you tears kept on popping up the whole of today. It has been overcast so went for walks on the beach went to sit on the rocks and talked to you thinking a lot and made a very conscious decision that I don't want a future without you. I have to have you a part of my life I can't picture it without your presence. We went shopping for the week and drove to Margate trying to find Kent as it is not a common brand to smokes and everywhere I go your absence was very prominent. I had your T-shirt on the whole day and after brunch had a nap and all that I dreamt about was you – me, dreaming we were just taking a stroll on the beach. No babe – I have never in my entire life been such a love sick puppy – what are you doing to me!! I am never going away again without you – this is enough! Missing you – love you – can't wait to see you again !! till tomorrow!!

10/03

My bedroom looks out onto the see and it just reminds me more of those couple of days we had in Durban. My first flight, my first waking in your arms and the passion the wild sex, all over the apartment. Remember standing on the table you made me cum so nicely then the lounge all over. The room, the supper, prawns, ice cream between my toes, the elevator, the window, the room... I want that now! Fuck babe I am missing you, the feel of you, to see you again, to talk to you face to face, your hands, your tongue, your body, my most favourite toy, I miss you!

As I put the phone down the fear of being just another statistic crept in! What makes me so special? so different to the other? and the way I was before?

Works of devotion, love and sexual pleasure partly reassuring. But what has changed from always being seen as a sex symbol that would make me any different now?

Sure it is fun, it is risky, it is living on the edge – but … what will it be? will my dream be fulfilled or should I just make peace with the fact that I am just another statistic?

Loving deeply – being loved in return, and having that just to turn around one day and say – I also experienced that in my life – another been there done that go the t-shirt.

Will I ever? Will it ever be?

Right now I cannot answer

Just have to wait and see

Just love me, that is all that matters and for as long as you are prepared to accredit it I shall give you unconditionally, just as long as there are no games, as I hate that, you know the hard to play, catch me if you can crap. The only thing I don't like, is seeing you stressed and under pressure – that I cannot help you with, unless we end in not seeing each other, but from my side I can handle it, as long as you are devoted and truthful which I want to believe you will never be the opposite. So babe – whatever happens I hope it works out for you because I love you anyway

4 more sleeps till I see you – can't wait!!

∞

I don't actually know how to say this but, this is just because I need to talk to you, and this the only way I can at this stage without having you get upset and ready to walk out, I end up feeling the shit for opening my mouth.

But let me start off by telling you how much I love you, never felt this way before, and thus far prepared as much as I can possibly be for accepting you and your children and emotions and the blame. Even facing the possibility of not having a child of my own.
As prepared as I am, because I know I am capable of handling anything as long as I can be with the person who truly makes me happy, and will return all the love I have to give, have fun, laugh, cry and enjoy life. Most of all be my best friend, lover and be the only person to share everything with, albeit it good or bad.

I have always professed that I'd never marry I'd have my two illegitimate children, as I shall never find a man to live up to my standards and ideals, and still respect me, love me, and be faithful to me. Yet now things are changing, as here I have the man, but I am not allowed to be with him…

I am dying – my spirit, free, cheerful, happy, dies when I am not with you.
I turn into something unbearable not only to others, but to myself.
From enjoying my life, I have become listless, unapproachable. Day in day out sitting in my house not speaking to anyone as I am running out of excuses, as to why I cannot go out with them, or visit, or have them come around for coffee.

On the one hand I am unsociable, as I don't know what to say, as my whole mind, soul and heart is with you. Clinging to my phones and pager. Constantly staring at the gate. Should it be a casual male friend I cannot speak to them, or see them, as I always think what would I do? Your words repeating, "what would you do if I had to go out with a female friend?"
So I just stay in, and it is killing me.
What I don't understand is if you are going through the same, who are you kidding? With these frustrations we are starting to argue, instead of talking about fun, life giving stuff, we are just talking about work and divorce issues, stuff that leaves a rather bad taste behind.

You say that there are 2 x things that still make you stay:
One is the financial side - short term you can sort out now, and I am prepared to give up anything to make that happen. Long term, now is not the right time to work out, as emotions are still a big factor. I am not suffering two years down the line due to rash decisions made now. I shall state again! Money is not important (I would have been playing in the 'Millionaire's boys club' if I was like that), but you know, that if you would not be able to spend money on your toys that bring you happiness, you will not be a happy boy.
Your children can have and must have everything they want as long as they don't use you and take advantage of you in an ungrateful manner.

The other reason is rightfully your children, and that I understand.
It is emotional, it does hurt, as much as you have those little faces in your head, they are in mine.
Remember, the only difference is, I have three faces, (wife and children) towards whom I carry the guilt.
I have been through the stretched out process as a child, and know what they are going through. Is Dad going tonight, or this weekend or when? Come home – Dad is still there … maybe this weekend? Dad is still there…. Everyday an emotional roller coaster till the day Dad is not there, then we can deal with that.
Mom can deal with that, Dad can deal with that, Ange can deal with that. Ange is scared, as now her shit starts, Dad being in his moods, Dad's guilt, tears, phone calls blame etc.,
Moms tears accusations hatred facing her…
The children's tears, blame hatred…

And all this I can handle and will handle, because making Dad happy and being loved by him as much as he does, is all that I need to give me the strength to handle. All Angie needs and thrives on is love, happiness and laughter.
The only thing she can't handle is the uncertainty of not knowing when, and her dying spirit.

Too shit scared to ask, too scared to say anything, so please, you tell me what must I do?
How long must I wait?
Must I still anxiously make plans to figure a way to be with you, what do I do?
I need to retain my spirit!! I need to smile again!!
As at this stage the only time I can be myself is when you are around and that is not much.

'50 shades of fucked up" is what Christian said in the Film I finally got to watch last night.

When everyone has been going on about this forever and still the many fantasies of just about every man I meet.

What is it I wondered that everyone has this deep-seated need for pain – inflicted or self-inflicting?
The little sentence that he uttered, which I doubt anyone had picked up, was that of a person with a false sense of self – a person that surrounds himself with all the power and riches – incapable of accepting or denying the simple basic = love and touch – why?
He tells it all – he was damaged as a child.

Yes, I was asked so many times to participate in BDSM or being spanked, hurt, forming part of circles, tribes or being dominated – being the sub.

My answer had always been – sure, but I am the Dominatrix – make me your Queen.

Yet, they all when with me, are gentle lovers.
All these outward fantasies – remember, 'I never said no' – but they all quiver at the thought that I might turn to be the Dom – they all change, when in the sexual situation as actually being that gentle lover.

Is that then the Dom as the male as they wish to call it – when I turn to say 'thank you, but don't fall in love with me' – the shock they show is amazing.
Why do they fantasise about being the powerful Dom, if they in that moment cannot display the power?
They want no strings attached, yet when you voice and show no strings attached they want more of you, they fall in love with you?

However, if they keep insisting on it, keep saying it and enact it if they are that true Dom – how much have they hurt as a child?

– as Christian had so said and the truth behind so many that hurt others deliberately.

∞

My thoughts are what keeps me company most of the time.
From absolutely thinking nothing to hopes, dreams, wondering off to the future, to the now and to the past.
I don't enjoy hankering in the past – I enjoy thinking of either nothing or creating, planning and finding new options, possibilities, designing, mapping, solutions and visions.

They dropped the boreholes at Mini-Tuscany, there are no real plans to develop that into an agri-project. I know how to turn this town – my land, mining, cell tower – Eskom, Telkom, Vodacom, MTN, Satellite, hydroponics, turbines.

∞

Here we go Adam:

If you should ever bother to contact me – which I will be highly surprised after this week in my absolute time of realisation, that you have been brilliant at making me realise that I am worth more than to grovel for your love – Allah salaam.

You will not have my time more than I give to everyone else! I opened up for you, to know to see what I am and who I am. You chose to take the sex route – therefore you can be another Dick, another Harry, another … List them.
Every man that I have had sex with and discarded me – some have come to the conclusion there will be no more. Some still play and when there is nothing, they want to come back. Some absolutely love me and want my every bit of me. Some just want to have fun. Some are married and want to fuck. Some are young. Some are single fathers and don't have the time. Some are just outright fun happy friends. Is what it is – various dynamics everyone has as we grow through our lives.

Who am I to judge?
What I know is that all start with their own intentions relevant to them, at that point in time in their lives.
I too have the choice to accept it, reject it or entertain it. Which bears relevance to where I am at in that specific point in time in my life.

It can be likened onto atoms colliding for the want of something scientifically explicit. Souls that pass are similar, some pass – some collide – some rub – some join – it is the current environment that makes it suitable, sustainable or temporary.

It's all very unique as some will re-engage or never engage.

It is like that – a seed planted, same seeds, from the same origin, in the same soil – some take – some don't – some start growing and die half way – some flourish.

Same as fertility – same as understanding, same as relationships – same as education.

∞

"MAGALIES MARDIGRAS IN MAY"
"DELETE 4 Letters in the alphabet"
"Cycle, Ride, Drive in"
"The organic Festival" – local farm
produce, local arts, theatre, choirs,
competitions, sports
"All non-profits benefit"
"Train between Magalies and
Cullinan?"
"Rovos rail, Department of Tourism,
Arts and culture, Mining"

∞

7 May 2019

It's called the 35 – 50 phase:

We are all questioning out livelihood.

Women look up from their breasts and realise – oh my god I have just done that feeding thing. Where am I? Where is my husband?
She realises – he is bald and fat and what has she achieved?
Other than feed, the children, and the man…. He is not that sexy hunk …

Men are out there just hunting to feed the family – then he looks up and says, I have been running away making sure I can feed the wife and family.
Where am I? Where is my wife?
He realises - her tits have sagged and what has he achieved?
Other than be a stranger in my own home, who is this woman and who are these children… she is not that cool hot chick…

He looks in the mirror – same as she does and thinks – 'hella no, this is shit' – I have not aged like this???

They both start looking for answers in what they think is the mid-path – the bridge crossing the river… to greener pastures.

They could either find a temporary solution, a permanent solution or none at all…
The Big D (affairs, infidelity, divorce)

We all work for days – we take a break to regroup. It's called WEEKEND
Work all work for weeks – we take a break to regroup. It's called HOLIDAY

Is that not how marriage and relationships should be?

It's called the 'LOVE-VACATION', as we all seek love and recognition at any destination we travel to.

Take a 'LOVE-VACATION', make in an institution in your relationships.

You don't own a person just because you are in a relationship with them.

Give them space, give them a 'LOVE-VACATION' to regroup.

∞

13 May 2019

There is no such a thing as unconditional regard or unconditional love.

You always have your frame of reference. You are according to you, learning as you grow to make your own way a reality to you. You are made from seed from fertile ground, however, you take your own reality and turn it from the various perceptions, into what is acceptable to you. Now from there create your own world and reality = your own conditional love and understanding to you!

As a parent you are a co-creator. You think you own that world you created in that person, that child, as you are at that specific point in your own growth and understanding. This however, is YOUR growth and understanding – is it not?

Unconditional – how? Because at that time – what you created was ideals …. Your ideals…
your understanding …
You always refer back to the time of your conception, when you grew up, of that little world that reminds you of that mind-set at the time, your own frame of reference. Based on this, you create your perception of what you want, or don't want, for that little world you created at the time.

Then you look at that world, through your eyes, ideals, understanding, frame of reference – you either accept or reject it – the T-junction – Yes/No, Ying/Yang, On/off, black/white.
So what do you do?

You raise your child according to the time in YOUR life! Which makes it??

? Un-conditional or Conditional?

∞

! Refocus Lady!

"Your focus is your studies – you need to complete this so you can qualify and move on! The cycle needs to end here!"

Your energy has been sapped by the people in your personal space. You have allowed their agenda to take over your daily function, your personal and emotional space!

With that still in your environment this will be challenging!
Let's see how we change this?

> "Egos above the cause the passion"
> "why is a woman's voice soothing?
> – brings you back to mommy's voice"
> "Boys vs Girls Labola, India girls vs boys – housing 6 months – NOW child trafficking – what have we created – human / animal barter = skin for clothes"
> "humanity is deborturated"
> "falling in love with visions of you"
> "perceptions – vs reading what you want to read – vs reading the story – vs reading behind the story"
> "26 – 30 = Vacant mother – edopuss, 30 – 40 = boss, 45 – 50 = virile awake – not young, 50 – 55 = longevity – young same old"
> "women being taken the child pose"
> "the drunk ladies tea party"

June 2019 – At the coast

The importance of silence is the time to reconnect with your own world.

That which you created as you begun your life on this plane. Nothing happened and nothing started without you.
Incarnation in the time that you began to where you are now in your life, was all because of what you needed to manifest, to learn and make a part of your home – the understanding to this point where you currently sit.

Be it on a rock next to the sea – looking over the ocean as the water crashes.
Be it on a side path next to a busy road in the middle of city lights.
Be it next to the sport field watching your children play their games.

At the boardroom table watching many people waste their time including you. When you sit around a boardroom table and you are not participating, not giving your input. You are wasting your time.
Being a student in a classroom, where you are not participating, you are wasting your time.

Re-evaluate your life and your journey. As time wasted can never be regained, therefore whatever your current position is in life, make the absolute most of it. As you are the master of your own life, your own journey, your choices. To be where you are, is your carnation – you have a choice to give it either life or death.

Life is inspiration – Death is frustration.
No one can be blamed for where you find yourself right this minute – embrace, love, life.

∞

Maybe I can manage with 6 months at the coast, and 6 months on the farm.
I love my farm the peace and tranquillity. Living on my own has taught me the respect of being, with me!
I do feel lonely – I do need company – but limited it is.
Living in the country where there is not water – water I mean that brings waves that you hear the deafening sounds of waves, is what I need to hear as it washed and cleanses with its robust movements, reminding you that you are not the power of all beings – it is humbling when you look across the ocean and realise just how powerful nature is.

How attractive the beauty of earth is, in the middle of the land, the country where I live – people destroy and forget the power of nature. With their designs and road that destroy. It is depressing when you look around you, and all you see is a rat race to nowhere. No one rebuilds the earth. They live on sewer pipes, under electrical pylons.
The noise of manmade creations, stuck to screens surrounded by electronic waves,

smoke filled air and no regard for the planet, humanity in general, frustration and anger surrounds every human.

– the crashing of waves – reminds me of the power of humility.

∞

I love the voices of children and the things they say – so intelligent so much reality and so much truth with absolute innocence they utter big words that often astonishes me.

The direct utterance is amazing – when they articulate their words with such profoundness and makes for no thinking of what the recipient would hear or how they would react.

Now, take that same child 20 years later, and see how that confidence is lost by the absolute heinous destruction of people. The 'don'ts', 'the rules', 'the cant's' - that destroy confidence and creativity.

'Child' – Remain confident.

'Adult' – allow the confidence to progress to the abilities that could change your world for the better. Allow greatness to continue in that confidence – All you need to do is allow freedom but teach Respect and NOT condemnation.

∞

To your majesty the sea:
Your waves are coming in with such beautiful anger that makes me feel so small.
I respected you Master.
I respect every word you speak to me.
You dominate my every peace. You dominate my world.
Your sound roaring to make us aware of the power you hold.
I was sitting at your level – when you raised your power above me that frightened me and made me realise with one raise – you could end me – my world that I think is so big – can be declared null and void.
My respect to you - my Majestic Master.

And then you shower me with fresh rain and water drops.

∞

AUTHENTICITY – Hermanus on the coast of Cape Town

I haven't been here since my eldest son was a mere 5 years old and my other, 18 months old. The area has grown beyond comprehension. As I was rained out in Sandbaai a drive 3 kms on, went from rain to sunshine.

Hermanus as I remember was a small little village with a quaint Waterfront – But now the brick factory has taken over with the modernised version of developers, that have obviously decided that modernisation and bricks are of more importance than to maintain the beautiful quaintness of the village – I feel lost in this city of modern bricks – why change the history with demolishing the old? Why not refurbish the old and maintain that history and rather build next to it?

Your ugly modern buildings that stand empty whilst, many opt for the older looking restaurants and buildings – but so many places with strong history gets lost in translation by modernisation!

The oldest will remain the best, as you cannot force tradition to move away, as even the tourist seek out the older – tradition is far more popular than your "ocean basket" or your "fusion café", which does not satisfy the pallet of the tourists that seek tradition of South Africa!

– Nothing special is served at the commercialised franchise – why are you doing this?

You stupid Architect, Town Planner?

∞

How important it is to take time to yourself is often misunderstood by so many.

You have to take that sabbatical – you have to nurture yourself to make that part of your existence, it is imperative to the soul.

You have to do the things you do not do in your everyday life, you have to walk into places that attracts your eye – it might disappoint you, but most of all it might just impress you.

You might just find that unique wine on the menu called GabrielsKloof, that makes the world of difference to that moment to your person named Gabriel – to say – "hey there is even a wine named after me"

– that as insignificant as it might sound to you when you walk into a place – the mere fact that you decided to drink that glass, it became part of your moment or day

– when you text and share it with your son, he could at that stage feel despondent, but you shared that with him, – that - made him feel extra special, -that- gave him that little bit of support or hope, although he is miles away from you, you thought of him – regained the courage to do something new.

You thought of him, you cared! Which is the ultimate love that's all that anyone wants to know in life is that they matter – that is love.

Insignificant to some – profound to others.

∞

As I drive through the coastal towns and see these amazing homes locked up for that once a year, maybe twice a year visit to the coast. Yes, there are agents rife in every town.

They don't care as much as you do, as they get paid to provide a service but not to care.

The thought that was brought to mind is

– who stocks up the fridge when you arrive, make sure there is wood in the fireplace and the first meal is prepared?

That is always the issue, people eat

– provide the first nights home cooked meal… what a lucrative business for the local resident that would be?

∞

FOR THE LOVE OF BEING DRESSED IN A RECOGNISABLE OUTFIT!

When walking through your child's school activities you are dressed in a Child-Welfare T-shit.
The power of the name, when people reprimand their child … to safe words when you walk by

– the fear and the stares!

"I best be the Good Parent, The Sweet Teacher"

The law enforcement agents like the Traffic cops, Police

– we should be visible as Child-Welfare and Social Workers.

∞

I manifest with my entirety

25 August 2019
25 8 2019
7 8 12
15 3
6 3
9
The end of a lifecycle
My end of Magaliesburg – Beginning of a New
12 12 2019
3 3 3
9

My year has many 3s which is the number that I find, is the number of healing and enlightenment.
I bring to this year my end of many cycles, beginning of many new beginnings.
As I transpire into a new awakening and new journey as 25 August 2019 is manifest as the end of Magaliesburg, which had brought me much pleasure in the journey of finding closure
– closure which one needs to begin afresh to start anew

– THE END

Michael, Uriel, Gabriel, Raphael as we move toward the beginning of a new!
We shall bring praise to God and the Universe, to assist in the transformation and allowing for everything to flow and happen as it should.
To allow this journey to come to an End, as we move towards a new Beginning!
That will bring enlightenment and fresh Start!
To the future of the journey which is manifested in the heart and soul and written in the sand.

∞

I shall no longer seek for answers in another, or wait for another to fulfil my dreams. I shall rather take the hand of another, to join me in this journey.

the path that will be one for me and one for the other… as I look back – I see only footprints of One engraved in the sand ….
Which is at this time – behind me
I am ready to walk next to another and make the footprints that of 2 rows
With no more doubts as I take the next steps toward my future fulfilment.

I do not feel that my journey will be without the hand of my Angels, God and the Universe. I know that the difference I have made, will remain sustained through the lives that I have changed. But I can no longer fight for those who wish not to seek the beauty of change.
I know my own worth and my own value – it is sometimes difficult to believe in it when all you do is fight. But Angelique why are you fighting? – this is not your nature to be in constant conflict.
You have set out to be and Angel of People and not a Fighter of Evil selfish ignorance.
You bring light and life to others, your journey is that of standing your ground for better or for worse In sickness and in health.
Your struggle to make this change in the area of Magaliesburg has come to an end. You will create and make – talk to the local council that will carry this forward. You are to just give them the opportunity to take the future path and make it theirs.
– to God be the Glory.

∞

On this day of 13 June 2019 when all my realisation and my writing in the sand the date.

I manifest with the Angels and God and the Universe. I am seated at Milkwood beach in Onrus – I never noticed that when I look up the seat where I find myself is no69 = 15 = 6 the numbers that represents the end.
The number 6 to me made up by 3 + 3 = 6
The number after 5 – the balancing number where you can decide to move to a 4 or a 6 – the path towards progress and learning.

13 6 2019
4 6 3
13
4
Leaving the past behind to engrave the future the 6 is what this day heralds!
4 + 6 = 9 – the end of a life cycle.

Manifestation of new beginnings:

13 September 2019
4 9 2019

13 3
4 3
7

Connect everyone and draw the map, join the dots, combine the efforts.
That is all you need to do – Create the Bigger Picture – SUSTAINABLE
DEVELOPMENT, Early Intervention Programs, Change Strategy.

∞

"Soos 2 duifies op Onrus se dak"
"it all happens in 3s"

"calendar selfie"

"when I look down I look old – when
I look up I look young"

"inside my story remains"

"sodra die icing afgeeet word – die
vrugte koek"

"I cannot begin to explain"

"you know me not"

"I had an epiphany"

"oh hella no"

"shit happens – life goes on"

"fuck me George"

"straight brother"

"makhulu umlungu"

"mama lekgua"

∞

"Sodra die icing afgeeet word, bly die vrugtekoek nogmaals "n vrugtekoek"

Jy kan hom versier, jy kan vir haar 'n rosie op sit.
Elke kersfees is daar 'n vrugte hoek – versier met missle toe – camel toe of prag
blaartjies
Onder dit is alles verdoesel
Die koek word vir maande voor die tyd bebak -
met bottels en bottels brandewyn
vele raad kom deur
vele vrugte – ou uitgevarste vrugte
Niemand wil eintlik se -
Dis mos 'n ou cherry
Dis mos 'n geputte dadel
Dis te veel sout, te min suiker
- solank daar genoeg brannewyn in is – verdoesel dit die smaak
En so wonder almal – as die kinders op kleins moet krismis koek eet -
wat de fok se ons -
Eet die vrot gemors en drink die ou wyn – Dis Jesus
Kom ons mors ons tyd
Kom ons mors ons geld
Kom ons maak vir 1 dag of ons almal lief het
en Ryk is en Kerk toe gaan
Wat van die ander 364 dae
Geniet die icing
Sluk, kou of spoeg die dadel put uit
- Jou keuse

∞

I don't want this day to end – I woke with such ….
No thoughts to name a date, to talk to meet to be….
I don't want this moment to end….
Everything of yesterday ended… it was amazing! I woke and all came to me!
New beginnings!!

∞

I am back to where I started a few days ago my Fairest Ocean. Where the land
meets the sea.
I give thanks to you as I will leave a piece of me behind while a take of all of you with
me – as memories are, what makes the soul and creates the heart.
You have taken me through the various forms of you through this week. I have seen
you be confused, be angry, be wild and come back to peace and calm.
Tranquillity is what you bring to my soul – I will always be thankful to you.
I have gone through all those emotions and have come to much realisation that I am
not alone – you are with me in my every being and that is my peace that I go with
– I am not alone – I am much loved!

∞

> Telepathic pheromones
>
> – chemistry – I want to fuck you –
> underlying explanation of sexuality
> – sub-conscious – do I look like a
> fuck machine – gift and arse – but
> receptive – the receptor or the
> communicator ….

∞

I am glad my "client" child is gone, my kids understand me, and this what I love about them. They don't recuse me, they take me as I am, as they understand that the things I do. It does not necessarily make me a billionaire, but it saves and helps so many children!
I, at some time, also know that I have to stand off!
Although I would wish to keep all the children, I can't. When people stand with a whole bread under the arm I need to bill them… how do you do that as someone that sees the pain of the child?
When the parents are just living for their own??

∞

24 June 2019

Being the mother of the divorced couple

Who were in any textbook will you find the perfect situation when faced with divorce. Every couple, family, children, circumstance is unique in its own making. I can only take my circumstances and situation as I am faced with and work with it in my own unique way to find the optimal solution – or not even solution, but all I can do is to be there in support of my children, as they in their lives go through their unique mechanisms of dealing with the environment that they have to face.

My only ever wish was to have children and to be a mother – but being a mother unless you have singularly adopted requires one to have a father. The dynamic that introduces more implications to having children.

In my life – I have a father for my children whom have made some decisions in his life which is not always well thought through, in consideration of the implications his choices have on the balance of his life, which in this case affects the children. Yes, he is a good provider financially, and he is a good father in the sense of making sure that the children's every day financial needs, care and home is in excellent condition. He is at home cooking and feeding them, makes sure that they attend school, never denies them any luxury or extra murals, does not abuse them in any physical way. He is always good to them.

The only little flaw is his choices in life partners, or should I say sexual choices he makes. The previous one, now let's just understand, he is close to retirement. He has two older sons whom had both fortunately at the time of our divorce, commenced with their adult lives. By this he really has gone out all the way physically and financially to give them all the necessary support and means to start their adult journey on a good levelled financial foundation. His next 2 boys being 14 and 10 at the stage will have a few years ahead having to complete school and university and also that first step towards financial freedom and adulthood. All and all +/- 14 year of commitment ahead to place them on their journey.

So what does he choose first … a 33-year-old with 3 children that are still very young – 2 just starting school, and another, I think aged 16? At the stage that they moved in together our little girl also became part of the family as she is now an orphan. Increasing the number of dependants and extending the years of financial responsibility with another minimum 4 years.

The house immediately filled with now a woman and total of 6 children. We are now having 2 x staff, 7 x dogs and a parrot. The first thing the new woman does is throw out furniture and starts redecorating … dynamics of children all in the same space in varying ages and still adds a new puppy. This was a disaster waiting to happen a matter of time for the bomb to explode.

In this time, I moved to the farm which was an important financial decision as I could not continue to afford the townhouse in Linden.

The bomb soon exploded – the fights commenced between the children, then the children and the other woman, then the adults, then the father forcing the children to accept the woman, then the boozing then the children and father then the woman and the children then the children and the children….

But there was no easing in of the situation or slow introduction, it was moving, engaged. It's like forcing the whole dynamic together 2 different worlds without allowing any time to heal. She divorced, he divorced and within months they moved 2 different worlds into one. Needless to say – this all came to an abrupt end.

The dust hardly settled – then the next young lady on the scene – this one is now 23 years old. Complete different culture, still a child and he is now 59 years old. The children 18, 14, 8 respect. A shock to everyone as the wounds have not every healed from the previous attack on the family. Pieces are still being gathered.

The first shock was the weird drinks in the fridge, the items of clothing around the house, the lies and the sneaky behaviour and texts. The jewellery in the bathroom. Then the big bang bomb, I have another woman, she is younger, she is black. All was acceptable until the introduction – she was a woman, she was black, no problem – but she is 23 years old and looks like a prostitute.

This was the biggest shock to the young kids. How could their father, a respected old business man with such sense, do something like this to a young girl. A giver/blesser is what he is called. A gold digger is what she is called.

The children are so embarrassed by their father's choice. Here it all starts. First they find all their sex toys – BDSM whips and chains. Then they have open sex in the open communal living area. Then she goes out dressing like a prostitute. Then my daughter gets left in a strange place with complete strangers for hours on her own without anyone she knows to have her hair braided. Then my son sniffs petrol. Then my son starts smoking. Then his little friend gets drunk. Then the lies about going on business trips when in the meantime it is an expensive weekend trips. Then it is the constant drinking of the two. Then it is sleeping till mid-day and lying in front of the television till night. Then it is the change in cuisine to meat, pap and chakalaka. Then it is the never home when the kids are home – going out when it is his weekend. The fights, the arguments between father and girl, children and father, children and girl. Children locking themselves away not to have to face the situation. Then my son losing his virginity to a trashy 16year old – while father is busy with his girl… son worried about pregnancy and contracting STI….

The choices he has made – hurts…. Yes – I step in every time to be there for my kids – but what does one do? Revoke parental rights? Grab children and have court cases? Have constant fights? Or be there for your children when they call in the middle of the night? humour his girlfriend – ask everyone to accept his shit and change their attitudes?? Threaten – scream – fight?

So I hold on tight to what I believe is that I cannot change him to realize that his actions are affecting his children… I can only be there for my children when they need to get away or to support or to listen. Financially it is not an option for me to move to Johannesburg, as I am living on a farm and my overheads are minimal right now as I complete the final year of my studies which is what I need to focus on to have a degree to fall back on this degree will always have a need. It is also my final year!

I have always set my studies and career aside for my husband, my children when they needed me. At the moment the options would be for me to go back to the gypsy life of being between Johannesburg and the farm. Studying right now allows me the flexibility to be there when they need me. Their father is a good man, always has been and the only other person that love my children as much as I do.

Currently they are learning from this lifestyle as to what is wrong or right in relationships with their women one day. What choices do you make and how do you behave? Which is also a good thing. They love their dad, but don't trust or respect him.

I am not perfect; I am sure they also have their gripes about me. I know my son did initially when we first divorced.

I am learning not to interfere too much not to make the decisions and not to take over all the control, as I can only control my life and journey as to where I am at the moment and give all the support I can that is in my power. At the end of the day I have to make choices about my life and have fears of my own that I need to deal with as I am not in a relationship and haven't been in one since I was married.

My path to healing has been intense as I did not only have to restart my life, I also had to deal with not being a fulltime mother. Learning to deal the hello and goodbye, with rejection with loneliness with nothingness. I had to learn to get to know me…

∞

24 July 2019

En route on the place from Durban. My father had just suddenly passed. I had always though that I would not react in the manner that I did. I always thought that the moment I would hear of his passing I would say my own goodbyes in my own way not have to deal the physical goodbye.

But then the call came on Sunday as I sat alone at a restaurant under the trees. I did have very uneasy feeling that day and the day before. But I thought it was because I had so much studying to do, so much being on my own — so many worries about the little time versus the amount of work versus the deadline.

But then I received that call. It was surreal I did not know what to do, how to react. But I did, I got into my car and drove home to pack, I was from that moment on even more in a haze of surreal. Do I drive, do I run, do I fly, do I hide … but it all just took over, it all I don't know what you would call "it" — as "it" took over. Pack, drive, brother, drive, fly … it was as though I lived in a hazy dream. Flying arriving, sorting, crying, sort, cry, clean, anger, pain, cry some more…

From going to the house he lived in, to hospital, the mortuary, the police station for affidavits to solemnly swear that I am his daughter (oh yes, I had to do that, because, I now have a married surname) to paperwork, documents, signatures, thumb prints, identifying body, watching it leave, documents, phone calls, shrine, clean, cry, money, documents, cremation, happy pills, more driving, crying, more cleaning, then he came to say "I am proud of you my son, thank - you pop" ... (yes, he spoke through me … I have this unfortunate for me, open channel to see, engage, feel souls, and for some reason or another they do love talking through me. I have blocked it in many ways. As the restless and passing souls have no boundaries, and can keep one awake and disturbed, beyond bounds.) more tears, more crying…. To absolute peace…

I closed the door behind me this morning… I closed a chapter….

Flying back — I say goodbye to it all — I say goodbye

In love and light —

I did what I could.

∞

22 July 2019

Dear Daisy

I tear a page out of my memoirs and write with your pen… we had both sincerely loved a person my Dad and your husband... he was a great man that I shall never every deny — we crossed 'our' that is, your and my paths at a very sensitive time in both our lives which neither can deny but he brought us together for whatever reason on purpose it might be?

All I can from the deepest and a sincere way is say thank you! Thank you for being there and looking after him through that journey — the journey of him still being what he needs to be — he is now released I know — I come, I clean, I sort, I sweep, - enjoy your new space — love Ange

∞

23 July 2019

So I sit here, my Father had just died, my Granny died, my Barbara died – I read all these fucking scriptures of what it means to pass, all these scriptures of prepare yourself all these scriptures of fuck whatever! Yet – none of them had ever come back to me and said – Ange – here darling – this is what it is – we had died – we had passed and I tell you – baby girl it's all real or it's all bullshit.

What 'you 'as Angelique experience is a dream or figment of your imagination. Fuck. I do good all day every day – so don't tell me I need to do more good! So mother fucking dead people that is Ouma, Pappa, Barbara, Who and what are we to believe – tell me for real!!

Sitting in the mortuary having to sort out the paperwork for the release of dad's body the last bit to say goodbye to the farther, my dad – it is administrative - it is so cold – what is your body really worth?

I slept on this couch last night and couldn't feel his presence. He is not an earthly being – it was not his place to remain, he is released and has peace, that no one will understand. Pappa is no longer part of this painful plane which is and never was for him, he is released, he is relieved. Thank you!

It is just to sit here and feel that one has come to a pure thumbprint, paper and signatures – I best sort the funeral plan

∞

16 August 2019 – fun with teens – sayings

- Shoof #touch
- Spliffy jiffy
- Find the grind that keeps your mind the game
- Happiness?
- Touch Ziggy
- Round #1 – puff straight
- A happy house – this is fund
- All I need is a brilliant bitch – touch brilliant bitch – you dig
- Boyzz
- Nother zig
- Really I now have to go into – passive slow love music? When woman want to go into hard-core music – men want to go into slow music
- Victimized, scrutinized, I am here to survive, how you live, how you die, all the time is really what you feel inside
- One percent or ninety-nine – I want it all, I swear they smell the blow on me, I hear them coming for me
- Sampha touches the soul
- Asking myself if what I am doing today is going to get me where I want to be???
- But of course!! – I am with my fam!!
- High hopes are getting low

- Amazing when you get to teach – pace yourself and gain the actual reality of experience
- Called the tequila sip
- Sip slow – enjoy the moment
- Bless the men and women who wake up with a smile
- No one knows me like the piano in my mother's home
- Mental cage – family
- Positive energy my god
- The truth will set you free, but first it will piss you off
- Dual magic
- Kiss me I wanna hot lock
- She's a bad lil diva
- When dynamics change, regardless of where you are @
- Just tryna zone – vice
- The most amazing is when your own child has things to say – just as you are a parent
- Men the underlying message is when the main honey say copt out
- You either control the moment, the thought, have conversation or the opportunity it is all about your moment of confidence – let them release – amazing what you learn
  ∞

23 august 2019

Here again in my old office my home away from home in the tranquil garden settings at Puputzis in Linden.

The days I spent here, ignoring what others said and just escaping form the noise of people, home and unhappiness with my life situation back then – I am now sitting here and just think how far I have come in the past 5 years of being the happiest divorced woman I know, enjoying every second of my single life, as a woman I have honestly come into my self – realisation and strengths taking my own power back, by not being that emotional 'slut' that could never say no to anyone.

Now sitting here without being rude, angry or self-absorbed. I realise my personal growth, and how amazing it is not to feel guilty for not doing this for others, but just being there for me and doing that which pleases me.

You don't need to let everyone know where you are and what you are doing – it is great to be alone!

∞

'TAKING BACK MY LIFE'

> Message from SAPS. Case registered on 2019-09-10 at LINDEN ref nr CAS 129/9/2019. Station contact detail: 011-8889211. Do NOT reply to this SMS.

TO MY #RAPIST, IN DECEMBER 1987, YOU REPEATEDLY TOOK AWAY MY INNOCENCE WITH YOUR CONTINUED ABUSE OF MY MOUTH AND VAGINA, REPEATED!! NON-STOP!! YOU LEFT ME WITH SUCH PAIN AND GUILT THAT I COMMITTED SUICIDE, TO BE REVIVED IN HOSPITAL! YOU LEFT ME HAVING TO BE COMMITTED TO A PSYCHIAATRIC WARD FOR WEEKS TRYING TO FIGURE OUT WHAT I DID WORNG TO DESERVE THIS! YOU LEFT ME VIOLATED WITH AN STD THAT DESTROYED MY WOMANHOOD TO THE POINT WHERE I COULD NOT HAVE CHILDREN NATURALLY! YOU LEFT ME WITH NIGHTMARES AND FLASHBACKS STILL OF YOUR FACE!! THE FEAR OF EVER HAVING TO SEE YOU AGAIN! BUT YOU KNOW WHAT MISTER! I WAS 14 YEARS OLD! YOU WERE MARRIED MAN! I AM NOW 46 YEARS OLD! I AM A #SURVIVOR AND YOU REMAIN A #RAPIST #RAPECULTURE! YOU REMAIN #GUILTY

<table><tr><td>

LETTER OF DEMAND

1. We confirm that we act on behalf of ("our client") who has instructed us to address this letter to you.
2. On or about the 8th of September 2019 you posted a column as well as photographs of our client on Facebook accusing our client of raping you when you were 14 years old. These are extremely serious allegations against our client.
3. To the best of our client's information, you have not approached the South African Police Service ('SAPS') at any given time with these allegations. Our client approached the SAPS to ascertain whether you have presses any form of charges against him but there are no pending cases against him.
4. Is is our client's instruction that these allegations against him are unfounded and amount to *crimen iniuaria* and defamation.
5. Your postings on Facebook, Twitter and Instagram have tarnished the reputation of our client and is reckless and harmful to say the least.
6. Some of your followers on your social media platforms have reposted your column, and they now stand as jury and have our client on trial without adhering to the doctrine "innocent until proven guilty" or *audi alteram partem.*

</td></tr></table>

9 September 2019 – my rape case notes

Board of healthcare 0115370200

011 7262184 Gerrit geldenhuys - psychologist at hospital that treated me

FCS head office 0123932363

NPA 012 845 6000

Victim Charter 012 315 1670

The FCS 9:20 – enter your mailbox nr

NPA I would like to report my own rape of when I was 14 years old – left a message 09:24

Email sent: to victim charter – no response

Finding my psychologist at the time – www.medpages.co.za – who, what and where of healthcare – search

Recommendation to go to Linden Police station to report

Board of healthcare 0115370200

16 September 2019

A week after I put my post on social media speaking up about my truth as rape survivor. Now in ENCA news studio to have a panel discussion as statutory rape survivor. With the same case as Minnow matter and Bob Hewitt

Research: -

12 % or fewer cases are reported, incident of rape 2018 -2019 based on 100 000 populations.
Rape = forced penetration

United States – sexual offences and rape = most unreported crimes. 80 000 American children are sexually abused every year.

10 – Belgium 27.9 per 100 000

9 – Panama 28.3 per 100 000

8 – Saint Kitts and Nevis 28.6 per 100 000

7 – Australia 28.6 per 100 0000

6 – Grenada 56.8 per 100 000

5 – Nicaragua 32 per 100 000

4 – Sweden 1 in every 3 women under age 15

3 – Lesotho 88 per 100 000

2 – Botswana 93 per 100 000

1 – South Africa 127.6 per 100 000

500 000 rapes in South Africa annually, 70 000 cases include children

1 in 5 girls and 1 in 20 boys

Non-contact abuse = exposure, pornography, voyeurism

Black African men think it's cool – white woman think it's okay

51.1% men – 33.8% of women

Optimus study SA:
41% rapes against children

55% by care givers

1.6 % rape before age 15

Sexual abuse – 39.1 % women 16.7% mend

Contact abuse

Physical abuse

Exposure abuse

Sexual harassment

Questions: - reasons for abuse

1 argues with him

2 neglects children

3 goes out without telling him

4 refuses to have sex

5 burns food

Sexual Offences Unit – 0117678000

Department of psychology – 011 5593130

Records at sandton clinic 0117092750

∞

∞

2019

The Affidavit

In December of 1987 I was doing a holiday job, doing filing for a window tinting company. My boss asked me to join him to Pretoria for a meeting. I call my Mom and asked her if this was okay, she said yes. We drove off in his car, but instead of going to Pretoria, he took me to the cable cars at Hartebeespoort dam. On the cable cars, he offered me dagga. I said no thanks. When we got off the cable cars we drove to which I thought would be the meeting in Pretoria. It was overcast that day.

He turned onto a dirt road, said he wanted to show me the place that he bought. In the middle of the dirt road amongst high grass he stopped the car. Told me to get out. We walked to the front of the car. He started kissing me. I felt uncomfortable and went back to the passenger side of the car. When I got back into the car, he also got back in and locked the door. Leaned over me and put the seat down. He got onto of me, forced his into me, on and on and on……

Then I remember him turning around and putting his penis into my mouth. He kept on and on and on…. We then drove back to the office. He put his and on my leg again. I remember driving back, crying. At the office, on the corner of Gordon Avenue and Blairgowrie Drive in Blairgowrie. My handbag was in the office. It was dark already. I said I need to phone home. When I put the phone down he pushed me onto his desk and put himself into me again. Then he pushed my head down and put his penis into my mouth again. Till he came into my mouth. I wanted to vomit and ran to the toilet…. Spitting out all that salty mess in my mouth. Drank water. We locked up the office.

He drove me home. I jumped out the car.

I was so scared that my parents were awake. I went to the bathroom. Turned on the shower and scrubbed and washed and scrubbed myself. And went to bed.

The next day, my neck and legs where full of bruises. I took my sisters base foundation and tried to cover all the bruises in my neck. Dad took me to work. I could not go back there. I hid behind the building the whole day, till Dad fetched me.

I never told anyone. I couldn't.

I tried to commit suicide…

∞

17 September 2019, 09:17

Message from SAPS.
CONST. JT will investigate your case
LINDEN ref nr CAS
129/9/2019. Unit contact
detail: 011-8018400. Do
NOT reply to ths SMS

………………………………..

I was called in by my Dad a few weeks later.

"you little slut, you sleep with married men. Your marks in your neck, after you come home late. Now this letter to some man……" I can't remember the rest as he went on and on and on……

(a letter which I had written to let a friend know where we were, so he could join us to lunch in Hillbrow, was misinterpreted by his girlfriend, which I never even knew existed)

Walking to my room – playing Depeche Mode… I can't … I am a disappointment… "only sixteen whole life ahead of her…"

First I walk to my Dad's Mini Panel van… there was a sharp cable knife… I tried to cut my wrists, but the blade was tooo blunt…

I walk to my Moms side table next to her bed. She had just received her scripts of her Medication. Lactogenic, Brufen and more...

Closed the bathroom door and started swallowing… swallowing … swallowing…

Took mom's lipstick and wrote on the mirror – 'Thank you Dad, know I know what I am'

Swallowing …. Swallowing … Swallowing…

I need to get back to my room, I don't want anyone to know or find me…

But – I passed out half way in the passage on the way to bed…

My Mom screaming – "Liefling!!! Help!!!"

… "Let her fucking Die – She is better off dead than in the gutters!! Let her fucking die"

…" Angelique…"

This horrible dry pipe down my throat – water and water gushing in my stomach….

"What's your name, what did you eat, what did you drink"

… "Where am I?"

"You are in hospital, ward 4"

∞

2014

Standing at the pay out in sportsman's warehouse cresta. I have my children with me and my husband. I look up… NO, I know that mouth, those cheeks, that face, under those sunglasses…. Right there in front of me…

My life flashed … I went cold… everything … everything dropped…!!!

"are you "K"??"

With a smile he looked up and said …"YES"

'Angelique?" he said

It was like my world … my safety net… my everything … disappeared!!!

All control – everything – left me !!!

I stood in front of my RAPIST!!!

The person that took away my innocence !!! the man that took away my womanhood!! Took away !!! my natural love!!! My natural trust!!! My Womb!!!!

'you raped me when I was 14 years old!'

…. I can't remember much from there on… other than … you raped me, I was a young little girl!... my husband and boys pushed him to the terrace… there where two boys, when my husband looked at the one and said, how old are you? I am 14.. your dad raped my wife when she was your age!

The children phoned their mother, I told my husband to calm and take the kids to car. no I did nothing the rapist said…arrogantly he said if I did, take me to the cops…

The mom arrived, I told her that he raped me when I was 14, her words where, I knew there was more about you, she immediately took her kids.

I said I will meet you at Fairland police station.

Dropped my children and husband at home and drove to the police station in Fairland.

I walked in and asked if "K" was there, the answer was No. I waited and waited for approximately 2 hours… no one arrived…. I went home…

Mom is it all sorted? Yes, my love…

The call from the prosecuting officer at Randburg Court

February 2020

I am nervously sitting waiting on the benches again. At the Magistrate's Court in Randburg. Not knowing what to expect. Is this the day of the hearing? Is this the day I need to face my reality and the perpetrator?

Getting called in to the office of the clerk of the court.

'Don't feel scared. You are safe here. We will be preparing you for the day of the court.

I look around the office, so dilapidated, the cream painted wall. Brown old furniture. It is only me and the clerk. People walking in and out all the time. I am an adult woman of 47 years old. I feel like I am the criminal. What must I say. I am so scared. My heart beating in my throat. My hands trembling. I am alone.

The prosecuting officer walks in to the office. Introduces herself and invites me to her office.

Another big office with files stacked all around. Broken furniture. Cream walls. Children's drawings stuck on the wall. I don't know where to sit. I am so scared. I don't know what to say.

Finally, I sat on this broken chair.

'I have your file in front of me. Tell me what happened?'

The fear. The lump in my throat. My hands shacking. My heart deafening my ears as it thumps away. Louder and lounder.

Telling my story….

She looks at me the whole time… not taking her eyes off me…

'why do you only come forward now, after all these years?'

'When it happened, I felt guilty. I felt I did something wrong. I disappointed my parents. That's why I decided to take my own life. Then growing up, I comforted myself by saying, "the wheel of life turns". It was much later, that in doing the work I do, in fending and fighting for children to not have to go through what I did. The law changing, that I am still able to lay charges. Protecting my own children. That I realised how much this person has destroyed my life. I am the one that tell the world to come forward. I am the person that tells the world to speak out. But I don't. I am hiding. I have lied to my own children since 2014, telling them, it is sorted. I am living the life of a hypocrite. Even starting #rapeculture. Being hosted on many radio talks about being a Survivor of Rape. Being part of Slut walk. Talking to children, youth about #metoo, #rapeculture. What have I done about me? What have I done about speaking out?'

'You know' she said. 'when I picked up your case file, there was something about your case. As I read through it, I felt that you were telling the truth. I feel that you are not the only one he has done this to. I want you to be strong. I want you to assist the investigating officer to find more that will come forward. Your case has merit.'

I could not believe what I was hearing.

I could not control my tears anymore. (Do you know how ugly I am when I cry? But I could not hold it back anymore…)

She held me for a while, whilst I could gain control over my emotions…

I don't know how I made it back to my home that day… But I did…

Tue, 25 February 2020, 12:31

Message from SAPS.
Serg. MJ will investigate you
case
LINDEN ref nr CAS
129/9/2019
Unit contact detail:
0118018400
Do NOT reply to this SMS

COVID – DISASTER – NATIONAL LOCKDOWN – SOUTH AFRICA

In the interim, I had gathered all the information in preparation for when I meet the new investigating officer. Reliving every moment as I gathered the pieces. It is my word against his. I need to track down anyone that can testify with me.

My mother had submitted her affidavit to the police, as part of the first phase of the investigations.

His children still trolling my social media pages. Making snide comments.

Trying to gather the strength in me to go to Hartebeespoort Dam Cable way where he took me that day. Perhaps it will bring back the memories and road he took me on. The road he turned right on. Perhaps the dirt road is still there. Perhaps I recognise the road markings. Perhaps the bushes that surround the area? Perhaps my guiding angels will open my eyes and lead me to where he did this to me…

"X" 2020/08/27
IN THE HIGH COURT OF SOUTH AFRICA
GAUTENG LOCAL DIVISION, JOHANNESBURG

CASE NO:42800/2019

Held on 27 AUGUST 2020 before the Honourable

In the matter between:

…………………………………   Applicant

And

MCADAM, ANGELIQUE   Respondent

DRAFT ORDER

It is ordered as follows:
1. That the settlement agreement marked 'X' is hereby made and order of Court.

2. Each party to pay their own costs.

………
WHEREFORE the parties agree that the matter between the Applicant and Respondent is being investigated by SAPS under case number 129/9/2019;

AND WHEREFORE the parties agree that the current status of the Respondent's Social media status commentary is acceptable to the Applicant and that it contains no defamatory or prejurious statements with regard to the matter under investigation.

………

INTERIM ORDER
This agreement shall remain in full force and effect as an Interim Order until such time as the Police Investigation under case number 129/9/2019 has been finalised and should the Applicant not be charged or convicted, then the Applicant may apply to Court for final relief.

………

3 September 2020

I have not followed up on my case. It is COVID 19 Lockdown. Since I have just received the Order of Court. Let me find out if the FCS has been operating during this time.

Good Day,
What is the status on my case?

Mrng mam….sorry I had to park aside in order text u… I took your Matter back to public prosecutor for decision and file withdrawn due to lack of evidence..no prospects to s successful conviction….

Noooo you must be kidding me
You have never even been in contact with anyone or never even spoke to me

I now have to escalate this to a higher rank
14 September 2020

Good morning. I have your case docket. You are welcome to make an appointment to come see me.

I went to see the Captain in charge. Explained again what I had been through….

Provided him with all the information that I have gathered. The meeting with the public prosecutor. The fact that I had never met the new investigating officer.

21 October 2020

Good morning
Hope you are well?
I would like to follow up on my case?
Any idea what is happening?

I sent it back to Honeydew FCS with a request for re-evaluation. Have you not heard anything from them?

Nothing at all

Okay I'm not in the office. I am going to send you're the number of the Captain.

Thank you

21 October 2020
Good morning Sir
I hope you are well
I just wish to follow up on my case that was brought to you.
Regards
Angelique

Will check and give feedback

Thank you kindly

You do realise that there is no Judge, No Jury, and No Interim, Nor Final Prosecution that will make a difference to what truly happened.

 I laugh at you; you piece of shit that wants to sue me for the possibility of defamation of character… what character? What character at the age of 31 takes a little 14-year-old girl to have sex… when you are married, a husband, a father of 2 little children, a business owner, a brother… you planned this!

As I am now older, and work with cases. As I am now older, and realised the concept of statutory rape. As I am now older, and realise the concept of a rapist does not only have one victim. As I am now older, and realise pre-meditated.

Let me tell YOU, you coward….

I have such a clear memory of you raping me!

'I have a meeting in Pretoria with a client. Have you ever been to Pretoria?'

'No'

'come with me'

'but I have to do the filing and answer the phones. N is not here.'

'it's okay, we can lock up the office.'

'are you sure?'

'yes'

'I have to call my mom and ask her first.'

'Mamma, my baas vra of ek saam met hom Pretoria toe kan gaan?'

'Solank jy betyds sal wees as Pappa jou kom oplaai.'

'will we be back for my Dad to fetch me?'

'Yes.'

'Hy se dit sal nie lank wees nie. Ons sal terug wees.'

'okay.'

'Dankie mamma.'

We locked up the office and got into your car.

We drove, to what I thought was the road to Pretoria, because it was far.

We drove into Hartebeespoort Cable way? I thought Pretoria was another built up area like Johannesburg?

You got out the car.

I was uncertain.

'the meeting is later; come I will take you up the cable cars.'

On the cable cars, you sat opposite me. You lit a joint.

'do you want some?'

'no thank you'

We got off the cable car.

Back into your car.

We drove out… it was overcast that day…

'I want to show you the place I just bought.'

'what about the meeting?'

'it was cancelled.'

We drove on the tar road. Then turned right…. It became a dirt road… you stopped… there was just long grass and bushes all around…

'get out, let me show you the place I bought.'

I got out the car.

We were standing in front of the car.

'I bought all this around us, what you see is what I bought.'

'that is nice, but we need to get back.'

'you know I am in love with you. Kiss me.'

'no, I can't'

'it's okay, no one will know'

'okay, just a quick kiss'

I gave you a quick closed lipped kiss and turned to go back to the car

You turned me around

'what are you afraid of, give me a longer kiss'

'no, I don't know how to'

'I will show you'

You put your tongue in my mouth, your beard and moustache… sis

I pushed you away and turned to get into the car.

I belted up

You got into the driver's seat.

'that was not fair, I showed you how to kiss'

'we must go home'

You leaned across me and put the seat down.

'kiss me again'

'no, can we please go'

'shhhhh'

You put your hands between my legs…

'please, I want to go'

'just be quiet'

Next you had my panties off. You put your penis in my face. Your balls and your hairs in my face. You put your penis in my mouth. I couldn't breathe. You put your fingers and mouth at my vagina… your whole body pushing down on me… then you turned around…… and put your penis inside me…

'stop please, it is sore..'

'shhh it will get better,…'

You kept on and on and on your penis in me, it is so sore, it hurts, it hurts… I want to vomit… your red beard in my face… the acne scars, the beard, the pain, I want to vomit… mamma, pappa …. Help my … eina… dit is seer… wat doen hy… pain, vomit, beard, hair…. I am nauseous… stop please stop… stink sweat… eina … stopppppp….

'please stop!!!'

You flipped me seat back up. Went back to your seat. Pulled up your pants. It was nearly dark. You lit us a cigarette.

We drove back.

I sat staring out the window. Tears rolling down my cheeks.

'I need to fetch my handbag. And phone home.'

You still tried to put your hand between my legs driving back.

We got to the office on the corner of Blairgowrie Drive and Gordon Drive. We went into the office so I can fetch my handbag.

How clearly I remember that office. front door, to the right was the front office where I sat to do filing and answer phones. Walk through the door, your office was to the left. To the right was where your brother's office was and the rolls of window tinting film.

Your office phone was according to you, the only phone that is unlocked at night. so I walked to your office to call home.

'hello mamma, ons is terug, 'k' sal my huistoe bring.'

'my kind, is jy veilig?'

'ja mamma'

I put the handset down.

You were right behind me. You pushed me down on the table, pulled down my panties again.

You put your penis into me again..

'please I need to get home'

'okay'

I pulled up my panties

And walked around the desk

You stopped me.

Pushed me down on my knees.

Forced your penis into my mouth and held my head so tight I could not get up or move.

You kept pushing your penis in my mouth, I could not breathe I could not get up.

I wanted to vomit…

The that shit stuff went into my mouth and throat .. I wanted to vomit… it burnt my throat…

'just swallow it'

you stopped hold me down

I got up and ran to the bathroom, I spat and vomited in the basin … couldn't stop drinking water… my throat burnt so much…

'please take me home.'

We got into the car…

Driving up Gordon road… I was so so scared…

When I saw the stop street in front of our house… my gates… I felt safe, I got out …

Please god, let my parents be in bed..

The house was quiet when I sneaked into the back door …

I went to the bathroom immediately opened the shower… I found everything, soap, facecloths, (my mom made loofahs out of plastic gem squash bags) I sat in the shower… scrubbing and scrubbing.. washing.. crying.. scrubbing….. crying…

Eventually I went to bed… what if I am pregnant… what …

The next morning… I got woke up.. ran to the bathroom… there was blue marks all down my neck, my legs, my arms… it is December, it is hot, it is summer…

I had sex… I have to go to work… I am pregnant.. I can't tell my parents…

Base – base - I emptied a whole bottle of my sister's base foundation on my neck, arms, legs to try cover up the scars…

'Kom pop, jy gaan laat wees vir werk.'

I could not, I could not walk back into your office…

I hid behind the building for the whole day. I did not want my parents to know… no one must know…

… but I plucked up the courage, and asked your next door neighbour. The Accountant, if I could work for him for a few days… so my parents would think… I am still working…

So yes you bastard! Your brother, the tall big guy, that shared offices with you, that was Canadian/American. He shared a house with you. As you walk into the front door, there was a couch to the left. The kitchen was to the right. Through the lounge, was a door to go to the outside. The passage to the bedrooms where on the left of the couch. The guest bathroom was on the left of the passage. Your brother's bedroom was diagonally across the bathroom.

DO YOU STILL WANT TO TELL ME – YOU DON'T KNOW WHAT YOU DID?

Is you AFFIDAVIT still – I don't know you !!!

Quite amazing when I saw you in Sportsman's when I asked you your name, and you said yes, it's me. You looked at me and said my name…. WOW!!

Yet in your police reports, and the legal letters, you claim you KNOW ME NOT???

YES – You actually KNOW ME NOT!

I WILL NOT BACK DOWN!!

As you KILLED my life for MANY more YEARS than you thought you DID!!!

How many more did you INJURE through your SICK FUCKING NEED to HURT YOUNG CHILDREN???

How many have you KILLED?

How many have you PAYED OFF to be QUIET?

ALLOW ME – To TELL YOU!!!

YOU HAVE NOT BROKEN ME !!!

Yes, you have made me QUESTION myself, QUESTION people, QUESTION trust, QUESTION humanity!!!

Left me in PAIN for 33 years!!!

BUT YOU WILL NEVER CLAIM – ANGELIQUE!!!!

I AM A SURVIVOR!!!

And I HAVE CLAIMED MY VOID!!!

With kind Regards

Love

Angelique

31/10/2020

19 October 2019

Nature, nurture, nurture, nature

So you are either an overbearing mother or overbearing father. The child was reincarnated to learn and their first teachers they chose are their parents from being conceived ... there would be either love, hatred or resentment

The triangle where love is either at the bottom or at the top with hatred and resentment on either side

A square as the foundation that everyone builds on! The base is a square and always ends in a pyramid of emotional / spiritual / material requirements and needs, that ultimately gives you conception to procreate either in love, resentment or hatred.

We ache for love – which is actually the world

∞

Listening to teen boys talk:

'Woman all have issue bra, but then they are easy'
'white boys always deflect'
'faithfulness – respect – I want she won't allow – respect wants as though it will be the death of you'
'Blacks cheat, coloureds won't commit, whites keep going on about his penis'
'I am staying with my chick cause she doesn't want sex'
'Babe marinade – marinating babes want dick so bad – they want dick together'
'that woman is such a bitch'
'bring her to my house'
'gents don't be like that the niggers will get you shagged'
'so can we just committing such'
'like like literally – my mom right, my mom drinks and my mom doesn't drink'
'get the fuck out dude'
'the early hun I fucked like oh wow'
'boy is so happy'
'girl get a load when she just when she just wants attention bro'
'20 minutes from here'
'not gonna lie'
'that hun is bad, I don't give a shit'
'I looked at this babe she had glasses and I literally just wanna fuck her dude'

∞

Some thoughts:
husband and wife – flip the coin the
3 second rule

Heads or tails = topic that either
wants to discuss

Flip the coin – that person starts
talking – before you respond, you
have to give it 3 seconds – think –
talk – stop – think – respond – all
works with an hour's glass or stop
watch

Flip the coin – gamble on me

"the corporate social worker"
"ice-tags to be incorporated into
anti-child trafficking"

∞

10 October 2019

The return from African travels

What an experience with taking the risk to take on an invitation from a person which had been my communique in exploring and exploiting words and emotions, esoteric to heart to nothingness – to testing from sex to physical to space – I took the plunge on an invite for exploring the unknown and the known … for what I thought was the known and the pseudonym which was always a sixth sense of questioning and querying – I took that plunge and flew away to an unknown country for an unknown as it came at the time when I could and felt like throwing caution to the wind in just saying fuckit! Even if at the time can't afford it in every aspect of work, study, finance etc. took that to experience and put much to rest ….

Uncertainty of words – uncertainty of self and so it started the 5-day journey of just – risk. Yes, I risked much as I took that leap of faith in the unknown at the fly. And it was beautiful – beautiful in learning so much about myself, to the point where it brought me to uncontrollable tears. That I could not stop crying last night as there was so much reality that came into my being so many truths that is deeply very deeply hurt. That even when we are adults we just don't trust the sincerity of the automatic innate human. That you need to question yourself of your own worth. Because of what in your growth you don't trust, you learn to distrust before you trust, that you constantly justify your worth through some form of power/strength. Vulnerability = hurt. Fake = cover strength / persona etc. to cover the hurt.

Yes, I met a beautiful man and amazing soul that also feels the same and it is to fucking painful that the beauty of the insecurity of reality has to have various masks. Uncontrollable tears came through as the reality set in … where we just want to feel safe and secure. The beauty of release was just too much that all had to come through. How we shifted it is scary!!! That the thought of have to say goodbye – make us build walls to protect. It was so surreal that the comfort with a person that you don't know felt so normal that you had to immediately do the right thing. To hope to extend the time. I don't want it to end… it is amazing…I will keep it going – I still smell you

∞

2 December 2019 –

My book title – 'ons soek almal fokking fireworks" of 'slyp 'n diamant'

2020 vision – rooi-kappie en die wolf vs don't cry wolf = lesson

Harties cable car ry…. Ek gaan daar staan en gaan die fokkin grond pad kry waar ek gerape was, want ek moet gelei word om 100% te glo dit gaan my heel maak van 32 jaar se gemors!

3+2 = 5 it could go either way – 5 = time to make decisions, stages of checking with everything

∞

Living cross-pollination:

It is all under our noses in a small section… the radius is literally within everyone's reach, why not share and make it beautiful – same as estate living… take the township block into the estate – take the estate into the block… it is the cost of a bus – everyone pays their R20 to see how other people live – give a real perspective to how the other side lives!!

The secret language and preparation of code –

We all communicate in subconscious code through:

- Music
- Body language
- Signals
- Punctuation
- Food

If something or someone does not relate to your exact moment it won't resonate so it translates into either – you ignore it or you react to it

It resonates – creating either a positive or a negative reaction.

∞

4 October 2019

You are under my skin Adam – what are you doing there and how have I allowed you to creep in, I love watching you read all my messages and send which means you feel the same, trying hard to not show this – I know my dear and I shall not give up as we go forward.

∞

24 December 2019

It was wonderful! as I lay on my floor at the kitchen door and just allowed myself to let go – no inhibitions – shit came out from me – out both ends – I vomited – I shat – I sweated – I cried – I snotted. It just would not stop – continued and continued…

Thank you – body, system and mind to just reach that point where you can say – enough! enough! the abuse of food, drink, mind, heart, body, soul, energy

The expectations you allow others to have for you, the expectations you hold and project on others and yourself…

A bubble can only hold so much air and travel only so far then it has to let go… so hello bubble Ange – thank you my body

1 August 2020

Pen to paper – I am writing today

I don't exactly know what the topic would be – it is my thoughts I think

This week has been all over in as far as turmoil, internal and external the outside influences has proved to be still, no answers, no healing, nothing but anger and frustration at the current circumstances that surround my world. This is 'my world' as I am the one living it.

My children are all around me, and not with me, which is my everything and I have to accept it. When they are living the way I have raised them, to make their choices to be who they want to be, and where they want to be, when they leave I am a lost bird - trying to find me! my nest, my everything! as though there is nothing but me! I feel completely lost, trying to fill me with every substance that serves of no intrinsic of tasting value – alcohol – smokes – people – party – internet – social media – shopping – sex - trying to fill that void!

Like grasping at straws with no lasting effect. It is a void that I want to explain to myself, searching through my mind, searching through labels, or words to give it some form of name and put It in a box that says ... depression, anxiety, fear... I google the meanings, but it does not fit the explanation of the void.

Trying to find meaning though trying to fill that void with fending, fighting and standing up, helping other children that I have not even met, to try fill that void to complete me... but it still remains nothing I touch turn into permanence nothing I do, who I speak, to what I do – fills that void it is a dark chasm that just is...

I understand now the true meaning and reality of why people with children in a situation of divorce behave in the manner that they do. It is not that they necessarily want their partner, that they did not get along with back into their lives – it is the deflection of that completely unknown void, they wish to fill when their children are not with them.

So what is the actual true effect that when you spawn and birth a child? It is a part of you that has been created the vested interest over and above the biological life science of mitosis. It is you that you have created and duplicated. Nothing in this world can take that away from you! It remains a part of you! So the moment it is not there it is gone – gone from your immediate space, time, interaction, life – so we walk around – well at least I do – trying to patch that with what? It is not a permanent solution; it will never be that ... child that little being.

Now if you are any bit like me, that have lived every second for the best in my children, that created my world, me my life for my babies, you would understand the magnitude of that hole/void/chasm.

So what do I do? As the reality that having a child in your home only lasts 18years! Although through the 18 years, I have prepared and adjusted 'me' accordingly – but never did I think, that the reality is so difficult to accept, I now want to fill that void – but how, where do I do that?

In addition to my 18 year leaving me, the reality of divorce and separation, was part of this life of having my babies, a major adjustment as at the time 18 was 14 that brought with it its own void, of not only being separated from home and onset of the temporary void. But within came the parenting versus teenage adjustments of allowing the 14 to become his own. The combination of divorce void, and maturation void, the tormenting experience of realising your baby is leaving your bed, your arms to becoming his own person.

 A wild bird I am – fighting for survival – on my own – the security of my own home, my own relationships my being – the acceptance of the secure home no longer being there, combined with acceptance of a maturing child.

Then 18 moves on and the next is 14 having to leave the mother bed to maturation. I am here now – alone with trying to find something to fill that void – and I feel lost

The truth for today!

"The ceremony of the void"

So I try to fill it with others that I think could potentially be "that" who fills the "void", but it is not the same! They are not that part of me that is no longer there! When they come through to fill that void and it does not fit exactly, or at the time and the way that I am needing – what do I do? Feeling angry, feeling disappointed, feel sad, feel hollow it what is it – hollow – as it is a void!

I try to patch it with, people, work, food, drink, party, sex, drugs in the attempt to fill that void. All of these that will never take the place not will it fit in exactly the same space. Nothing will fit that 'void'.

It is not the fault of the patches it is not the patch that is wrong. It is the difficulty and the reality that the 'void' is a part of you. It is to accept that and find a means to embrace it – which is the difficult part, and "yes" it is not easy and you cannot escape it. It is real, it is a part of you it is real.

So don't blame those around you, or anger, or need, or it is 'your void', 'your life' and 'your reality'.

Deflecting is not going to assist in the adjustments required to embrace and accept. Acknowledge the' reality', face the' void', give it a 'special name', 'celebrate it' and allow it as this is a 'part of you'... this is 'your void', 'this is you'

August 2020

So I watch my children, they are all just being themselves! I do feel and believe as they continue through their life's journeys that at least for the sake of being a Mother I have given them their basics.

My one little friend – what does Rasta mean – the purity amongst people? He is lost amongst religious conformity. Why do you want people to sleep and wake? I want to be an anaesthetist mama Ange…

I have lost another man to the ballet of life and the only constant remains – my children! Hello mother – there is simply no contest!

Aa you are Angelique – it is not just one thing! It is a culmination of what you have to put out to the universe! accept it! work it! you have the influence, knowledge and power to do it! #unitethefight

Mining + cell + farming + rural + off the grid/windfarm – 3000 children education = 2 x high schools 2 x primary schools 1 x college – entrepreneur!! 26 August 2020 commemorates – I don't need anyone I need to make it work.

"There is a certain part in the party that everyone feels awkward"
"it's only when respect ends – is when those underlying issues come out"

July 2020

I feel that it is time to write

Under my trees in the middle of winter cold breeze freshly sweeping around me. What is going through my own thoughts right now? Today as I am –

I don't really know and can't say to be honest… today is just one of those neither here nor there days. I know that I am surrounded by my children and animals, but I somehow feel goddamn lonely, I think that is the feeling? Or is it – I am not quite sure… I do know that it is one of those days that just has no value of feeling or meaning just a sense of numb – listless – pointless – that feeling of what the fuck have you actually got in store for me today and if there is something, maybe I don't want to participate in it… nothing really inspires or triggers me today…

Trying to eat – nope
trying to work – nope
trying to read – nope

Just a fabulously useless day of what the fuck ever

So now I am just sitting under my tree on a chair if have never sat on for 6 years. It has been standing in my garden – in a place that I have never sat before… semi – cool I think…

A miracle I want a miracle of some sort – I think, don't ask me what – just a miracle. I can certainly factually say without a doubt I want to fuck – have sex – be touched and loved again. That is no maybe! That is a goddamn fact! Yes that's it! I want that miracle on my doorstep ! Now!

2020/09/03

 Where were you mom and dad? So caught up in your own lives, that you never realised that your daughter was being raped! That your little angel that you placed on that satin pillow was the one that kept the family together, the one that stood by your mom while you lived through life and death, Dad the satin pillow that saw you through your multiple affairs. Sister the one that stood by your side when you dealt with your not wanting to deal, brother the one that still remains your guardian brother, the one that still entertains you. At the end of all of this… I stay strong! No one will break me!

My wings are stronger through my lessons! I am still the mother – and I need no man to prove who I am!

I shall continue to say – I want the children! but I don't want the man!

Why do I say that?

Because – men are like children! They think they own the world, but because of what society had done to them, they don't understand the reality.. hence they seek! That is why, I am soo happy and glad that I am divorced, because now, I have the opportunity to teach my children to be real without having to deal with their father, before I have to deal, teach and educate them about life and accepting who they are.

Ek is so kwaad so ontsettend kwaad hoe kan jy as n pa weg stap van jou dogter wat jou nog altyd hoogagting gegee het, not the benefit of the doubt so as very few kids I probably did more than anyone else did, I am so angry but got to keep going

19 August 2020

"it might be out of place for you, because you are new to the already lived in space"
– Angelique

12 April 2020

The art of basic instructions

we learn to read without comprehending

we learn to hear without listening

we learn to look without seeing

We are amidst the world saying Enough is Enough. Come to a halt and just be still my soul. Be still and take this time to reflect on absolutely everything. "I am sick" she says, "I am in pain" she says. "I gave you everything, I have and I give you my core, my food, my breath."

"I am sick she says" – I send you messages; I send you signs.

"I am sick she says" – I send you angels that walk amongst you share the messages with you

"I am sick she says" – enough! I am sick can't you see, can't you read, can't you hear

"I am sick "– and cannot continue like this.

I don't know how much longer I have to keep feeding you.

My name is Mother Earth

And watching my children all destroying each other, to have what I give you what there is enough of for everyone to share in peace.

I will take the gluttons that keep everything to themselves and find a means to force them to share.

I will take those pieces that knows no harmony and discrimination and ills and will clean up.

I will show those that do not take responsibility, accountability and ownership of what I provided them with, back to their basics, their homes, their roots.

I will clear their heads, their homes, their hearts and allow them to find harmony.

I will take away those that cannot find peace, cannot speak peace, cannot think peace and replace them with my new born light workers.

There will remain one language, one nation, one race and that will be my light workers.

Those that know the meaning of respect, care, love and gracefully allow the sun to shine for every organism, the ground to feed every organism and the air to breathe for every organism.

You don't realize my power, my abilities as the Mother.

I AM MOTHER EARTH

6 May 2020

Change = emotional combustion

It all just works and happens as it should

At the exact minute and time when you are faced with the possibility of change or the introduction of anything different or new. What exactly happens to you. The immediate reaction is that of fight or flight. When choosing to fight it is also placed into different categories of positive or negative as before you go into the decision of flight the assessment, albeit 1 second or 2 years is and instant explosion

'I want somebody to share, share the rest of my life. Share my innermost thoughts, know my intimate details.' – Depeche Mode

20 June 2020

Adam

Where do I begin to tell you that I have fallen in love with you, with your being – my heart my internal soul my being feels it so deeply it has gone to a level of deep touch that I cannot transcribe into words – what the connection is I don't know, it is confusing and burning, is actually burns so much that how do I even put it into any form of words or expression or dream or – it is a sick feeling of heart, mind, soul, passion – the kind that inspires and the kind that makes you sick, happy and sad – a mixture of everything that I cannot explain it is amazing yet it hurts – brings life but brings emptiness at the same time. I want to tell you; I want to express it to you – but at the same time if I do I fear that you would not accept it. That you would fear what I want to say and block it.

I am afraid of opening my heart again, of feeling and falling in love and loving – I don't want to hurt I don't want to have to go through the recovery process again, as it is a pain that I would rather ward and guard myself from ...
I have this backup plan that every time I feel uncertain that you do not see or feel the same way, that my love will be unreciprocated, or that I am just being played, I download Tinder and make myself want to feel – wanted – but then it lasts for a second, I am over it or I seek for something out there that would give me that false sense of acceptance. More and more I have felt no need to easy patch my scratches, more and more I have felt that it is okay. I do not want to try build that wall or keep it built, I want to let it down. I want to show my vulnerability, I want to have that soul connection and deep touch again. I feel somehow it is with you, that I will have that again. That you are that person that will make this prayer heard and come to fruition – to make me feel life, alive, love and laugh again. That I need to not hide anything that I have a means, a person, a soul that I can and want to connect with again, or for the first time or just allow all the facades, the guards, the walls to drop and fade away and be free, be so free that I can dance around and be and feel inspired again – to explore and exploit and run and create brilliant energies and colours and smells with. Design, create, think, express. Say hello to the new, with new inspiration make love to me – to you – to the universe.

"the winning confidence"

"combining SA and USA with concept learning"

"Children's future"

"Series – Madeleine"

"Billionaire kevin"

"another child welfare in the states"

"research – Columbus, North Carolina, Hughston, Texas, Canada – South Africa"

"die een sit jou in die kak – die ander maak jou arm"

Epiphany Ange 8 June 2020

Do I have to sell myself?

Yes you do – you have to sell yourself all the time to get where you want to be in life – male male male – female female female

If you triggered something in me – a passion a picture a thought

It is all the fucking shame

Do I want a man …yes - is he the same place as me "underlying contract" – YES

Does is co-inside with me and my minute or hour – NO

Do I want to accept it … this minute - YES in 2 hours NO

My perceptions - we pour OUR needs and limits onto other people and expect them to be the same.

People love challenges – the moment you feel unchallenged you seek a challenge – excitement – fun albeit education, anger, fight, knowledge, sex … that is the human and developing psyche – we all experienced intrigued about how we tick as humans the mind / brain etc.

That we end up in the rhetorical maize and we all go back to the research of others and all of a sudden we give that person a name – classification.

God – Jesus, Buddha, Siddhartha

123, ABC, alpha beta omega

Balancing the mind and soul, air sky moon stars

Alpha = I
Beta = others
if you are alone you are alone or the other person they refer to it as you

2020

"CELEBRATING THE VOID"

The parent from the moment you wish to fill to what is the human being birthed. In the psyche there is a void when entering this plane, you are part of a human x2 the mother and the father created you. It takes a sperm and egg that came together so you are created. From there you grow closely within the mother hearing the heartbeat, the voice and so continue to develop in warmth closeness to the mother's heartbeat. From there on born – always seeking the closeness that warmth and heartbeat the attempt to fill the void. The moment you are born, that void now exists in the mother, and father is celebrated by your birth as the product of the void he has through providing you with that sperm that created you.

Can you return? Can she place you back? But now you meet your other half – your father. The other creator in your existence – relate to that voice and that dynamics of the cell that created you. You are now filling and celebrating that void.

Parents, children, work, divorce, house, animals, nature, spiritual, life, death

"take your hands off me for the last time, I never belonged to you, you see, take a look at my face for the last time" – soft cell

You know
That years of my life that I dedicated to you is not wasted
Never is and never will be
I have learnt a lot about me during this time
I have learnt a lot about humanity
I have learnt a lot about men, about woman

It gave me as Angelique the time to pause
Time to think
Time to reflect

As I was yet again caught in the hope and the dream that someone out there
Someone truly understands
Someone truly believes
Someone truly loves
Someone truly realistically

Just wants Angelique,
For her
For what she is

And without any weight of a doubt

God knows -

She IS someone's QUEEN 🐵

I thought and hoped it is YOU

I thought and hoped

Please God

May my prayer 🙇 not be unheard

If it is unheard ... may the Answer come NOW
May my prayers NOT be filled with MORE hopes of empty wishes

AMEN

I say in many forms what I feel
I say in so many ways what I live and who I am
There has not been one moment that throughout the years of engagement with you
that I have exposed who and what I am ... enough to allow you to decide ...

You say I am yours, you tell the world I am yours, you want me to believe I am yours
..
You speak of me as yours ..
But am I ?
Have you asked me ?

Have you truly showed me ?

When you are with your own ... do I exist?
Have I been introduced - or the concept of me - been introduced to any part of your
life? Your family? Your immediate?
Have you been asked? Have you been honest to them?

These are all questions I have...

And the only one that could first and foremost answer that .. is you to you .. before
you answer that to me
Because- if it is not to me - it would be to the next and the next after me ...
or
Do you go back and work on the relationship/marriage that you have ?

Know that either way ... this is ultimately about you, as you have to be convinced in your own of your own convictions, as there is only one person that will make you happy and that is you...

Before you can bring anyone to understand your love, your smile, your brilliance - you need to understand what you want 💕

Just know - I as Angelique have seen, and she, this lady has developed what I would call a deep seated understanding and love for ... What you wish to do with it - crush it, develop it - that is ultimately in your hands ...

as for me - it will always be there - regardless - it's called "MY A" chamber

There is just something about you, about us, about whatever this is ...

Hello 🖐 my fabulous

Sitting in my favourite seat in my kitchen
Dressed in my Hugh Hefner
Sipping my wine
I think of you

I cannot help but wonder ..
What is this we have ?
It intrigues me ...
I hate it ...
Yet I love it ...
It's such a strange addiction
I cannot explain

I know I am done:
Done with lies
Done with empty promises
Done with untruth
Done with no trust
Done with seconds of words
Done with memes
Done with stock saved pics
Done with stock saved videos

I know you are one amazing person
Very misunderstood
Extremely underestimated

There is much more to you that somehow i believe neither you nor others in your immediate surroundings see
So my absolute amazing person
How much more can I say to you

I cannot and will not be the SECRET
I cannot and Will not be the OTHER WOMAN
The KARMA of that is NOT what I want to build ANYTHING on ...

You are my absolute... and that is without any doubt ... that I am saying this
Clean up and clear up your life
You know where to find me
When you are ready

But you have to realize that everyone and everything has a limit ...

The question posed ... why do you sound Insecure ...

What is insecurity?

Is that within yourself as the person?

Is that with your surroundings?

Is that with your relationships?

And so we can continue defining and breaking it into bits as you take every circle ○ of life ... outside ... YOU

The first component/layer Is ME ... NO
The 2nd is my immediate children .. NO
The 3rd is my house/home ... NO/yes
The 4th is my family ... NO
The 5th is my friends .. NO/yes
The 6th is my ... person ... the one that would understand the above and would love live and share the above, trust, respect, the above

When it gets to the first ... 2 - 5 is what is ...
If 1 + 6 wants to equal 7 ... which is the factor that takes you forth on the journey of fulfilment then it can't be denied

If you are my 6 and I am your 6 (as you know when I speak me, it also mirrors you) then the journey will continue...

And that my absolute love ♥ is true truth and trust ... I always ask for ..

I want to TRUST... what I have in you .. that every word, every lyric, every song, every meme ... is real

I NEVER EVER EVER want to HURT another 🙈

Please don't put me into that position because I as Angelique found MY person ... MY nr 6 in YOU

We all wish to place those that we encounter.
Enthralled we are when we endure the suspense of the release ... slowly
We feel that there is time .. to play
We all play ... the game or life
Continuously testing ...

What if .. the games we play
Holds reality for some ..
it actually does - when the game involves people...

As they are not pawns on a chessboard that could be shuffled according to a clock set on the side
But - are they ? .... mmmm
Can you call checkmate when the board is still full?

Be careful of the games you play ...
be certain that you know the game ...
Be assured that you know the game players ...

Remember you are the master when you seat yourself to the play ...
you set yourself up when you take on the game ...
You know ... you either win ... or loose ... regardless of the amount of times you play the game ..

Result - your decision

You know I feel you

I can't explain...

It might be a new to you .. as the intensity and passion that - in perhaps your frame of reference is not what has ever been experienced...
Multi-facetted (yes.. that is my angeliqism) as I make up my own terms and language as I go along ☺

To have an extreme passion for life
Passion for the moment
Passion for what is in the NOW is what is important

We cannot reframe the past .. we lived it - we took that picture - we placed it on the
wall ... in a book ... on the pedestal ... it is a beautiful memory

We take what is in our current- the life, that which is in our present- what gives us joy
- makes us feel alive - brings us clarity - passion- participation - energy - light - life -
inspiration- that is soul food ...

Do we plant seeds on tried and tested grounds ... that brought fruit ... yes
Did we nurture the ground whilst we were plucking the fruits ... no/yes
Does the ground need to be reworked to bear more fruit ... yes
Do we have the capacity to wait for the ground to be nourished with the - hope that it
would perhaps regain ...???

Do we pass the ground on to another... to nourish and bear fruit ...??
Do we hold on... in the hope to perhaps maybe find that 1 little seed that is lying
waiting ...???
Wrinkles - broken body - broken soul - says .... why??? What was I holding on to?

... that's how I see life -

No broken soul - no winkles
Everyday has brilliant opportunities...
passion passion passion

May I NEVER hide in the shadows of a wrinkle ... may I live on the layer that sees
the sun ☀

Oft times one is left at not knowing why?
We sit amongst so many people
So much materialistic belongings

We meet new
We live with what we have
We say goodbye to the old

We continue to question?

We laugh because it is expected
We dance because it is expected

... then what ??

All those clichés that the world brought to you ... your world .. disappears...

You try to make sense of it
Because it is something you never wanted to end .. it is something you thought would be a forever…

But then ... it's gone ..
Is it really gone?
No ... it is NEVER gone - because it MADE you - YES .... YOU ! As you ARE!!
Part of YOUR journey !

How you wished to have entered onto this plane... who you meet .. what you do - what you choose and decide - it remains

Eventually it becomes a VOID - you choose to fill that void with something that is ... mediocre / temporary... or celebratory / permanent...

Mediocre = passing time (play)
Permanent = fulfilment (decisions)

The latter is what many fear ... for the simple reason that they have to commit to THEMSELVES

"You are born alone; you die alone" (c) Angelique

What you do in between - is your life's journey, how you wish to live and enjoy it or with whom you wish to share it - that's Your decisions □🙊

The universe will conspire to continuously remind you of the reasons why you chose to return to this plane ..

We ALL carry an intuitive and innate message regardless of the audience and the time spent

,"I'm not asking you to kiss me, nor apologize to me when I think you're wrong.
 I won't even ask you to hug me when I need it most.
I don't ask you to tell me how beautiful I am, even if it's a lie, nor write me anything beautiful.
 I won't even ask you to call me to tell me how your day went, nor tell me you miss me.
 I won't ask you to thank me for everything I do for you, nor to care about me when my soul is down, and of course, I won't ask you to support me in my decisions.
I won't even ask you to listen to me when I have a thousand stories to tell you.
I won't ask you to do anything, not even be by my side forever. Because I don't want to have to ask you."

I don't know what is going on
I am left confused
I am left with many questions but know answers

As you know I respect you
And have grown to feel for you
But I can't force you

So if it is that I need to set you free
Then I will
If you are mine you will come back
If you were never mine,
You won't return

My feelings toward you
And what we have built
They are real
Very real

So I shall set you free
My absolute amazing person
You know where to find me
Should you wish to be

From me to you
As I am going now where
I am here

So many clichés
'Do what you need to do'
'Live the life you want'
'Be who you are'
'If you love someone…'

So I am setting your free

Dear Master

My thoughts will not dissipate:

I love every moment in time that I have had to experience with you,
From the moment that you without a moment of doubt from your side pounced me on the site,
Continued to lure me into your words,
Persistently continued to make me meet with you,
I was not at my perfectly dressed for the occasion,

You were at your lookout,
Yet you continued to pursue …
You blatantly continued to lie to me,
The pretense of a persona
Which goes against my every grain
Yet – I did not allow that to interfere
About to enter into another season
Testing – I believe

Why continue testing?
Is it not about time to make concrete decisions?

I do believe that at this given play / test / call it for what it's worth
That somewhere along the line the truth be told

Games are amazing – that will truly never end
Excitement is fabulous – mundane is not my forte
Adventure is the future – that is my outlook
Inspiration is life – that is my every moment
Optimism is air – that is what I breathe
LIfe is to be lived – that is what wakes me

 So I ask you Master
Don't you think it is about time that you make a call on what you want?
Another Dating Site ?
Another Porn Site?
Or
Go back to what you had and make it work?
Or
Know what you have found and make it work?

You know I love 3s ….. everything in life happens in 3s ….
Left – right – forward
Left – right – backward
God the father - God the son - God the holy ghost

 !!! you have to make a decision !!!

To allow yourself to move forward

With indecisiveness lurking, you can never be free. There will always be some form
of guilt hanging... There will always be ... a hold that will not allow you the freedom to
be ... which will always be the underlying uncertainty... which you know is the current
burden and in reality...
The only thing that is truthfully keeping you apart from living your life to the full
potential ...

Release yourself from that which you don't want ...
Release the person that you don't want ...

I know what I want - I know it is right here

She continues her journey, through what she thought would be simple, her quest continues to endure what brings about much fear as she unravels through every layer, healing the lifetimes of enduring to the undulated code carried through.

A term of endearment he says in the fleeting moment. With such intensity her body reacts to the mere thought of possibility, whilst she is decoding. Innumerable layers already depleted, could it be she wonders…

The intensity grows, that makes her limbs weaken the motion of fear works its way, exhilarating trembles finds its way passively to the point that makes her soften, with a subtle warmth growing moist.

Her muse has found his way to her soul. Is this possible she wonders to herself, that words in fleeting can bring so much to affect her physical to react with such intensity. Has her layers been excoriated to leave her centre so open that with the touch of his thought has the power to bedew her petals as the core is revealed.

I walk Amongst many
Be it whichever they decide to project
The absolute brilliance of being me
Is that given what I am surrounded by

When quietly deciding which part I wish to play

To provoke or to release
That remains my decision
For now my decision is ...
to release ...

As that which comes back to be a part
That which comes back to find me
That which will continue
Will come back
Or
As they perceive continue

For now - this is it - for me
To take a breath
To regain

What I call Ange Angel Angelique

As my days of manic starts coming to closure
I find myself more taking back what is me
Rather than what is expected of me
That being said also requires the bar that I set

To create expectations

Which we all thrive for and also in turn thrive on

There is a set reminder ... be it commercial, be it religious .. be it family ... be it ultimately economically inclined which was introduced by the socio-religious norms ...
Regardless of - thanks to all - as it gives many the opportunity to set aside the ego to recap ..

As whatever one wishes to do - it is a world renowned useless time - hence the much one wishes to argue the masses in not reforming to this time ....

There is just a world that dooms and demands routine of some sort
Therefore- as a non-conformist being forced to conform

This will be my last letter to you for the year ... as this platform forms part of my - what I wish to call - social media

Oft we find ourselves at the moment
Yet we perceive the other to understand our current yet fleeting moment ...
Can they?

The answer is profoundly NO!!

As neither are presented with the current circumstances

We oft wish to prevent / protect the other from seeing or living that side - cause that is our part of control "hide away" where respect remains different

But - we want to go "home" in the end ...
What does "home" mean?

She asks her co-actor ....

The script closed for now..::

She lays back
Her dark locks brace Some
As she looks up to seek his gaze
She want to be seen to have him reach so deep
As she lays back
Awaiting
She quivers in her yearning
Does he know
The touch she so awaits Does he know how to slip his hand down the nape of her
neck
Take it down her back
And lift her

She gyrates her hips to steer
He lifts her pelvis with his hands
With much control whilst he looks deep into her eyes
Towards his lips
She smiles to submit
As he brings her crevice to his mouth
His tongue beginning to explore
She gently placed her feet on his shoulders
As he finds his way with his lips
His tongue seeking
Guiding his Teeth to a gentle bite
She moans
As the vigour and exhilarating pressure of the tongue
Becomes more
He slips his thumb into her and firmly presses down
He as she believes he is not so naive
The pretence places more questions to her...
As he slowly releases
Which she loves without ridicule ...

He knows the gem ♦
Yet he questions himself
She will not entertain
Yet
She won't give in

She knows the gem ♦
Yet She questions herself
He will not entertain

Yet
He won't give in

Both have reasons
Again
They look at each other

It's surreal
Again I say
As she moves motionlessly through her place
Vigorously her mind moves through many scenes
Does that necessarily project reality
She sits back and cries .. she has her own to deal ...
Not with her new incumbent. oh no ...

Some would wish to - as that would mean they could fall within those traps of self
But she chooses to not have her new incumbent ever engage

Image - she has to continue the new with the past ever lagging ...
that is never ever the new ..
Certain parts .. of course and indeed will remain a part of her forming - but does it dictate?

Unconditional love dictates - with absolute significance-
But what is that? She asks ??

Trust me .... she will not ask a question until she has an answer that she believes is the truth ..
What is unconditional love ??

(The co-actor to respond.....) as they continue writing their script

The capture
Does that not depend on the audience?

As the mind processes
The audience will always perceive
Dependent on their frames 🖼

When art in which ever form it is presented
Could take so many forms
It all depends on the recipient
Whilst I prepare for my virgin script

Much happens Around me
Some could be shared
But most remain hidden
Intrigue of the unknown is
What keeps us captured

Start composing
That surreal art
As no artist
The true artist to life
Want the norm

With limbs entangled the settings will change as the deeper they explore the intrinsic trust and exhilaration of not only the flesh but considering the depths that their souls could ignite as they continue to script and deeply scribe without inhibited freedom of creativity as they will stand without a cloth that keeps those many facets and layers from truth …. True exposure will bring that play to a reality ….. as they write together

I write you a letter as a year had come from the moment you seeked my acknowledgement

At first it was with scepticism that I accepted and engaged, however you continued to pursue me although with much doubt I gave you the benefit without haste and ongoing persuasion although underlyingly I knew the person being introduced is not the real – it still remained as if neither you nor me would want to give up.

Much doubt as the layers started peeling away the feat in both was obvious as the more the curtains opened to what could either be a spectacular or disastrous play.

But how would we know if the audience does not see the play to critique.

Warily we draw back the curtains to peek through to first test the script, the actors, the writer.

Testing the ability to perform on stage together.

The after effects of each performance during practise to acknowledge their own roles in the play to find comfort.

As not play is successful if the main characters do not complement each other in the roles as it is scripted.

So fat it is still a script, so far the actors have only practised in their own dress rooms behind the scenes.

As the play is about life every lasting reality the importance is for the characters to carefully read and understand the script. Evaluate their own roles to ensure that they complement their partner when they both stand on stage to give a captivating performance to their audience with conviction, that will sell out the theatre and requests for more is deafening and awe inspiring that they don't want to leave the stage, but start scripting another scene, the second the third as they continue to capture each moment and enhance each other as characters as leading actors in a star performance that inspires the script, the writers, the audience. Adding lyrics, music, poetry, paintings, art to their screenplay that no one wants to stop creating, no one wants the story to end.

But they know …. To get to that ultimate goal they first need to practise in their own showroom as they peel away at their own, layer by layer till they feel comfortable in their own role with their own script. That as virgins to the new stage they will join together to bring out only the best in themselves and their co-actor.

To choreograph their performance, write their script, compose their music together that will be unique to the play, their performance, their work of art.

Let the show continue as they find their being.

I sit here

In awe of what had transpired in 24 hours

It's very few that can sincerely translate the quirks ...

In my makeup I honestly love every moment.. as I am the recipient..

I CELEBRATE THE VOID

In many ways we think we have concluded the cycle of abuse, but have we really? When you are broken as a child, wanting and seeking that safety guard. And continuously being let down by the ones that you think will protect you. Which is first and foremost your parents that brought you into this life. That has let you down, perhaps not by their own making or decisions. Perhaps by their own circumstances as it produces itself. So be it.....

The bottom line is – an adult is supposed to be mature enough to make the decision to bring a child into this life....

Stop trying to fill the void, to keep the man, to keep the woman – by bearing a child!

Once that penis – goes into that vagina it = a child!!

When that child is created …. It equals responsibility! It is the glue that keeps Man and Woman together!

That child is a product of the two people that decided to be in that pro-creative partnership...

You did that through a moment of attraction …

Sperm leaves scrotum via penis …. Egg leaves ovary via vagina … (if it was left intact … there will be no void)

It did …. And it created… YOU

Why?

You wanted to be created… you needed to be created…

Unless you realise your OWN worth

YOU will DIE

YOU will BEAR NO FRUIT

YOU will PROCRASTINATE

YOU will TRY and TRY and TRY again

OR

YOU will BLOSSOM

YOU will BEAR FRUIT

YOU will GROW

CELEBRATE THAT VOID – UNDERSTAND YOU!!

NO ONE ELSE BUT YOU!!!

You can love all you want, you can hope all you want, you can hate all you want, you can kill all you want

Until YOU realise and CELEBRATE YOU as YOU are!!

You are going to CONTINUE to create MANY VOIDS

In MANY lives.

So STOP!!!

STOP TRYING to fill YOUR VOID with TEMPORARY PLEASURES!!!

Understand YOU and realise what it TRULY is that you YOU want FROM YOU!!

Not from anyone else

Yes I can blame my FATHER for not protecting me….

Yes I can blame my MOTHER for not protecting me ….

Yes I can blame my SIBLINGS for not protecting me ….

Yes I can blame my GRANDPARENTS for not protecting me…

Yes I can blame my HUSBAND for not protecting me…

Yes I can blame my BOYFRIENDS, GIRLFRIENDS for not protecting me…

You know what – I made in my OWN the decisions to MAKE more CHILDREN – to FILL that VOID…

Because – I did not FEEL PROTECTED – I wanted to show and prove to the WORLD and to ME – I CAN, I SHALL and I WILL be BETTER!!

I WANT TO FILL THAT VOID FOR ANOTHER!

What was the result???

I created MORE VOIDS!!!

INSTEAD – I SHOULD HAVE JUST –

CELEBRATED MY VOID

That is –

LOVE THINE SELF

If you truly accept who you are

You will NOT force YOU onto others,

NOT your CHILD

NOT your LOVER

NOT your PARTNER

NOT your FRIENDS

NOT YOU and MOST OF ALL !!!!!!

NOT YOU

No parent, no institution, no teacher, no preacher can EVER teach you and NOTHING will sink in, as you will go through life, day after day, year after year until you have actually learnt

YOU are THE VOID

CELEBRATE IT !!!

CELEBRATE

YOU!!!

EVERY YEAR that YOUS grace this EARTH this PLANE with your presence

YOU have either NOT completed your journey and learning

OR

YOU still have a MESSAGE to SHARE

EVERY day you wake – there is a reason for your waking

'Open your EYES and SEE, your eyes are OPEN' – Erasure

Amazing the sounds that keeps on returning

Here am I alone again ,,, a quiet town where life begins,,

Should I ever explain… David sylvain

Not I need not explain, I need not have to explain to any other who I am nor what I am … da da da de da !!!

I have braced my life with mirrors that surrounded every corner of my house. Have danced to every mirror to say …. Angelique you are wholesome….

In my kitchen I had a life size mirror to which I danced clothed, naked … I added another mirror… they all broke … why? Because I need not their approval

Because I am friggen brilliant

I stand for seconds in front of the mirrors in my bathroom ,,,,,, I have 4 mirrors – if they can hold my pose whilst sitting on the toilet, brushing my teeth, rubbing cream on my body, getting dressed, then hail Selassie …. You did not break whilst I did that? From there on … my life and day begins… my next mirror happens to be at my kettle making coffee – hello beautiful

The balance happens to be my windows – which I have a choice – I either focus on the reflections of me… or I see beyond to what is outside… and embrace

I watched for a sign…. We wait for signs all the time, yet there is no sign … we are our own celebration, I am as selfish as it might sound… we come into this world alone – we die alone

Nothing and no one will die with us nor will it be birthed with us

That channel remains

What we learn in between remains

What we reject in between remains

We continue to learn to find the means to celebrate the void

Search the void

Find meaning to the void

What is the void

The ultimate void is

YOU

So simple so stupid…. We all try to make a difference… try to find meaning ,,,

In the end….

When I die – I will be mourned, for maybe a day, perhaps a week………..

And then?

I am NOTHING…

So really …

If you want to make something, be something, make a difference … do what you need to do! believe what you need to believe! change what you need to change –

It's about YOU – you are the VOID

The VOID is YOU

CELEBRATE IT !!!

Blasphemous rumours … Depeche mode

Only 16 whole ahead of her

Slashed her wrists bored with life

Didn't succeed thank the lord for small mercies

Fighting back the tears mother reads the notes again

16 candles burning in her mind

She takes the blame its always the same

She goes down on her knees in prays

When you can see your children pass through these years

You have made it!

They are fucked up – and you as parents are fucked up!

The kids realise it and start asking questions, you are through that feeding, stage, they ask questions, you say thank god they can feed themselves. But they can't but put you on the spot, because they ask questions to find themselves, your answers need to be honest and real… because you too where 16 … you too experimented with cigarettes, alcohol, sex… music… call it the second phase of potty training

This time around… baby oil turns into KY jelly…. And condoms … instead of nappies and nappy rash cream… cigarettes and alcohol instead of bottles and breast or milk formula… real cars and bikes instead of Lego… internet and porn …. Instead of Shaun the sheep,,, rap and nigger ass pussy songs instead of ,, Beethoven rock a bye baby…

They start asking real questions… answer them honestly, don't hide, they love learning the truth… because they think you are old and don't understand. You do understand, you have done it, been there and lived it. The more honest you are, the more your children respect you. The more you lie and hide the truth, the more they look for that hidden chocolate in your cupboard. If they find that hidden chocolate …. They will always question you – and distrust you FOREVER
If your child is disgusted with you – it will be – because you LIED!!

LIVE WHO YOU ARE!

'don't worry, it's all taken care of, you will never have to deal with him again'

I look at my husband…

'don't worry, it's all taken care of, you will never have to deal with him again' – these were the words in 1998…

Don't forget he was the Reccy … the boy in SA army recognisance, the excuse for his abusive behaviour and having the contacts to take out the person that would harm me in any way….

The years I had to deal with his asthma … rushed to the ER and his turning blue purple and pink … waking with frights … talking in his sleep … falling to dead sleep.. waking and wanting to fuck me like I was a puppet… shag doll… if I did not Immediately respond, I was a slut and useless whore… that fucked men before him… pulled me by my hair.. threw me against the wall… accused me of being worthless….

Yes I googled... reckies … how to deal with them, how to live with them, what to do…

The journey began, I was going to be that woman, that wife, that mother, that will work and help and change him … counselling, psychologists, psychiatrists….

You are proper missing it babe.. you are the problem…

the next day… there are flowers, the whole of impala fruiterers are bought out of every lily .. every tiger lily and jiffsophola ?? and Carnations?? Really… I hate carnations and jiff… anyway… I will make a loose arrangement…

and so every time he did wrong the gifts would increase in some form of price…

the tickets to the various countries of travel.. UK, Zurich, Namibia

The cars where upgraded.. Renault to Jeep, then Hudayi SUV

Rings, watches,, more jewellery

My plea …don't buy me anything… just spend time… have a picnic .. pick me a flower when you walk …I don't want anything … I want you to be with us

… but what was it in the end… money, sex… sex… money…

I would not ask for a cent… if I wanted to buy something for me, I would first ask.. if I did, he would constantly remind me of what he spent…. Buying me…

Then … I decided – fuck that, every time you lie to me, every time you fuck another woman, I will and I shall buy things for the house and kids… I will not ask; I will just spend the card to the max. because your love language is money… I will hurt you where it hurts most… card, money, house, kids, money, card…buy food only at Woolworths, redecorate the children's rooms, buy kids clothes, buy more toys and Lego, have greater and bigger kid's parties, buy more stuff for the house. The house was amazing! The kids where so spoilt! They got everything their hearts desired!!

God I was silly – I should have bought stuff for me… too late she cries

Oh do I recall the day when I was successful in pulling off the showroom launch … lest you forget, my successes are never to be embraced.

Art works displayed, the cocktail party, people engaging… your jealousy rage… attacking me in front of people, clients, strangers…

Then attacking my brother… my success … ended in a Jerry Springer … when I had to end up calling out the local security to have you removed from the premises.

Why? why would you not allow me to have something that makes me Angelique?

My evenings with my girls … at home.. art evenings.. where we were at home, in my studio, just having time together. Girls doing art, right next to my children. I was not going out, I was there. At home. Yet you found a way to even destroy that. Constantly telling me the kids where an attended to. Constantly phoning me to say the kids where crying. I was 1 meter away, on the same premises. Then when you finally got drunk enough you would … so called attend to letting my friends out….as I needed to lie with the kids because you could not calm them? I lost my friends because you rubbed them up.. whilst I had to lay with my kids…

Hello Marie from Kenya, I was not angry that he shagged you. I was angry at him for promising you a life in South Africa. For the fact that he probably never told you he is married and have children. That you would give up your life and family in Kenya, for this man that is semi-promising you a future in South Africa…. I am upset with you.. I could have travelled Kenya… silly girl

Hello lily from London, you have an amazing husband and beautiful children. I don't want to buy your house. Thank you for the offer. I did however enjoy my travels. Saw London, wales, Scotland and my favourite the Cotswolds and Buckinghamshire

Thank you dear Alya the secretary, I don't want to participate in your beauty products. I am au natural… thanks for the offer darling…

Ooops thank you… Katie .. ktm … I loved my travels.. saw Zurich and Italy, and my boys are captured in their Ktm bikes… and my baby boy still has Tomas tank engine and bob the builder.

But thank you Anelia from Namibia… my absolute heroin… I solute you. Not only did we travel Namibia. You also released me from having to deal with more… you beaaauty!!! Just such a pity – that you introduced downhill from there on forward for my children… thank you for shnaaffing cocaine in their presence, and getting so drunk, whilst throwing what they saw as home… all the furniture out, and also introducing your older daughter to my younger son… that started cutting… You go go girl…

Hello Magosha, I do feel sorry for you from the bottom of my heart, you were 23 when you were introduced to this old man… with his whips and chains… my girl, where do you think your life will end up? Yes, he is paying for your schooling, upgraded your shack to a home. But you live in a room, only to be let out for food and drink? Actually if I listen to what my children are telling me, you are actually living the life… you sleep all day, drink, eat, watch Netflix, go shopping, spend time with friends… wow!!! You got it made darling… all you need to do is shag the old man. What a life ... you go girl .. he is an alcoholic, and you will not receive a cent when he dies… but who cares.. ya … you are living the dream…

His 4 sons have lost all respect for him … which is a bit sad… but they fortunately have Mother that will keep them going, thank god my daughter is still too young to realise what is going on. But the pain in my sons.

Celebrate the VOID my SONS

Celebrate the VOID my DAUGHTER

The MA will NEVER let you down!!!

I never let myself down, regardless

of what I had been through, I shall never let you down!

sometimes you need to realise that making decisions is a hard call…

it all still remains in 3s

mother – father – child

every child has its own dynamic to you as a person…

the time you bore that child was within that own dynamic and time of your life that has its own uniqueness… as the exact time and place within your being, within your realm and within your own awareness … was also the time that child needed to be birthed…

the same is with the time the animal… the business… the career choice… the tinder… (please give it a name) had to be part of you…

the moment it flows and remains… it is meant to be and it will continue growing. Bearing fruit and be with you

the moment you have to fight for it.. it is not meant to be.. it will hurt you, or it will hurt the recipient… so let it go…

oft we have this preconceived idea that because of our own agenda or desperation that we need to hold on to something, because if we let it go, we feel like we have lost, like we have failed...

you know what – the answer to that – is NO

you actually haven't failed, you have not, for the pure and simple reason is… you cannot control another's world, nor their destiny…

you could perhaps influence it through your interaction, but you cannot ever control it … it is not your journey, it is not your being, and it will never ever be YOU

you are merely a conduit for those who are birthed through you. You are merely and influencer, based on your own realities, perceptions and learnings. You have experienced your life at your lifetime through your own frame of reference. You shared that, from YOUR own perspective.

The other person has their own realities, perceptions and learnings from THEIR perspective. As they too were created from their co-incidence of their own frames of reference.

Mother + father = Child 1

Mother + father = Child 2

So Child 1 meets Child 2 regardless of the point in time.

Same family, same sex, different families, different sex.

What do you get?

Two completely different frames of references … making a combined Third

You see …. Everything happens in 3s

You are the result of:

An egg…. Leaving the mother – creating a void

A sperm …. Leaving a father – creating a void

You are gestating – close to a heartbeat, and feeding and growing in that womb.

You are birthed – You leave a void in the mother,

yet you are celebrated by the father that meets the void that he never met – the sperm

You now enter into this world – Product of Egg, Sperm – Celebration

But now what?

There is no heartbeat, not food, no protection –

It is cold, it is harsh, moving from one hand to another, no warmth, no heartbeat, no food….

What do you do? your security of the 3 basics is gone…

The VOID…. has just been created!!!

For the rest of your life you will seek to fulfil those 3 basics ….

Warmth – the home

Heartbeat – the love

Food – the security

Celebration – the acceptance –

I AM ME – I AM ALIVE – I AM THE ONE THAT BREATHES ON MY OWN!!!

The PRODUCT and CREATION of LIFE!!!

MOM

+

DAD

=

ME

It all happens in 3s

CREATE the VOID or CELEBRATE the VOID

You are either the Survivor or the victim of life

There is no other choice

Life or death

If you wake in the morning – you have a reason to be alive

You have 24 hours to prove it -

24hr day

-

8 sleep

=

16 awake

1 + 6 = 7

The scale can tip either way

In 24 hours

2 + 4 = 6

You have a choice to CELEBRATE your day

Or

………

You learn from yesterday

You live today

You dream/hope/plan for tomorrow

…. So I fucked up yesterday

How am I fixing it today because I am awake…?

…. So I can manifest something new for tomorrow

I WANT YOU TO KNOW

The only means of communication due to our life

As it is currently, is through writing

I do get frustrated most of the time

As I do believe you don't understand me

It might be intriguing to get to know the multi facets of how I operate

Oft I too wonder if the periphery   of me coincides with my core

Which is brilliant as I too go through the many layers of me

I can play, so many games to satisfy those outside of me

As the many buildings of layers and bricks

Walls display many paintings

Ceilings many lights

The core of the structure remains

When it Is built on solid foundations

Of the self, the builder, the architect

Not many realise what that means

You build your foundation at birth

Those that wish to give input are the decorators

Those that wish to restructure are the architects

Those that wish to find play are the landscapers

Everyone wishes to change you

They bring in their directors, their creatives, their visions

At the end of the day

You are you

You need to decide

As you grow through your life

Which brick, layer, mortar, decoration, plant

Will make you

Once you have decided and realised that

You will never

Be able to

Love

Celebrate

Be

I hope you understand my words and thinking ...

If not

I shall translate in blatancy

The true reality behind this is: I am tired of being played, I am tired of people

Send me another porn pic, send me another meme, I will kill you.

Tell me what you want and who you are. Make a true effort to be with me, talk to me, live with me, understand me

'I am so tired, tired of playing with this bow and arrow …. Give me a reason to love you, give me a reason to be… a woman, I just wanna be … a woman '- Portishead

What does that truly mean..

We all actually just want to be..

But …. But …. But…

There is the constant weighing above our heads…

Love – god is love they say

But you are raised to fear God

Which inherently say – you need to fear Love

Love others as you love thine self

So you fear god – so you fear self – so you fear others

See it boils down to the 3

God, self, others

Fear

Or

Love

God, self, others

I know who I am,

I know who others are

So

Who is G O D ??

Same is the transvers – replace GOD with SATAN (Love with Hate, Life with Death, Peace with War, Food with starvation)

Fear? Or Love?

Love? or Fear?

Full or empty

Celebrating the void is understanding that you need to find the balance between.

The moment you understand that you cannot and will not be able to change the world for others. You will not be able to build their reality, nor will you be able to try change their life path, their journey.

You need to realise that you come into this world… alone… you will die … alone

What happens in-between – you can either Fear = VICTIM

OR

You can Love = SURVIVOR

The balance is that you need to embrace and learn from everything that comes to you… as it is either a stumbling block or a learning curve…and you know what?

'Every stumbling block is actually a learning curve', it is up to you to learn, from it, embrace it, and say thank you for teaching me who I am right now.

Somewhere earlier on in my life I came up with the above that kept me going.

Somewhere earlier on in my life I also came up with 'fuck the people, I am the people'

Somewhere earlier on in my life I came up with 'you come into this world alone, you die alone'

'is what it is' make the bloody best of it!!

'you won't die, until you have done, what you came here to do, embrace it'

Embrace your journey – CELEBRATE the VOID that YOU created BY BEING BORN

As you are the PRODUCT of SOMEONES egg that left their body

And

As you are the PRODUCT of SOMEONES sperm that left their body

YOU ARE THE VOID

CELEBRATE IT!!!

Every step of the way – when you walk

Every sound – when you talk

Every move – when you dance

Every note – when you sing

Every letter – when you write

Is You

It is no one else but

You

When you get to the realisation and acceptance

Of THE SELF

Of YOU

The ability to love

The ability to be free

Is Acceptance in Celebrating

THE VOID

THE REALISATION IS LIBERATING

YES – I AM READY!

I don't want to re-read my script…

As I OWN every word I have written

No Book shall every be complete. No Journal shall ever end. No script has and end.

The mere fact that you are able to put any words to paper. The mere fact that you are granted another day to live, to share, to be part of this plane.

You are blessed. You still have a lesson to learn. A story to tell. A journey to live. An impact to make.

Regardless of how big or small.

You are here for a reason.

Live it.

Celebrate it.

You are amazing, you are fabulous.

You are you.

JUST BE FUCKEN

'A'

Last but not least.

I wish to thank every person that I know.

Every person that has ever been a part of my life and my journey.

There is not one person that have walked into my life that has not made a difference to who I am.

To how I see and perceive life.

You have all taught me some lesson. A unique lesson.

I thank you from the absolute bottom of my Soul and my Heart.

You made me who I am Today.

Bless you

pureskiing
AUSTRIA
THIS IS TO CERTIFY THAT
ANGE

Crime in Progress?
There IS an exchange rate
on your child!
STOP
CHILD TRAFFICKING!
#CWSAGauteng
#CWSAICETAGG
#SickenamoreCapital
#SASCG

Fundraising at CWSA Roodepoort

ACHIEVEMENT

CERTIFICATE OF COMPLETION